N. C EDSALL
1990

COUNTRY LIFE

COUNTRY LIFE

A Social History of Rural England

Howard Newby

Barnes & Noble Books
Totowa, New Jersey

© Howard Newby 1987

First published in the USA 1987 by
Barnes & Noble Books
81 Adams Drive
Totowa, New Jersey, 07512

ISBN 0–389–20720–9

Printed in England

CONTENTS

PREFACE

This book took far longer to write than either I or the publisher had hoped. Its gestation coincided with my holding the position of Dean of Comparative Studies at the University of Essex during the difficult period following the expenditure cuts announced in 1981. To have completed a manuscript at all under these circumstances was something of a personal triumph, but I am particularly thankful for the patience of the publisher, in the form of Robert Baldock, Juliet Gardiner and Faith Glasgow, which went far beyond customary endurance.

My thanks are also due to others who made it possible: to Frances Kelly, my literary agent, for suggesting the project in the first place and for harassing me to complete it; and to Jill Scott, Linda George, Carole Allington, Mary Girling and Sandra Dyson for bullying their IBMs until they made sense of my steam-age production technology.

HOWARD NEWBY
Great Bentley, Essex
1986

INTRODUCTION

'A man cannot be busied in the offices of husbandry', wrote Edward Lisle, a Hampshire farmer, at the beginning of the eighteenth century, 'but many things will come under his observation, from which divine, moral and philosophical conclusions are so natural and obvious, that, if he will avoid making them, he must shut his eyes against the light of the sun.' In the chapters which follow, many aspects of social changes in rural England from the time in which Lisle wrote his *Observations in Husbandry* will certainly come under observation. The purpose will be to construct a narrative sociological history of rural England from the emergence of a fully-fledged commercial farming system in the eighteenth century up until the present day. This history will be sharply critical of the stereotypes and myths which surround the popular image of the rural world: the pastoralism of merrie rustics, safely-grazing sheep and stolid yeomanry. The reader will, however, be left to formulate his or her own divine, moral and philosophical conclusions.

The conventions which surround a romantic view of the countryside are not the only ones which need to be cleared aside. An equally pervasive evaluation of rural life is that nothing of importance ever happens there: that arcadian virtues exist beneath a pall of tedium. Those prospective readers who share this conception might be reassured by Lisle's own corrective:

Can they propose a nobler entertainment for the mind of man that he would find in the inquiries he must make into all the powers and operations of nature wherein husbandry is concerned? The subject is so vast it can never be exhausted; could he live, and spend ages in agriculture, he might still go on in his searches, and still make fresh discoveries, that would excite afresh his admiration of the riches of God's wisdom. Add to, that scene of nature, which the country lays before us, has I know not what charms to calm a man's passions, and so to compose his mind, and fix his thoughts, that his soul seems to be got clear of the world; and the further his education enables him to carry his inquiries, the higher are his reflections raised.

One can only agree with Lisle that the subject-matter of this book is indeed so vast that it can never be exhausted. It is therefore necessary at the outset to place a boundary around it: to indicate what it is – and, equally important, what it is not – trying to achieve. The purpose of this book might best be described as to provide an historical companion to my *Green and Pleasant Land?* (see Further Reading). The latter was primarily concerned with social change in rural England during the period since the end of the Second World War, although by way of background it occasionally delved as far back as the mid-nineteenth century. In this book a much broader historical sweep has been taken, but in most other respects the purpose remains the same: to furnish a heightened awareness of the changes which are occurring in English rural society and their historical antecedents.

This may seem unnecessary in view of the plethora of books which have been published in recent years on various aspects of English rural life. Popular books based on such diverse topics as country diaries, rural reminiscences, rustic crafts, village life and the rural landscape have regularly filled the bestseller lists; some have, indeed, achieved unprecedented commercial success. Yet these have frequently obscured as much as clarified our perceptions of rural social change, reflecting the past, as they so often do, through the distorted mirror of nostalgia. When so many individuals feel alienated from the unpleasant realities of modern society, such nostalgia is understandable. Moreover nostalgia is an extremely powerful emotion. But such nostalgic conceptions of English rural life rarely constitute an accurate assessment of it, for in reality they offer a comment which applies neither to the past nor to rural society but to the infinitely more squalid urban industrial present. Taken as a literal description of the past they can, indeed, be positively unhelpful, presenting a sentimental and idyllic evocation of a rural past which never existed. In this sense a fallacious conception of rural life has become one of the major protecting illusions of our time.

The destruction of illusions is not a particularly pleasant exercise, but here it is an essential one. A proper understanding of English rural life requires a dismissal of the prevailing cultural myths which surround it. Indeed this is perhaps the single most important task which this book hopes to accomplish. With this end in view, a number of separate but interrelated themes will be developed which, it will be argued, are helpful in understanding the history of rural England over the last three centuries. Predominant among these will be the argument that most of the changes which are associated with the transformation of rural society during this period can be traced, directly or indirectly, to changes which have occurred in agriculture. This is not to say that this is the only way of approaching this transformation, but rather that it is a particularly helpful way of doing so. It helps to redress the balance of writing on rural England in which the role of agriculture has all too often been underemphasized. It also helps to define the period covered by this book, for it then makes sense to begin with the decades during which agriculture came to be dominated by a new form of social and economic organization: capitalism. From the eighteenth century onwards English rural society became a capitalist society – the first in the world – and a system of agrarian capitalist development was set in train that continues to have a widespread impact upon the nature of rural life today. This does not mean that the changes which have occurred were inevitable, for no such determinism is intended, but it does place at the centre of the analysis a consideration of the commercial rationalization of agriculture, organized around profitable production for the urban market, and the social consequences of this process, both in terms of the quality of social relationships in the countryside and the changes in the structure of these relationships.

3

A further theme is the changing class structure of English rural society. The transition from the feudal social order of the medieval world to the hitherto unique arrangements of a capitalist agrarian society constituted a profound break in the history not merely of rural England but of Western civilization. From the predominantly landlord/peasant class structure of the manorial system there eventually emerged the tripartite class structure which typified Victorian high farming: landowner, tenant farmer and landless farm labourer. During the twentieth century this transformed in turn into a predominantly bipartite structure of owner-occupying farmers and farm workers. However, this has itself been modified by the arrival of ex-urban newcomers to the countryside, particularly since the Second World War, whose presence has provided a new, and often disruptive, element in rural social relations. This new population symbolizes an important aspect of contemporary rural society, namely that it is no longer only, or even predominantly, an agrarian society. Notwithstanding agriculture's traditional role as the mainspring of rural social change, the non-agrarian character of the rural population today demands that other factors now need to be taken into account.

The ex-urban newcomers to the countryside are frequently represented as the harbingers of another important aspect of rural social change: the gradual assimilation of local, rural 'ways of life' into a nationally-based 'mass society' in which differences between rural and urban lifestyles are negligible. In the 1780s, according to this perception, village children sang traditional rhymes and danced around the maypole; but by the 1980s they were playing rock music and watching *Top of the Pops* like anyone else. Although on occasions this dangerously over-simplifies the degree of cultural homogeneity present in modern English society, it is nevertheless entirely valid to point out that there have been strong homogenizing influences: education, the welfare state, the mass media, the extension of public and private transport, etc. The extent to which 'rural England' still represents a distinctive and meaningful 'way of life' will also be an underlying theme in the following chapters.

4

In extending the historical scope of this book beyond that encompassed by *Green and Pleasant Land?*, the dangers inherent in trespassing across disciplinary boundaries have been of considerable concern. As a sociologist invading the preserves of social and agrarian historians, I admit to a certain professional nervousness. However, no disciplinary axe is being ground and this task has been undertaken with a well-developed sense of humility concerning the professional competence of the historian. A book of this kind inevitably involves some generalization, but there has been no desire to reduce the enterprise of history to a sub-species of sociology; indeed personal philosophical predilections tend towards the reverse. In any case this book is written for the general reader and not for the academic specialist. It therefore dispenses with the conventional academic etiquette of footnotes and citations, although due acknowledgement is made of the work of others in the section on Further Reading.

One final point: the reference to 'England' in this introduction is deliberate. Attention will be given to Wales, Scotland and Ireland where their experience is relevant to an understanding of English rural affairs. However, the social history of these nations is so complex, and in some cases so distinctive, that it cannot easily be assimilated into a history focused predominantly upon England. Thus, while English rural history cannot be considered entirely separately from that of Wales, Scotland and Ireland (or, for that matter, Canada, Australia and Argentina) it is not suggested that this book offers a systematic social history of these countries.

CHAPTER I

THE FIRST AGRICULTURAL REVOLUTION

By the middle of the eighteenth century English agriculture was well on the way to becoming a fully commercialized economic activity, organized and administered according to the needs of the market. This constituted a decisive change from the medieval economy which had been based largely upon farming for subsistence, and governed by tradition and custom rather than by the calculation of profit. The development of a capitalist agriculture was pivotal for the economy of England as a whole, since agriculture accounted for between 40 and 45 per cent of national income and, of course, it dominated the rural economy, despite the continued presence of much small-scale manufacture and handicraft. The growth of the system was unique in the world: rural England contained the first capitalist economy. While the 'English model' was never to be repeated elsewhere in its exact form, it did represent in a general sense a prototype – the economic system that had developed in rural England by the latter half of the eighteenth century was destined to become global in its extent.

Unfortunately any attempt to move beyond these very preliminary generalizations runs into a minefield of conflicting historical claims. Indeed to consider in any detail the course and causes of the transition from the feudal system of medieval agriculture to the capitalist farming economy which has developed down to the present day is to step into one of the most polemical of controversies in recent English historiography. The arguments revolve around two very different perspectives on this period, each of which has found its way into the popular conception of what is frequently referred to as the 'First Agricultural Revolution'. In the first perspective – popularized initially by the Hammonds and R. H. Tawney – emphasis is placed upon the disappearance of an independent peasantry, dispossessed by the legalized theft of enclosure and reduced to pauperism and destitution by the removal of their customary rights over common land. Rendered landless and poverty-stricken, they became factory fodder for the new industrial towns. The second perspective – to be found in the work of historians such as Kerridge and Mingay – emphasizes instead the technological innovations of this period. The eighteenth century was a century of agricultural 'improvement' characterized by new machines (Jethro Tull's seed drill), new methods of stock-breeding, new husbandry techniques ('Turnip' Townshend and the Norfolk four-course rotation) and new forms of estate management (including enclosure). It was a period of unprecedented entrepreneurial success, increases in productivity and yields sufficient to feed a growing urban population. Moreover, so far as the 'independent yeomanry' were concerned, the number of small farmers actually increased. Far from representing a social and cultural loss, the Agricultural Revolution was a period of burgeoning technological and economic advance.

Fortunately more recent historical research has demonstrated that each of these contrasting views is over-simplistic and, in many respects, positively misleading. In part, the differences stem from divergences of purpose and method. The more pessimistic interpretations of the period stress the unequal *distribution* of the benefits gained from commercialization, and emphasize the social and cultural dislocation which the rise of capitalism entailed. The more optimistic perspective stresses the *gross gains* in productivity which the new innovations provoked. The emphasis is placed upon necessary economic advance in order to achieve the modernization of medieval agriculture. The latter employs estate records and views agrarian change through the eyes of the 'improvers'; the former elaborates the view from the village rather than the estate, pays considerable attention to forms of social protest and develops a 'history from below'.

A further complicating factor concerns dates. Conventionally the Agricultural Revolution was placed between 1750 and 1815, but few historians would now be so restrictive. Further research into the commercialization of agriculture has pushed the onset of enclosure, new husbandry techniques and even the introduction of new implements back into the seventeenth and the latter part of the sixteenth centuries, while others have discovered elements of a peasantry as late as the last quarter of the nineteenth century. In part these are accounted for by local and regional variations in the pace and extent of the transition. But they also indicate that the changes were much more gradual than the term 'revolution' might suggest. Nevertheless, the significance of these changes was indeed revolutionary: once they had run their course English rural society had undergone a fundamental, qualitative and decisive break. For whatever the perspective that is taken on the Agricultural Revolution, and despite their differences, few historians would wish to deny its long-term significance.

A SOCIAL UPHEAVAL

What, then, was the Agricultural Revolution? And what was the nature of the transition which it represented? The first, and most important, point to make is that we are discussing the transition between two completely different types of society. It is not simply a question of the disappearance of the English peasantry, agricultural innovation, increases in productivity or even the growing influence of urban centres: it is a question of the whole social, economic and cultural basis upon which society was constituted. The medieval economy and society were different in kind from the aggressively capitalist system which supplanted it – and currently popular conceptions concerning the timeless continuity of rural life in the past should not be allowed to disguise this.

The origins of feudal society were militaristic rather than economic, but the lengthy period of absence of any foreign conquest ensured that a reasonably stable economic system was able to establish itself which was, to some extent, peculiar to Britain: the manorial system. In its purest form the manorial estate epitomized the society and economy of the feudal era. The economic basis was agriculture and if it was not entirely self-sufficient, then it was reasonably self-contained: feudal society was a conglomeration of *local* communities. The manor was also a unit of social and political authority and, whatever their origins in military protection and service, there is little doubt that by the late medieval period this authority stemmed from the functions and powers which attached to landownership.

In this respect the manorial estate consisted of two distinct parts. One part of the land was cultivated by the lord of the manor himself and was known as 'demesne', while the remainder was rented to tenants and was cultivated by them. The income of the landlord was thus partly derived from the produce of the demesne land and partly from the rents – either in kind, in the form of labour service on the lord's demesne, or, increasingly towards the end of the feudal period, in money – from his tenants. The proportion of demesne land to tenanted land was clearly important – and it varied enormously, with consequences for the precise balance of social forces in each locality. Moreover few manorial estates corresponded exactly to this 'pure' model and no one locality was 'typical'. There were similar complications relating to the composition of the field system which comprised the tenanted land. 'Open fields' consisted of unenclosed land subdivided into strips for cultivation by individuals and their families, according to their own requirements. 'Common fields' were similarly divided, but were managed and used according to communal practice and custom. Once more there were extreme variations in field systems from one locality to another. Nor was the system a static one: a gradual evolution of 'open' and 'common' field systems occurred throughout the medieval period in response to a number of factors connected with fluctuations in population, patterns of inheritance, changes in society and the accessibility of markets for disposing of the surplus over and above subsistence needs. Beyond direct manorial control there also existed the highly significant amounts of common land (not to be confused with common fields), marginal land and land not yet colonized, which were an important resource – often through common rights over grazing, turf-cutting, firewood, etc. – for the sizeable number of smallholders and labourers constantly living on the margins of subsistence.

The presence of common fields and common rights signifies the importance and – in theory at least – the legal force of customary practice. Such communal customs were regulated not merely through the institutions of the manorial estate, but through the village, the inhabitants of which forged an alternative set of ties, rights and obligations. If the manor represented one essential reference point in the medieval economy and society, then the village represented the other. Villages, like manors, varied enormously in their social structure and composition from one area to another. Equally significantly the relationship *between* the manor and the village was also highly variable. The distinguished medieval historian M. M. Postan has characterized the feudal village as follows:

The most obvious characteristic of the village was its topography. It was a collective, i.e. grouped settlement; and the form of grouping most characteristic of the medieval countryside was that of a 'nucleated' village consisting of a cluster of households round a natural centre, topographical or economic – a well, a pond, a village green – which would also include or be contiguous with the site of the village church. . . . The inhabitants of a typical village formed a village community collectively administered and possessing formal and informal bodies, courts, assemblies, 'chests' and guilds, which issued and administered the rules of husbandry, watched over local customs of tenure and inheritance, and enforced local peace and order.

This model is something of an historical abstraction, but villages of this type could certainly be found all over medieval England. The most important variation was a result of topography and village layout and here there was a significant divergence between the nucleated villages of the arable (i.e. crop-growing) areas and the more scattered hamlets and farmsteads of the pastoral (i.e. stock-rearing) areas. This distinction is one which will run throughout this book and is at least one element of visible continuity between the medieval and the modern rural world.

The relationship between the village and the manor was, then, by no means a uniform one. Some manors embraced more than one village; some villages, on the other hand, contained the holdings of several manors, even entire manors. Consequently the extent to which it was the village or the manor which controlled the local economic and social life varied quite widely. And this in turn had important repercussions for the villagers, since it affected the balance between serfdom and freedom in their everyday lives. From the thirteenth century onwards, the evidence suggests that, whatever the position in legal theory, it was the economic standing of the villager – the size of his holding and the income it yielded – which was more salient than his or her legal status. Particularly towards the end of the medieval period, growing economic differentiation was more important than progress towards the universal manumission of serfdom.

The system of agrarian capitalism which eventually emerged from the medieval feudal order differed in almost every important respect. The processes of consumption were separated from those of production, with an opaque, complex, but nevertheless identifiable set of impersonal 'market forces' linking the two together. What accounted for the nature of production was not the subsistence needs of the producers but calculations of profitability.

The inputs into the productive process – land, labour, fixed and working capital – also become commodities, bought and sold under conditions of market competition and according to a calculation of profitable return. Such changes not only involve the creation of conditions of profitable production – access to markets, ease of transport, continual advances in productivity and cost-efficiency – but the creation of new *social* arrangements which facilitate these. In much of Britain this meant that (in the classic form) the capitalist farmer leased land from a landowner and employed landless labourers, hired on a contractual basis, to work it. These three groups (which became known in the latter half of the eighteenth century as 'classes') regulated their relationship not according to traditionally-defined customs, rights and obligations, but according to contractual negotiations conducted by formally free individuals, with outcomes based upon the balance of market conditions.

From the medieval manorial system there emerged the new commercial landed estates. The function of the landowner was that of estate management, rather than husbandry – the creation of those conditions which would enhance the prospects of profitable farming, and thereby his rental income. As *The Economist* was to put it trenchantly in 1857:

The business of a landowner – the management of land as property in the best manner – is something quite distinct from farming. It consists in rendering the land attractive to the best class of farmers, the men of skill and capital, by means of permanent outlays combined with conditions of lettings which are consistent with profitable farming.

Tenant farmers were the true entrepreneurs, for, as *The Economist* clearly recognized, it was they who controlled the productive unit of capitalist enterprise: the farm. Their skill lay in the provision of capital and the management and supervision of labour. As a succession of continental visitors who came to England to learn from the 'improvements' of the eighteenth century were to recognize with astonishment, this 'best class' of farmers did not work. Manual labour was a matter exclusively for the farm labourers, some hired by the day, others on an annual basis, but all supporting themselves by the power of their labour in return for a wage.

At each level of society the moral rights and legal obligations of the feudal system had been pared down to the impersonally economic. This removed from the village community the customary control over the regulation of traditional rights. However, the village remained an important centre of opposition to the economic changes which were taking place. Social protest could act as a temporary brake on change, but much depended upon its relationship with the local estate. Villages which remained under the effective control of the local landlord became known as 'closed' villages, where the size of settlement and the construction of cottages was carefully regulated in order to avoid the possible burden of paupers (see Chapters 2 and 4). 'Open' villages, on the other hand, were under the control of no single landowner and acted as a reservoir for casual labour for the surrounding farms. In the nature of things they were much more likely to be centres of resistance and social protest – many of them notoriously so – but they were also frequently slum villages of the worst kind, where the effects of pauperization of large numbers of the rural working population were readily to be seen. By the early nineteenth century the village population – whether in 'open' or 'closed' villages – had become primarily a proletarian one. In this respect the villager was little removed from the status of the urban dweller, whose numbers were growing so rapidly during this period.

In the broadest sense the 'First Agricultural Revolution' merely marks the transition between these two kinds of rural economy and society. However, the precise nature of the processes which underlay this transition – their causes, timing and extent – is that which has created greater controversy and which still needs to be examined in detail. It is convenient to consider this in three parts: (1) the emergence of a fully commercialized estate system; (2) the process of enclosure; and (3) the management and technology of the farming enterprise.

ESTATE MANAGEMENT: LANDSCAPES AND FIGURES

I have already mentioned that, until fairly recently, the conventional view of the Agricultural Revolution has associated it with the new technology introduced by eighteenth-century landowners such as Coke of Holkham and Townshend of Raynham. Perhaps as a result of this, the convention has since swung towards the opposing view: that the role of the 'improving' landlords was a minor one compared with the more mundane improvements in husbandry technique undertaken by a multitude of commercial farmers. Now it is common for historians once more to acknowledge the importance of 'improvement', including the role of landlords in estate reorganization, but at the same time to emphasize their much broader role in creating a set of conditions beneficial to the new farming economy. In other words, the crucial role of the landowner was in estate management rather than in the introduction of new techniques of production. The landlord who 'improved' his estate during the eighteenth century therefore played a crucial role in the transformation of rural England, but it was not limited to such matters as crop rotations and new breeds of stock.

At the heart of the changes in estate management which occurred during the transition to the new agrarian economy lay an essential change in the access to, and rights over, property. In feudal law these property rights were extremely complex and usually incompatible with the emerging capitalist economy. In order that landed property should be freed from the encumbrance of customary rights and obligations which characterized it in the Middle Ages, there had to be new capitalist definitions of property rights. What this involved, from the seventeenth century onwards, was a definition of property which today we take for granted: landed property became a thing, a discrete physical commodity, which could be bought and sold like any other commodity and was freed of any social obligations which had hitherto rested upon its ownership. During the feudal period the law had specified rights and obligations that were attached to landed property; now these were entirely stripped away and the law merely defined the process whereby the ownership of land (i.e. title) could be claimed. What the owner *did* with the landed property once the legal process of acquisition had been completed was now up to him; the law remained silent. Thus an owner was entirely free to clear, hedge, fence, sub-divide or sell land, without reference to *any* social obligations, customs or traditional rights. Moreover the acquisition of ownership now granted *exclusive* rights of access to the land. Customary rights of access for such matters as gleaning, grazing, the gathering of fuel or the killing of game were proscribed. Thus emerged that most familiar of contemporary threats: 'Trespassers Will Be Prosecuted'.

The modern mind, which is so accustomed to a particular definition of property for it to be 'obvious', can find it difficult to grasp what this change of property rights entailed and why it was so significant. Hitherto the land had not been merely a 'thing' to be bought and sold like any other commodity, nor could it be separated from a network of social and economic relationships that surrounded it: land was, indeed, these relationships as much as the physical commodity itself. Thus when rights over land were changed, the social and economic consequences were far-reaching. Once the legal framework of property rights had been altered – which it was after the Civil War and particularly after 1688 – then the pace of 'improvement' was largely influenced by the dictates of the landowners on the one hand and the strength of popular resistance on the other. As the eighteenth century progressed, so this conflict deepened, often reflected in the widening gap between what the law allowed and what local custom and practice determined. As will become clearer in the discussion of enclosure in the following section, what was abrogated was rarely, therefore, the *legal* rights of the peasantry, but the *customary practice* embedded in the social fabric of the local community. E. P. Thompson, in a discussion of eighteenth-century property rights, summarizes these points by noting that:

. . . it is not helpful to discuss inheritance systems unless we keep always in mind what it is that is being inherited. . . . What [the farmer] inherited was a place within a hierarchy of use-rights; the rights to send his beasts, with a follower, down the lane-sides, to tether his horse in the sykes or on the baulks, the right to unloose his stock for lammas grazing, or for the cottager the right to glean and to get away with some timber-foraging and casual grazing. All this made up into a delicate agrarian equilibrium. It depended not only upon the inherited right but also upon the inherited grid of customs and controls within which that right was exercised.

It follows from this that different groups in English rural society at this time were concerned about different aspects of customary property rights and were anxious to change – or not to change – them in different ways. For example, the landowners themselves were not unduly worried by the kinds of factors listed by Thompson above. What concerned them was that land, having been transformed into a form of economic capital, could be accumulated in a well-regulated manner and could be transmitted intact from one generation to the next. This too needs to be stressed, for the landowner was also embedded within an 'inherited grid of customs and controls' which in this case consisted of the family. It was the landowning *family* which was the relevant economic unit in the control of estates and for which suitable mechanisms of inheritance and accumulation had therefore to be arranged. Two essential legal mechanisms emerged in the seventeenth century which facilitated this: the strict settlement and the mortgage, which allowed the widespread changes in estate management for which the eighteenth century is noted. Under the terms of strict settlement, the control of inheritance of landed property was placed in the hands of trustees, guaranteeing the descent of property to unborn heirs and limiting the role of the eldest son to that of life-tenant. This enabled other relatives excluded from direct inheritance of the estate to obtain incomes for themselves, and also prevented the heir from selling off parts of the estate in order to meet current expenditure. All that then remained was to arrange propitious marriages with the object of accumulating more land and/or wealth. In the transactions which surrounded the marriage contract, future wives brought with them a dowry and were in return assigned a portion of the estate so that they should have some security should their husbands predecease them. The financing of such transactions could only function effectively given a market for mortgages – and *this* could only function under the stable and predictable conditions which strict settlement guaranteed. Mortgages also became important in providing access to secure credit and as a means of further financing the expansion and consolidation of the estate's holdings.

The conditions which surrounded the commercialization and expansion of the landed estates during the eighteenth century thus represented a combination of legal, social and economic factors, rather than any one of these in isolation. By the end of the eighteenth century, as Keith Tribe has pointed out:

. . . capitalist tenant farmers dominated English agriculture, not because the tenancy system represented the most efficient and progressive contemporary framework for the development of agriculture, but as a consequence of a social and political system which led to the concentration of blocks of land in the hands of a few landowners who both lived in the countryside and depended on farming rents for their income. This stimulated an interest on the part of the landlord in having 'good' tenants. . . .

Good tenants became a favoured category – courted when leases were renewed and aided during times of recession – and these tenants themselves expanded and flourished through a mixture of commercial acumen and judicious marriage. The contribution of the landlord was to provide the conditions under which they could prosper rather than by direct capital investment.

However, while the basis of the landed estate was its economic viability, it was never *merely* a commercial unit. It was also a political and administrative centre, a status symbol, the embodiment of a family lineage and – most directly and visibly – an artistic creation. Hand-in-hand with the commercial reorganization of the estate went the remodelling of the Big House, its gardens and surrounding parkland. Despite the drain on available resources that this represented, there were few landowners who did not recognize that the house and its surrounding acres symbolized and immortalized the standing and the accomplishments of the family which laid claim to it. Calculations of social prestige and political influence demanded an imposing physical presence in the countryside. Furthermore, a conspicuous display of 'good taste' was a necessary accoutrement to the calculations of profit and loss. From these sentiments sprang one of the indisputably great English contributions to Western art and aesthetics – eighteenth-century landscape architecture. The estate was reorganized in order to provide a flourishing commercial enterprise; but it was also reorganized in order to reflect prevailing aesthetic judgements.

The 'improving' landowner set about creating landscapes which conformed to a formal set of compositional rules, known as the 'picturesque', which were represented in the works of eighteenth-century Romantic artists such as Claude and Poussin. To display a correct knowledge of these rules, and thus a correct taste in landscape, became a valuable social accomplishment. Thus the eighteenth-century landowner, through the agency of his hired landscapers, fashioned 'pleasing prospects' which conformed to patterns of composition which hitherto only a landscape painter would have used on his canvas. Nature having thus been rearranged, a working countryside had a picturesque order imposed upon it, whereby fields, hedgerows, trees, even complete villages, were cleared in order to provide a 'pleasing prospect' from window or terrace. Landscape architects like William Kent, Lancelot ('Capability') Brown and Humphry Repton changed actual landscapes into pictures instead of painting landscapes on canvas. Their creations were to give the English landed estate a significance in the history of art which its commercial activities were to grant it in the development of agrarian capitalism.

This distinction between aesthetics and commerce was itself a division which the new landscape architecture reinforced. The eighteenth century thus provided a decisive break between ideas about nature and beauty on the one hand and a functional countryside on the other – a divergence which has remained until the present day. Agriculture and the making of money became an *intrusion* into the picturesque composition and so was banished beyond the park boundary or hidden away behind newly planted belts of trees or artificially constructed mounds and knolls. The landscape artists who

were responsible for this separation understood these principles very well. Repton, for example, in his manual,
Observations on the Theory and Practice of Landscape Gardening,
was adamant that 'the beauty of pleasure-ground, and the
profit of a farm, are incompatible. . . . I disclaim all idea of
making that which is most beautiful also most profitable: a
ploughed field and a field of grass are as distinct objects as a
flower-garden and a potato-ground.' Repton and his fellow
architects established and then disseminated these principles in
the many thousands of acres which they remodelled for the
newly commercialized estate owners. Profitability and beauty
were thus separated and the new commercial rural economy
was not allowed to disfigure the pleasing prospects of those
who ultimately benefited from it. Again Repton expressed
this sentiment succinctly: 'The difficulty of uniting a park and
a farm arises from this material circumstance, that the one is an
object of beauty, the other of profit.' Or, as William Gilpin,
the eighteenth-century observer of English rural life, put it:
'Land which is merely fertile is a barren prospect.'

Once the principles of Brown and Repton were established,
through such masterpieces as Chatsworth in Derbyshire
(Brown) and Stourhead in Wiltshire (Repton), then hundreds
of estates up and down the country were transformed by the
leading landscape architects of the eighteenth century, their
followers and imitators. Selected aspects of the farming
economy were only readmitted as rustic embellishments to
enliven an otherwise sterile scene – landscape furniture such as
grazing animals (at a distance) or a vertical dimension to offset
undulating horizontal contours, such as the smoke rising from
a 'picturesque' cottage. People were allowed in only as 'figures
in a landscape', including locally-recruited 'hermits' to inhabit
purpose-built classical 'ruins' and grottoes.

It is one of the ironies of the 'picturesque' movement in
landscape design that it represented a rejection of the earlier
formality of the Tudor period and embraced the desire to
create a more 'natural' landscape. Of course, nothing could be
less 'natural' than the artificial lakes, dammed and diverted
rivers and streams, newly-planted woodland, excavated

'ha-has' and resited villages and farmsteads which created this landscape. In imposing their aesthetic tastes on the remainder of rural society in this way the 'improving' landowners were expressing not merely a confidence in their own judgements, but their ability to impose a new social and economic order on the locality within their jurisdiction. In other words the imposing beauty of the English country house and its surrounding park also symbolized an enduring social dominance.

ENCLOSURE

It was not only around the house that 'improving' landowners were busily reorganizing the landscape. Beyond the park boundary the agricultural landscape was also being recast by transforming the scattered strips of the open field system into contiguous fields, enclosed by hedges, fences or walls, and grouped together into discrete farms. Ostensibly enclosure was no more than this – a regrouping of holdings which allowed a more efficient use of land and capital. In fact the process of enclosure symbolized much more, being as it was in most cases a measure of the new commercial farming economy. The process of enclosure thus went hand-in-hand with the social and economic changes which characterized the new capitalist system. It was much more than the rearrangement of field systems.

There has been much dispute about the precise timing of the enclosure movement, but it is now generally accepted that it was a continuous process beginning in the late sixteenth century and ending in the early nineteenth century. The means by which enclosure took place varied a great deal through time and according to the area and type of land involved. Much, though by no means all, was effected by Act of Parliament or through the courts, but some was also carried out by agreement with varying degrees of voluntary co-operation. The earlier enclosures, in particular, were carried out by agreement, often so that arable land could be better cultivated.

But the earlier period of enclosure, especially during the sixteenth century, was also undertaken in order to create sheep walks, and this was responsible for a great deal of depopulation. Enclosure during the eighteenth century, on the other hand, was largely effected through Act of Parliament, and was a direct response to rising corn prices and the associated commercial opportunities. During this later period it is often difficult to assess the precise contribution of enclosure, as opposed to other elements of agrarian change, in the marginalization of many small producers and the growing ascendency of the large farmers.

As I have already shown, enclosure was not a simple reorganization of holdings and landscape. Nor was it only open and common fields that were enclosed, but also common land, permanent meadows and waste. The repercussions which this had on the local community have been summarized by the historian Joan Thirsk:

To enclose land was to extinguish common rights over it, thus putting an end to all common grazing. To effect this, it was usual for the encloser to hedge or fence the land. Thus in contemporary controversy anger was directed mainly at the hedges and fences – the outward and visible signs of enclosure. To make it economically worthwhile, enclosure was often preceded by the amalgamation of several strips by exchange or purchase. If the enclosed land lay in the common arable fields or in the meadows, the encloser now had complete freedom to do what he pleased with his land throughout the year, instead of having to surrender the stubble or aftermath after harvest to the use of the whole township. On the pasture commons, enclosure by an individual signified the appropriation to one person of land which had previously been at the disposal of the whole community throughout the year. All enclosures, then, whether they concerned land in the common fields, in the meadows, or in the common pastures, deprived the community of common rights.

While the effects of these changes were severe, as far as the least privileged members of the community were concerned, the contention that enclosure was *directly* responsible for the eviction of the peasantry and other small farmers is now discredited. The peasantry did indeed disappear, but the

processes which led to its disappearance were not as straightforward as this. To begin with, there is the awkward fact that
the number of small farmers actually *increased* during the
eighteenth century, and although this requires careful
interpretation, it is hardly compatible with the view that
enclosure was part of a consciously directed programme of
peasant expropriation. Modern accounts emphasize the ways
in which peasant proprietors struggled to adapt to market
conditions and were most often bought out by the 'improving' landlords. Other factors also slowly eroded their commercial position. Economies of scale, especially in the arable
counties, could be significant and the larger producers were
also able to withstand bad seasons and periods of poor prices.
In some ways the process was not unlike that which occurs
today: the larger producers flourished and expanded at the
expense of the small cultivators. Those small proprietors who
survived did so by adapting to the changed circumstances: by
becoming part-time farmers, by specializing in forms of
husbandry where small size was not a constraint, etc. In other
words, they survived by adapting to the changing market
conditions and this rendered them a very different *kind* of
small farmer to the medieval peasant. Not only were the
remaining small farmers qualitatively different, but their
significance in the agrarian economy had also changed. By the
end of the eighteenth century the number of small farmers
may have increased, but their contribution to overall production was increasingly insignificant. English agriculture
was passing – as far as the quantity and value of production
were concerned – into the hands of large tenant farmers with
their aggressively entrepreneurial attitude towards the development of capital.

Modern historiography thus tends to place enclosure alongside a number of managerial, technological and organizational
changes, each of which contributed to the development of
agrarian capitalism in England. The new commercial conditions favoured the consolidation and amalgamation of
farms, and thus a long-term tendency towards larger units of
production. Enclosure hastened this process, but was often as

much a symptom as a cause. Changes in estate management ensured that these larger farms were tenanted, while those taken over were frequently freeholders: thus differential rates of attrition contributed to the newly emerging agrarian class structure. This complex and gradual process can be summed up by quoting from the agricultural historian, E. L. Jones:

> Nevertheless, the small farmer was neither swept away by enclosure nor entirely bought out of existence by the bigger landowners. The growth of population from the mid-eighteenth century actually increased the demand for small farms, which (since quite high rents were offered) it often paid to satisfy. Very large and very small tenanted holdings may have been increasing at the expense of the intermediate range. At the upper end of the scale the amalgamation of farms into larger units operated by a smaller number of more capable tenants was not, however, always accompanied by the thorough consolidation of their newly enclosed fields. The process of building larger farm units and bringing them within ring fences was being accomplished by the buying-out of small freeholders, by private exchanges and by enclosure. Since larger enclosed farms were more progressive technically the drift was advantageous. Yet it was slow. It has not always reached its goals today.

So much for the economic significance of enclosure; a much more difficult issue to assess, however, is what enclosure *meant* for the bulk of the rural population. It is by now apparent that enclosure was part of a more general tendency towards the economic and social marginalization of the small cultivators in English rural society. The vulnerability to pauperization of many of the rural population was strikingly increased by these trends, particularly as those who were below the level of self-sufficiency were exposed increasingly to the vagaries of the market for food, rather than being able to rely upon ostensibly trivial, but actually crucial, rights to some patch of common or waste land. If nothing else, enclosure destroyed a myth of independence which occasionally compensated for economic misery and social subjection. It left the propertyless labourer starkly aware of his lack of real political rights and his actual poverty. Certainly the folk memory of the old village community could no longer be sustained. Instead of mutual aid and a general recognition of rights and obligations, there was now a society governed by the impersonal calculation of profit and loss. Enclosure could not be said to have caused this, but it was its most tangible and observable manifestation. The hand which directed the new market economy was hidden; but that which directed the process of enclosure was only too visible.

FARMING IMPROVEMENTS

I have already shown that the conventional view of an abrupt technological revolution having occurred during the second half of the eighteenth century is no longer compatible with the findings of recent historical research. The pace of agrarian change certainly quickened during this period, but the processes involved were both more complex and less tangible than the now discarded version would allow. To some extent an earlier generation of historians were influenced by the propaganda of the late eighteenth-century publicists of the progressive husbandry techniques. The most famous of these was Arthur Young, whose series of county reports on the state of agriculture and whose tireless proselytizing of innovative methods of agricultural improvement did much to spread information among the more enterprising farmers of the period. Young, like many effective journalists, often sought an 'angle' in order to interest his readers. By associating husbandry techniques with particular individuals he was able to create 'human interest' and thereby increase the effectiveness of his propaganda. Beneficial husbandry regimes – such as the Norfolk four-course rotation of wheat/turnips/barley/ clover – were associated with individual farmers ('Turnip' Townshend), while in other cases legitimate commercial interest was abetted by persistent self-publicity – as in the case of Robert Bakewell's renowned stock-breeding methods. In this context, associating an 'agricultural revolution' with these individuals became a retrospective collaboration in what was sometimes self-aggrandizing publicity.

Many of the most significant innovations during this period were in fact more mundane and perforce anonymous. Before turnips became popular as a field crop, the supply of fodder had been greatly improved by the first widespread cultivation of clover, sainfoin and rye grass and the development of irrigating pasture adjacent to streams and rivers – and so-called 'floating' meadows. Innovations of this kind spread at a fairly sedate pace from the mid-seventeenth century onwards, and by the mid-eighteenth century were already employed across considerable areas of the country. These techniques were diffused less through the didactic literature epitomized by Young, than through the pragmatic example of progressive landlords and their more enterprising – usually larger – tenant farmers. Though less eye-catching than the innovations for which the eighteenth century is now best remembered, these techniques were frequently decisive in increasing yields and output, thus contributing to the prosperity of those who employed them.

In the encouragement of these techniques, responsive and adaptable estate management became essential. Improvements in farm accounts and new methods of book-keeping allowed a more rational administration of estate practice to be undertaken. Alongside the progressive landowner there was therefore created an apparatus of efficient estate management whose smooth and profitable running was in the day-to-day hands of an agent. The estate agent symbolized the period of agricultural 'improvement' as much as the better-known innovators. For the rise of a commercial agrarian system brought with it the rudiments of modern cost-accounting management. Although ultimate authority was vested in the landowner, typically it was the agent who was delegated to deal with drawing up leases and tenancy agreements, ensuring that they were observed, collecting rents, supervising the home farm, keeping accounts and ensuring the payment of wages, taxes, tithes, rates, etc. With the development of capitalist farming by the tenants of landed estates, administration not only emerged as a separate – and frequently complex – function, but a recognizable professional stratum emerged in order to perform it. Thus a complex structure of managerial authority was being created whereby the estate itself was managed by professional administrators, while individual farms were frequently managed by tenants who rarely involved themselves in any manual labour.

The landlord and his agent attempted to pursue an economically rational system of administration by obtaining the maximum rent from the most progressive tenants and by arranging tenancies in such a fashion as to encourage the most profitable production by farmers. Tenant farmers were, if anything, more directly profit-conscious, with the larger tenant farmers, as we have seen, making the running both economically and technologically. As Hobsbawn and Rudé have indicated in their appraisal of English agriculture at the end of the eighteenth century, the large tenant farmer:

... played a disproportionately large part in farming, and he was the man the visiting foreign experts had in mind when they talked about the novelty and progress of English farming. From the labourers' point of view he was a remote – an increasingly remote – boss. For, as overseas observers noted with amazement, used as they were to European peasants and American working farmers, *he did not work*. 'They rarely do any personal labour whatsoever', said that knowledgeable reporter of comparative agriculture, Henry Colman. They supervised and gave the proverbial pig the proverbial prod while leaning over the proverbial gate. Economically their importance was capital.

Thus an important criterion of the ideal farm was its optimal size in terms of managerial and supervisory efficiency as much as economies which might be derived from the system of husbandry *per se*. This in turn had repercussions on the desired configuration of holdings on an estate – for example, the desire for consolidated rather than dispersed holdings – and the design and layout of the farmyard and farmstead, which frequently were constructed in a manner that afforded as good a view of the working of the farm as possible.

Efficient management could not proceed adequately without the proper keeping of accurate records and accounts – if only in order to calculate the limits permissible to the rent negotiated with the landlord's agent. Arthur Young helpfully explained the purpose of this exercise in his *Rural Oeconomy and Farmer's Kalender*, published in 1770:

The grand object is to keep a ledger, or account for every article in the farm; in which an account should be opened for every field in the farm, or at least for every arable field, and one for all the grass. The farmer should in this book directly without the intervention of a waste-book or a journal, enter all his expenses; but, for doing this, he must take the trouble of dividing his rent to every field, so that the account may be complete, and not have an article for rent alone, unless it be a mere memorandum; and, before he balances his books at the end of the year, it is necessary for him first to cast up the sundry accounts, such as tythe – poor levy – various expenses – and divide them in the same manner as rent.

Such careful, methodical calculation would have been incomprehensible to the medieval peasant, who was primarily supporting a household, rather than running a business concern. Even amongst the commercial farmers, few probably lived up to Young's ideal, for the poor quality of farm accounts has remained a persistent complaint of critics from that day to this. Nevertheless, Young's model was one to which the progressive tenant could aspire, and sufficient farmers were sufficiently attuned to the necessity of keeping accounts to allow comparisons of profitability to be monitored. It enabled them to establish a system of capitalist farming in which various factors of production could be costed, calculated and organized, according to the most effective and efficient means of making a profit.

By the end of the eighteenth century, England had come to possess an agriculture which was self-consciously innovative, progressive and attuned to the needs of the growing market in food commodities. Uniquely in the 'civilized' world, the peasantry had all but disappeared. Taking the longer view we can see that this was, indeed, a revolutionary process. It may now be conceded that it was neither as sudden nor as straightforward as has sometimes been assumed, but its historical significance cannot be over-emphasized. The agricultural revolution of the eighteenth century was not only a matter of new husbandry techniques, but also of social reorganization. A new class structure emerged; relations between these classes were conducted on a new basis; rural society was effectively reconstituted. The transition was not, however, smooth. Resistance and protest, though ultimately impotent, regulated the pace of change. This was particularly the case in the early nineteenth century, when widespread and concerted attempts were made, perhaps too late, to enforce the customary rights and obligations of a now obsolete social order.

CHAPTER 2

POOR LAWS AND CORN LAWS

By the end of the eighteenth century the widespread effects of
the Agricultural Revolution were becoming clearly discernible. Output and productivity had increased dramatically and
had enabled the expanding commercialized farming sector to
supply the burgeoning urban market and to feed an overall
population which grew by 50 per cent in the latter half of the
century alone. But the benefits were distributed very
unevenly. Improving landlords and their aggressively commercial tenants prospered. Small farmers, though they increased in number, found themselves comparatively disad-
vantaged. The farm labourer fared worst of all. His standard
of living declined after the 1760s, as the surplus rural
population depressed wage rates and enclosure removed most
of his customary rights. His wife, too, was less able to
supplement his wages from domestic handicraft and manufacture as the new industrial system gained a foothold.
Unemployment, underemployment and pauperism became a
way of life for many rural working-class families.

These difficulties were made worse by the rise in food prices
over the same period. As agriculture moved from a subsistence to a commercial basis, so the *price* of food became a
matter of concern to the rural, as well as the urban, working
population. Although perquisites of various kinds were still
available, the growing specialization of agriculture, new
forms of technology and the loss of traditional rights meant
that it was the cash-wage economy which mattered most.
Purchases of bread, which had accounted for 44 per cent of
total family expenditure in the 1760s, constituted 60 per cent

by 1790. Bread prices began to assume a totemic political significance and during the next thirty years were to be an important causal factor in rural social unrest. The irony was that the rural working population, still overwhelmingly engaged in the production of food, was as dependent upon the impersonal mechanisms of the market in regulating what it could or could not afford, as the urban, industrial population which had no involvement in agriculture whatsoever.

This was also the period of the Revolutionary and Napoleonic Wars. From 1793 to 1815 Britain was effectively cut off from continental supplies of grain, which, from the 1770s onwards, had been used to supplement home-grown produce. The distortions which the wartime economy engendered were, moreover, continued into the post-war aftermath. As far as the structure of rural society was concerned, the result was a culmination – and to some extent an acceleration – of the prevailing trends of the latter half of the eighteenth century. Equally, it is possible to look forward and note that the ramifications of continental war on the rural economy at home during this period provide a foretaste of not entirely dissimilar trends in 1914 and 1939. History was not to repeat itself, nevertheless the impact of war on rural England reveals a number of continuities which cannot be put down to mere coincidence.

UNMERRIE RUSTICS

The immediate impact of war was one which is quite familiar to twentieth-century observers: prices went up. The grain shortage brought about by disruptions in continental supplies were compounded by bad harvests at home. The price of a loaf, which had fluctuated between 6d and 8d between 1765 and 1794, doubled in price during 1795 alone, reached 1s 3¼d in 1801 and 1s 5d by 1812. To workers dependent upon cash wages, these increases were devastating. Various attempts were made to contain the situation, including the offer of bounties on imported grain, prohibitions on the use of grain for distilling and encouraging the consumption of potatoes, but the effect was at best marginal. The response of the poor and the newly-impoverished was emphatic: they rioted. Unable to buy, they had little to lose in attempting to seize supplies by force. For those in authority food riots became a hazard of contemporary life, a sensitive barometer of fluctuating grain prices and a threat to established order in a number of localities.

Sporadic rioting also represented an attempt to reassert the precepts of the old 'moral economy' of the medieval world – to fix a 'fair price' at which produce was to be sold. By the beginning of the nineteenth century, however, such a moral economy was already an anachronism and prices were regulated by market conditions alone. In recognition of this, many of the riots were aimed at influencing market conditions – to intimidate farmers and millers, for example, to bring more of their stocks of grain on to the market, or to interrupt the movement of grain around the country. In general the outbreaks of unrest were spontaneous and mercurial. There is little evidence of any lasting organization beyond the ability to write anonymous letters or placards threatening the locally rich and powerful with violence and arson. Few overtly political demands were made, and the riots – which were always localized and sporadic – never cohered into any organized movement. Nevertheless, the propensity to riot was by no means ineffective as a regulator of prices, at least in the short-term. Riots occasionally established, albeit temporarily, an informal scale of minimum prices to be charged in local markets, and by the summer of 1795 the resistance to the movement of foodstuffs around the country had become so severe that Parliament agreed to compensate farmers for losses up to £100. At the local level, however, landowners and magistrates were not always unsympathetic – in some cases compelling farmers to bring their surplus stock on to the market. On the other hand, those engaged in rioting were concerned only to establish a fair price, not to overturn the economic system, effect political revolution or engage in theft for its own sake. Even when in control the mob rarely turned to looting, preferring instead to organize their own sales and distribution and turn over the proceeds to the owners.

The immediate demand of the rioters was therefore 'bread or blood'. The riot was a form of pre-political collective bargaining aimed at mitigating the impoverishment brought about by rising food prices. Just beneath the surface, however, was the demand for equity and justice, the attempt to reassert the traditional obligations expected of those in positions of power and influence. In this sense the riots were, literally, reactionary, expressing a desire to go back to the rural society based on custom and tradition that was by now obsolete. Underlying the immediate causes of unrest – rising food prices and a falling standard of living – there was, then, a series of factors brought about by the changing nature of rural society itself. Many of the rural poor were only too aware of these changes – and did not like what they saw. The only alternative of which they could conceive was a way of life which had existed before these changes had taken place, often elevated by a powerful sense of nostalgia into a somewhat mythical pre-capitalist 'Golden Age'. A merrie England composed of happy beef-eating rustics may have had little basis in fact, but it was a fiction with sufficient influence to act as a rallying point for rural protest throughout the period. It found literary expression in the poetry of Clare, Goldsmith and Crabbe, and its apotheosis in the observations of the most influential writer of them all: William Cobbett. At the heart of all this protest was the recognition that social relations between the component classes of rural society had been transformed. No longer were they regulated by tradition and custom, nor even a benevolent sense of social obligation, but by the impersonal, and increasingly harsh, reality of the market.

The clearest indication of this involved the decline of farm service. Until the beginning of the nineteenth century the hired agricultural labour force had been divided into two groups: 'labourers', hired usually by the day or by the week, and 'servants', hired by the year. Farm servants not only enjoyed greater security, but they mostly 'lived in' the farmer's household, eating meals alongside the farmer and his family and thereby receiving their wages largely in kind, rather than in cash. Although such close proximity could have its drawbacks – most notably the extent to which farm servants were always at the beck and call of the farmer – their lives were closely intertwined to that of the employer and his family. Most significantly, farmer and farm servant both worked together and ate together. Farm servants were hired annually at hiring fairs, themselves one of the great festivities of the rural calendar and the pretext for a good deal of celebrating with varying degrees of sobriety. Once the hiring was agreed the farm servant could rely upon board and lodging for the year and to participate in the daily life of the farming household. Socially such a pattern of hire fitted best with a society in which distinctions of wealth and status between employer and employee were not very great; economically it fitted best when prices for farm products were low, stable or declining, rather than high and rising, and where casual labour was in short supply. All of these conditions were affected by developments in the latter half of the eighteenth century. The experience of war and its immediate aftermath supplied the *coup de grace* to the system of farm service.

The emergence of a chronic surplus of population in the countryside depressed wages and undermined the traditional labour relations of farmers and farm servants. Quite simply, it became much cheaper to hire labour on a cash-wage basis than to underwrite the cost of their board and lodging. The distortions introduced by the wartime economy encouraged the substitution of labourers for servants. Not only were wages depressed, but prices of foodstuffs were rising. Furthermore, as grain prices rose, so farmers were encouraged to extend their tillage and specialize in cereals production. Across the south and east of England, land disappeared under the plough at an unprecedented rate. This in turn altered the labour requirements of the arable farms, for cereals production minimizes the need for year-round labour and maximizes the peaks of labour demand at seed-time and harvest. Labour thus became casual, and the farm servant turned into the day-labourer who was paid in cash rather than kind and thus faced the unnerving prospect of inflationary food prices. As Cobbett was to observe: 'Why do not farmers now feed and lodge their workpeople, as they did formerly? Because they cannot keep them upon so little as they give them in wages. This is the real cause of the change.' Following the Agricultural Revolution there could be few farmers unable to make the necessary calculations. During the wartime period, failure to make these changes would have been positively irrational.

At the same time there were social reasons for these changes. As farmers prospered during the wartime economy on the basis of rising grain prices, so an increasing gulf opened up in the standard of living of the farmer and his workers. Inevitably this had social repercussions. The standing of the progressive tenant farmer was rising in rural society. It was not only grain prices that were inflating – so was the farmer's own estimation of his status. This quickly expressed itself in that most primordial of taboos, the desire not to break bread at the same table as those to whom might attach some social stigma. From being intertwined, the lives of farmer and labourer became differentiated. Fewer farmers worked alongside their labourers and those that did so worked less often. Farmers and workers no longer ate and lived together. Their relationship, which had never been equal but which had been close and personal, was now reduced to a simple cash-nexus – the payment of an increasingly inadequate wage. Labourers were no longer people but 'hands'. Farmers no longer espoused a paternalistic concern for their well-being but were content effectively to pauperize them. The instrument selected to carry out this task was the Poor Law.

SPEENHAMLAND AND AFTER

For centuries the Poor Law had been an integral part of the way in which social class relationships in the countryside were administered. Since 1601 overseers of the poor (who in rural areas were almost invariably farmers) had levied a poor rate for the relief of the sick, the aged and the unemployed. The depressed wages of the latter half of the eighteenth century, followed by the inflationary pressures of the Revolutionary and Napoleonic Wars, soon precipitated a crisis as an unprecedented number of poor people applied for relief and there began a commensurate rise in poor rates. This was not merely a fiscal crisis; what was at stake was the whole basis of labour control in the countryside – and with it the entire social fabric of rural society.

In order to appreciate this it is necessary to recount something of the history of the English Poor Law in so far as it affected rural areas. In its origins the Poor Law was bound up with the legal duty of all men to labour. Those who were unable to do so were to be cared for ('from cradle to the grave', if necessary) by their community. The Act of Settlement of 1662 confined such relief strictly to natives of the parish in which they applied or to those who could establish 'settlement' there. The system was essentially a local, communal one, very much reflecting the structure of medieval rural society. At one and the same time it guaranteed farmers a local pool of labour (by providing strong disincentives for labourers to move outside the parish and risk ineligibility for relief) and controlled the liability of ratepayers (by providing checks on any influx of paupers through the conditions attached to 'settlement'). During the eighteenth century the Poor Law became modified in practice in a number of ways. There was a tendency for parishes to combine into 'unions' for the purposes of administration and, in keeping with the emergence of a free market in labour, the Poor Law ceased to be used as an instrument of labour compulsion. After 1782 outdoor relief was permitted for the able-bodied and the poorhouse became a refuge for the aged, the sick and the disabled. All of this worked reasonably well as long as the number of paupers remained within manageable bounds. Wartime inflation changed all that.

In 1795 – the year in which bread prices doubled and food riots threatened mass unrest – the system teetered on the brink of total collapse, overwhelmed by the sheer numbers of those applying for relief. In May the magistrates of Berkshire held their famous meeting at Speenhamland in order to decide on what to do. The climate of crisis called for emergency measures. They sought refuge by attempting to turn the clock back once more to the system of parochial responsibility which had characterized the pre-capitalist rural world. First they established minimum wages linked to the price of bread on a sliding scale, so that when the

. . . Gallon Loaf of Second Flour, weighing 8 lbs 11 ozs shall cost 1s . . . every poor and industrious man shall have for his own support 3s weekly, either produced by his own or his family's labour, or an allowance from the poor rates, and for the support of his wife and every other of his family, 1s 6d.

As bread prices moved upwards so did wages along this sliding scale. Over the next two decades the Speenhamland system spread to virtually every county in England, although its significance in the North was reduced by the growth of industrial employment there. The second important feature of the Speenhamland system was that it reinforced the local basis of poor relief. Only a very confident or a very foolish labourer would now venture beyond the area in which he was eligible for relief. Speenhamland thus produced a strange hybrid of medieval obligation to the poor of the parish with the new market economy which regulated bread prices according to supply and demand.

As an emergency measure this might have sufficed. What the magistrates meeting at Speenhamland could not have foreseen was the continuation of high food prices for the next twenty years, their perpetuation by legislation after 1815, and the continuation of a rural pool of labour which remained chronically in excess of local requirements. Thus a reasonable short-term palliative turned into a long-term disaster. This latter-day family income supplement succeeded in pauperizing a whole generation of the rural working population. As Hobsbawn and Rudé have pointed out, it achieved the worst of both worlds:

The traditional social order degenerated into a universal pauperism of demoralised men who could not fall below the relief scale whatever they did, who could not rise above it, who had not even the nominal guarantee of a living since the 'scale' could be – and with the increasing expense of rates was – reduced to as little as the village rich thought fit for a labourer. Agrarian capitalism degenerated into a general lunacy, in which farmers were encouraged to pay as little as they could (since wages would be supplemented by the parish) and used the mass of pauper labour as an excuse for not raising their productivity; while their most rational calculations would be how to get the maximum subsidy for their wage-bill from the rest of the ratepayers. Labourers, conversely, were encouraged to do as little work as they possibly could, since nothing would get them more than the official minimum of subsistence. If they worked at all, it was only because their fathers had done so before them, and because a man's self-respect required him to.

This is the context within which the growing separation of farmer and farm worker during this period has to be seen. Whatever the humane intentions from which Speenhamland sprang, the outcome was intensely dehumanizing. As parish expenditure soared, so the temptation to reduce *per capita* spending could not be resisted. The parochial basis of relief delivered the poor into the hands of their local rulers, upon whom they remained utterly dependent. Although the stigma of applying for relief was effectively removed, poverty and pauperism became a way of life in the overwhelming majority of parishes in southern England, with virtually no prospect of improvement. With the return of peace in 1815, matters went from bad to worse. The wartime boom in agricultural prices quickly turned to depression as continental trade was once more resumed. The outlay on poor relief actually reached its peak between 1817 and 1819 as still further members of the rural population were rendered unemployed and under-employed by agricultural depression. In rural areas, levels of poor relief remained high throughout the 1820s. Eventually, however, the system offended prevailing sensibilities sufficiently to engender wholesale reform. Ratepayers demanded relief from *their* burden, while accumulating evidence of a rapid fall in farming productivity alarmed agricultural observers. By the end of the 1820s it was also clear that the Speenhamland system had failed in another of its purposes.

Far from heading off social unrest, it had contributed to the creation of a rural population that was rife for rioting. Poor relief payments were indeed correlated with unrest – but positively rather than inversely. Parish overseers were singled out for attack in many areas. By 1830 if widespread violence were to be averted it seemed that the current system of poor relief would have to be scrapped rather than extended.

THE ROAD TO CAPTAIN SWING

The end of war signalled the termination of the artificial wartime boom and the onset of a correspondingly acute recession. The rural labour market, already suffering a surfeit of labour, was swamped by demobilization. As I have already shown, the rural society which emerged into peacetime was by no means similar to that which had entered the wars. By now the rural labour force was rendered particularly vulnerable by the combination of casualization, pauperization and the effects of enclosure. The new agricultural technology did little to relieve the prevalent deprivation of rural areas. Indeed, the symbol of the farm labourer's misery was the threshing machine, which deprived him of winter employment and thrust him onto poor relief at the harshest time of the year. It was a visible, tangible – and destructible – symbol, unlike the 'hidden hand' of market forces. Thus threshing machines attracted a deep and abiding sense of hatred; by wrecking a new threshing machine, the farm labourer could give vent to all the pent-up emotion and frustration engendered by his impoverishment.

Such acts of sabotage had to be undertaken with care, however. The complete dependence of farm labourers upon the locally powerful was such that overt conflict and resistance could rarely be contemplated. Instead a rural underworld of social crime became endemic. During the first two decades of the nineteenth century there was a noticeable correlation between outbreaks of crimes such as arson, machine-breaking and cattle-maiming, and the level of economic distress in the

countryside. Poaching came into its own as the rural underworld activity *par excellence*. It encapsulated many of the
hidden class tensions of this period – both directly by proving
to be an economic necessity for many families, and indirectly
in terms of what it was that poaching symbolized. The taking
of game was not regarded as criminal activity within many, if
not most, rural villages, but as a 'crime' created by the
abrogation of common property rights associated with
enclosure. Poaching was thus an act of defiance against the
established order, a reassertion of lost communal rights – and,
more prosaically, a convenient and habitual way of filling an
empty stomach. It was simultaneously a reaction to economic
distress and a barometer of rising social tensions. Although by
definition the historical evidence is patchy, all the indications
are that poaching was on the increase, with prosecutions
nearly doubling during the 1820s. In retrospect this trend
appears ominous. More overt forms of rebellion were on the
way.

Discontent, however, rarely broke through the placid
exterior which the rural underworld displayed to those
outside. The first two decades of the nineteenth century were
characterized by sullen resentment, rather than open acts of
rebelliousness, and even during the 1820s there was no sign of
any organized opposition to those who controlled rural
affairs. Although criminal activity was increasing, it consisted
of individual, local and isolated acts which form a pattern only
in retrospect. The farm labourer seemed too afflicted by the
daily grind of poverty, unemployment and dependency to
organize any widespread and collective form of rebellion.
Nevertheless, rebellion came – and it came with a sudden
ferocity which startled and alarmed the propertied classes in
rural society. In the autumn of 1830 a general uprising took
place; it began in Kent in late August, but by November had
engulfed virtually the whole of southern England. The
'Labourer's Revolt' (as it is sometimes known) had no
recognized leader, but became associated with a mythical
character whose name the machine-breakers and rick-burners
frequently invoked: 'Captain Swing'. By the end of the year

there were few who had not heard of this bucolic Robin Hood
or who were not familiar with some local act of machine-
breaking or incendiarism which he was alleged to have
instigated.

As far as can be discovered, it all began at Lower Hardres,
near Canterbury in Kent, where on the night of 28 August
1830 a threshing machine was destroyed. The next day
another one was demolished at Newington, near Hythe. At
the time, little notice was taken of either act. The authorities
were much more preoccupied with an outbreak of arson
which had engulfed the Kent–Surrey area between Caterham
and Orpington since June. By the third week in October,
however, something like one hundred machines had been
broken in East Kent, gangs were said to be roaming the
countryside at night in search of the despised threshing
machines, and seven rioters were subsequently brought to
trial. Soon after, the isolated acts of arson and destruction
entered a new phase, and a more visible and coherent
movement emerged. Large numbers of labourers assembled
in broad daylight and began to demand higher wages. Local
farmers were not always unsympathetic, sometimes refrain-
ing from hiring machines, more often deflecting the labourers'
demands towards the reduction of tithes and rents. In this
form the movement spread quickly, and by mid-November
'tumultuous assemblies' – sometimes accompanied by the
smashing of machines – were commonplace in Kent and
Sussex. From here the movement spread with extraordinary
rapidity. By 18 November there were outbreaks in Hampshire; by the 19th in Berkshire and Wiltshire; and on the 21st
the first outbreak was reported in Oxfordshire. The movement now had a momentum of its own. The Midlands and
East Anglia quickly joined in, and by December the whole of
southern England was affected. Several northern and midland
counties were also recipients of 'Swing', and the outbreak of
rick-burning reached its northernmost point around Carlisle
by the end of November. For a short time the whole of the
English countryside appeared to be on the verge of open
rebellion.

Although rural England seemed to teeter on the brink of total conflagration, it never quite occurred. To begin with, the pastoral counties of the north and west, though touched by the passage of 'Swing', were comparatively quiescent. A number of economic and social reasons account for this. Hired labour was less common in the pastoral areas, wages were higher (due partly to industrial expansion) and were regulated by annual hiring fairs. Settlement was more scattered and there were fewer working-class villages to act as hotbeds of resentment and underworld activity. The Swing movement was thus centred on the arable counties of the south and east, recognizing that it was by no means confined to such. In this respect the county of Wiltshire formed an instructive microcosm of the national situation: the 'chalk' part of the county was riotous, while the 'cheese' was quiet. Only high-wage areas within the arable counties avoided the full impact of Swing – a point best exemplified by its virtual absence within a 25-mile radius of London. Within this broad regional pattern there was considerable variation from one area – and even one village – to another. This was often associated with such factors as the size of the village, the pattern of landownership, the presence or absence of a history of conflict over such issues as enclosure, and so on. In many ways this variability reflects the essence of Swing. It was not a nationally co-ordinated movement, organized and directed from a central location. It was a grass-roots movement which emerged spontaneously in villages across the country and which remained stubbornly local in its emphasis and in its demands. The towns were untouched and revolution was not on the labourers' agenda – despite exemplary instances across the Channel.

The spontaneous and variable character of the Swing movement is also reflected in the wide range of activities and tactics which were undertaken by those who were involved. Rick-burning and machine-breaking characterized the uprising, but the labourers frequently resorted to any suitable tactic that was at hand. Before any property was actually damaged, handbills, posters and threatening letters frequently made an appearance, signed by the elusive Captain Swing.

Assemblies, wages meetings and petitions also played a part, but so too did assaults on overseers, parsons and landlords. The most common pattern was a judicious mixture of a number of activities, depending upon local circumstances. Sometimes the demands were made in a defamatory, but polite, style, as in the following example from Romsey in Hampshire:

Gentlemen Farmers we do insist upon your paying every man in your parish 2 shillings per day for his labour – every single man between the ages of 16 and 20 eighteen pence per day – every child above 2 – to receive a loaf and sixpence per week – the aged and infirm to receive 4s per week. Landlords – we do also insist upon your reducing their rents so as to enable them to meet our demands. Rectors – you must also lower your tithes down to £100 per year in every parish but we wish to do away with the tithe altogether.

On other occasions they could be more intimidatory, such as the following letter received by a bailiff on an estate in Essex:

Mr Brockis, I send this to you to let you know that if you Do not give 100 Shillins A Day Every thing shall come to Ashes We have come from Kent in that intention And so we mene to go through Essex We brought this to yore dore Becaus we Dont like to put you to No exspence And we ment to Burn up the Pash nige up first.

Frequently, letters of this kind, whether polite requests or thinly-disguised blackmail, were the prelude to machine-breaking and arson. The notoriety of 'Captain Swing' was due to the eponymous signatory of such letters, and for a time the hunt was on to capture and try the 'agitator' who was responsible for the rebellion. But Captain Swing was not a recent version of Sir John Hampden, the seventeenth-century defender of common rights, nor was Swing a *nom de guerre* of William Cobbett, despite the suspicions to the contrary. Swing was not a person but a cry of outrage. In the closed and dependent world of village society it was only through the disguise of a mythical leader that such demands could be expressed.

By the end of November 1830, with southern England apparently in flames, the rebelliousness could no longer be put down to the disgruntled actions of a few petty criminals. An organized rebellion appeared to be taking place and, equally alarming, was receiving some sympathy from certain local farmers and magistrates. Once the riots spread beyond east Kent, the Government intervened. Sir Robert Peel, the Home Secretary, despatched troops to Sussex and Hampshire. They were intended as a deterrent and a warning against future disorder. Given the spontaneous and unpredictable nature of Swing, however, they were of little other use. An essentially localized – even though widespread – movement required local knowledge and local measures to put it down. Magistrates thus set up a variety of policing methods, ranging from night watches on vulnerable farm property to organizing private armies of vigilantes to hunt down those responsible. As the Duke of Wellington, for one, later boasted:

I induced the magistrates to put themselves on horseback, each at the head of his own servants and retainers, grooms, huntsmen, gamekeepers, armed with horsewhips, pistols, fowling pieces and what they could get, and to attack in concert, if necessary, or singly, these mobs, disperse them, and take and put in confinement those who could not escape. This was done in a spirited manner, in many instances, and it is astonishing how soon the country was tranquilised, and that in the best way, by the activity and spirit of the gentlemen.

Thus did the antidote to the Swing rebellion become a more homespun version of big-game hunting. The most successful method was, however, the so-called 'Sussex Plan' instigated by the Duke of Richmond. He enrolled a constabulary of shopkeepers, yeomen and 'respectable' labourers, organized them into sections and districts under local commanders and sent them out as mobile units to occupy rebellious, or potentially rebellious, villages.

Beneath the determination to meet intimidation with force there lay the more complicated issue of how to deal with the leniency and sympathy for the rioters which was sometimes expressed at the local level. One such case in Norfolk in December, 1830, attracted the attention of the new Home

Secretary, Lord Melbourne, who promptly castigated the local magistrates for their failure to defend the principles of order and property:

It is my Duty therefore to recommend in the strongest Manner, that for the future all Justices of the Peace, and other Magistrates, will oppose a firm Resistance to all Demands of the Nature above described, more especially when accompanied with Violence and Menace; and that they will deem it their Duty to maintain and uphold the Rights of Property, of every Description, against Violence and Aggression.

If local magistrates could not be trusted, then the Government should intervene. Consequently a Special Commission was set up to try the prisoners awaiting trial in the most affected counties, and by December the 1,900 or so people involved began to be dealt with. Melbourne's determination to take a strong line has to be seen in the light of the fact that, under Acts passed in 1827 and 1828, machine-breaking and arson carried the death penalty. Moreoever, any person who, unwillingly or not, was part of a crowd whose action led to extortion, violence or physical assault was also liable to be hung. When the Special Commission sat for the first time at Winchester on 18 December to try the 185 prisoners indicted in Hampshire, it was made clear that recognized grievances were not to be regarded as extenuating circumstances: 101 were capitally convicted, of whom six were left for execution and 69 commuted to transportation. By the time the Commission had concluded its work in the other counties it had tried 992 cases. It had passed 227 sentences of death, although only eleven had been left for execution, and of these all but three were later reprieved. This still left nearly 1,000 cases to be dealt with in the normal way. Their example having been set, the Commissioners could now observe this with more confidence. In the event, 1,976 prisoners were tried by ninety courts in thirty-four counties. Of these, nineteen were executed, 481 transported to Australia, 644 imprisoned, seven fined and one was whipped. The ferocity of this punishment was greater than that exacted on either the Luddites or the

Chartists, to take two contemporaneous urban examples. For some villages the loss of their most active and able-bodied men was a blow from which they could not recover – and it was not forgotten. The resentment was stored away in the folk memory, to re-emerge later in the century when the labouring population was once again stirred.

In the short term, however, repression worked. By the end of December the Swing rebellion was virtually finished, notwithstanding some further minor outbreaks in Kent and Norfolk in the summer of 1831. The draconian punishment of the Special Commission had the effect of bringing the rioting to a halt and of leaving the labourer demoralized and disillusioned. Rightly or wrongly a generation of rural working families believed that they had learned the lesson of open confrontation. Henceforward it was imperative that opposition should be covert, even secretive, for the result of outright conflict could now be anticipated. Rural opposition thus reverted to type and the rural underworld of poaching and rick-burning flourished, now fed by a shared sense of hatred and revenge. But the limits of violence and crimes against property were now known and could not be over-stepped. The labourer sought solace not in the brief ex-hilaration of Captain Swing, but in a Primitive Methodist millenium, in the better-paid employment of the towns – and in the maudlin compensations of the four-ale bar.

The authorities had had a fright. However unlikely it may appear in retrospect, for a short time the propertied classes were forced to contemplate the spectre of rural revolution. This partly accounts for the severity of the response, but there was more to it than this. The rural upper class felt not only opposed, but betrayed by such a widespread display of insubordination. The economic basis of rural society may have passed from paternalism to cash nexus, but the ideology of benevolence was unalloyed. The outrage of those in control of rural society was provoked not only by the demands for higher wages, but by the attempt to assert rights – the 'natural' rights to work and earn a living wage – thereby implying that the authority of their local 'betters' was in some sense illegitimate. Appeals to legitimate authority – to 'justice', the king, God, etc. – served only to exacerbate the sense of betrayal. Repression was thus partly fuelled by a sense of moral outrage which rendered the immediate reaction all the more extreme. A more considered view was tinged by class guilt. Many landowners acknowledged some degree of culpability and began to repair their authority by applying an analgesic to the problems of rural distress. This came in the form of private charitable activity, which increased noticeably in the period after Swing. A somewhat self-conscious attempt to recreate a rural 'community' from above was undertaken – as will be seen in the following chapter. For another forty years the countryside at least appeared to be pacified, and a reconstructed sense of community could be celebrated. How far this community extended to the reality of labouring life will be examined further in chapter 4.

There is one postscript to the Swing movement which has achieved greater fame than the anonymous machine-breakers and rick-burners of the autumn of 1830, and which demonstrates that not all farm labourers were demoralized by the Special Commissions. Towards the end of 1833 two delegates of the newly-formed Grand National Consolidated Trades Union visited the village of Tolpuddle in Dorset, where for some months the local farm labourers had been in dispute over wages with their employers. As a result there was founded the Tolpuddle Lodge of the Friendly Society of Agricultural Labourers. From this point onwards the repression of the farm labourer becomes a brief part of what every schoolchild knows. On 24 February, 1834, six of the leading Tolpuddle trade unionists were arrested and taken to Dorchester gaol. Before a packed jury and a hostile judge they were subsequently tried and found guilty of illegal oath-taking. Under conditions of great hardship, the six were transported to Australia. The significance of the Tolpuddle Martyrs lies in the development of urban British trade unionism, rather than in the history of unionism in the countryside – which was still forty years away. The public outcry that ensued, the collections of money to finance eventual repatriation and the assertion of the rights of combination were orchestrated entirely by the *urban* trade union movement as part of its own struggle for legality – and not in order to improve the conditions of the rural worker. Were it not for its urban repercussions it would be placed alongside the many isolated acts of agitation which occurred in the aftermath of Swing. Indeed, in some ways the experience of George Loveless and his fellow martyrs can be contrasted with the experience of Swing. The Swing movement did *not* take a 'modern', organized, trade union form – and, significantly, it is doubtful if the Tolpuddle agitation would have either, were it not for outside intervention. The farm labourer of the 1830s was still a long way from developing a collective organization which could represent its interests. But if the significance of the Tolpuddle Martyrs is almost entirely symbolic, then at least they secured for the farm worker a special place in the history of British trade unionism.

THE NEW POOR LAW

The Swing rebellion did, however, achieve something less symbolic and of more immediate relevance than the presence of the farm labourer in the iconography of trade union history. In 1834 Parliament passed the Poor Law Amendment Act, which completely overhauled the creaking system of poor relief and ushered in the 'New Poor Law' which remained in place for the rest of the century and, as far as the farm worker was concerned, until 1936. The Swing riots had clearly demonstrated the hatred of the poor-relief system prevalent among many rural workers by the way in which parish overseers were frequently singled out for attack. The mal-administration of the Poor Law was often cited as a cause of discontent, and once the riots had subsided the Government acknowledged this by establishing a Royal Commission on the Poor Laws in 1832. The Commission collected evidence from 3,000 parishes, with a pronounced bias towards the rural areas, and to some extent it sought that evidence which might be expected to justify the case for reform.

The Commission recommended a uniform system of relief administered through a central board. Outdoor relief was to be abolished for the able-bodied, who were henceforth to be given indoor relief only in workhouses built for that purpose. The workhouse regime was to be deliberately harsh in order to deter all but the most desperate from seeking relief. Families were to be separated. In general, conditions were to be more uncomfortable or 'less eligible' than that of anyone in work. The 1834 Act allowed parishes to form Poor Law unions in order to finance and administer the workhouse in their area. They were administered through a board of guardians consisting of all local justices of the peace and members elected by local ratepayers and property owners. In practice the rural guardians were overwhelmingly farmers so that the role of poor relief in regulating class relations in rural areas was barely affected. Moreover individual parishes within each union continued to be responsible for the cost of the relief of its 'settled' inhabitants. The incentive thus remained for parishes with few landowners (and thus ratepayers) to carefully limit the number of inhabitants (by limiting the number of dwellings) who might at some future stage become a burden on the rates. An attempt to help the poor by clarifying the issue of settlement under the Poor Removal Act of 1846 only made matters worse, for irremovability was conferred upon any family who had continuously inhabited a parish for five years – and this provided an even greater incentive to keep the number of houses to a bare minimum. Not until the 1865 Union Chargeability Act were these problems finally sorted out.

Meanwhile, under the 1834 Act assistant commissioners were appointed by the Poor Law Commission in London to organize over 15,000 parishes into 600 Poor Law Unions. This was a somewhat delicate task, given the pattern of local sensibilities and the variations in custom and practice between different parishes. Since the Poor Law played such a central role in the system of rural social control it could not be easily tinkered with unless the authority of local landowners were to be undermined. For this reason the 1834 Act is often cited as the first major attack upon the hegemony of the rural landowner in organizing the concerns of his parish. For the first time, local Poor Law guardians could be instructed from outside on how the system was to operate. In a broader context it marks the first harbinger of the incipient decline of the landed interest in the social and political control of English society and the related growth of the influence of the industrial and commercial middle classes. It also represents a major shift in the balance between central state control and local autonomy – an absorption of local and regional idiosyncrasies into a system of national uniformity. All of this was not, however, readily apparent at the time. The immediate purpose was to save money and to eradicate pauperism by invoking the principle of less eligibility – and in these aims the Act succeeded.

The long-term consequences were also lost on the poor themselves. For them the workhouse was a prison and the New Poor Law epitomized the harsh impersonality of agrarian capitalism. Sporadic outbreaks of unrest occurred once more, but after the experiences of 1830 there was to be no sustained or planned campaign to halt the progress of the new system in rural areas. The threat of unrest was, however, sufficient to provide a check upon the complete implementation of the new measures and upon the speed with which they were adopted. In some areas they were introduced only cautiously and hesitantly. Despite the pressure for uniformity from London there remained a degree of local variability. Outdoor relief, for example, was never completely eliminated, if only because it turned out to be cheaper under certain circumstances. Even by 1850, of the one million people who were aided, only 110,000 were inmates of workhouses. Similarly, the conditions of the elderly, the sick and the disabled – to whom 'less eligibility' was not meant to be applied – varied considerably. In some areas they were treated in the same way as the able-bodied poor, but in others they continued to be granted outdoor relief.

Whatever the outcome, the prevailing philosophy behind the 1834 Act could not have been in greater contrast to that which had characterized Speenhamland. The latter, however anachronistically, had acknowledged a communal responsibility for the poor which belonged to the shared assumptions of the pre-capitalist world. The New Poor Law placed the moral responsibility for pauperism on the poor themselves, who, unless they could demonstrably prove otherwise, were to be regarded as 'less eligible' for help than those to whom relief was due because they were less than able-bodied. There could be no better illustration of the new individualism nor of the more impersonal way in which economic and social relationships were now to be conducted. This may have contrasted with the ideology of benevolent paternalism which characterized the self-conception of rural landowners and farmers – and which accounted for the continuation of so much outdoor relief – but the two were reconciled through the notion of less eligibility. Those who applied for relief were to be placed – literally and figuratively – outside society. As Disraeli was to comment, to be poor was now officially recognized as a social crime. Those who applied for relief were thus, by definition, 'undeserving'. Their plight was thus of no concern to the benevolent patriarch.

Despite the implied resistance of the rural underworld, these values were absorbed by a sufficiently large proportion of the rural working class to affect the long-term consequences of the new system. The poor certainly detested the workhouse and in this sense 'less eligibility' worked, and labour discipline was restored. Equally pervasively, poverty became a matter of personal shame and to remain outside the workhouse was not only a matter of good fortune but a sign of working-class respectability. And with respectability came thrift, sobriety and passivity. By mid-century this was achieved – at least to the satisfaction of the propertied classes. The Act also succeeded in lowering the cost of relief – another matter for self-congratulation among middle-class ratepayers. For at least another generation the New Poor Law thus provided a satisfactory solution to the crisis in class relations that had developed between 1795 and 1830. To the rural landowner the interference in local affairs by the embryonic bureaucracy of central government seemed a small price to pay for the pacification of the labouring classes. The 1834 Act put the finishing touches to the ultimately successful transition from one means of regulating rural class relationships to another. This success was a precondition of the economic prosperity of mid-Victorian agriculture which was to follow.

REPEAL OF THE CORN LAWS

If the long-term effects of the Poor Law Amendment Act on the landowning classes were not immediately apparent, then few could fail to understand the significance of a much more potent symbol of their declining omnipotence: the repeal of the Corn Laws in 1846. The Corn Laws were an old-established expedient for controlling the prices of home-grown grain by taxing (positively or negatively) imports from continental Europe. They took on a new significance in 1815 when, in the immediate aftermath of the Napoleonic War, a much higher rate of protection was introduced in an attempt to perpetuate the artificially inflated prices which had been brought about by the peculiarities of wartime conditions. This began a new phase in the history of the Corn Laws since the degree of protection granted by an as yet unreformed Parliament was so blatantly self-regarding as to provoke riots in London and unrest in a number of other cities. Whatever their precise economic effects (which were variable) the Corn Laws became a symbol of the greed of the landowning interest. Byron, for one, could not resist pouring out his scorn:

> The peace has made our general malcontent
> Of these high market patriots; war was rent!
> Their love of country, millions all misspent,
> How reconcile? by reconciling rent!
> And will they not repay the treasures lent?
> No: down with everything, and up with rent!
> Their good, ill, health, wealth, joy or discontent,
> Being, end, aim, religion – rent, rent, rent!

In their actual influence on prices the role of the Corn Laws was much exaggerated, since other factors had a greater effect than the level of imports. Increasing productivity, the extension of cultivation and the quality of the weather were far more decisive. But it was what the Corn Laws stood for which mattered politically. In 1840 the Report of the Select Committee on Import Duties had concluded that the repeal of the Corn Laws would pose no immediate threat to English agriculture because even in the years of bad harvest and high prices the level of imports was relatively low. The Anti-Corn Law League, founded in 1838, seized upon such arguments to press the case for free trade.

The campaign for repeal was not, of course, concerned with the arcane details of removing this or that tariff on imported cereals. What was at stake was the adjustment of political power in accordance with the changes that had occurred in the economy, a wresting of power from the landed interest and the transfer to the hands of those who represented industry and commerce. By 1846, Sir Robert Peel, now Prime Minister, had become convinced of the case for repeal. He was himself a progressive landowner who had come round to the view that the Corn Laws were not necessary for agricultural prosperity. In terms of an overall class interest, repeal was a necessary tactical retreat in order to maintain the authority of an hereditary nobility and to allow the landed interest to retain public respect for, and even acquiescence in, their political leadership. In these aims Peel was largely vindicated. The middle classes did not aim to undermine the landed interest, but to redress the economic balance; socially and politically they remained happy to defer to the institutions of aristocratic power. Economically agriculture flourished as never before and the full effects of repeal were delayed for thirty years (see chapter 3). Once it had recovered from the short-lived depression immediately after repeal, agriculture was generally and increasingly prosperous. From 1846 to 1873 repeal was an entirely spurious issue as far as agriculture was concerned. Britain entered a period of 'high farming' – high in the cost of inputs, high in output, and high in profitability. Far from being swept aside by the forces of free trade and political reform, the landed interest appeared to be at its zenith.

CHAPTER 3

HIGH FARMING AND HIGH SOCIETY

Confounding the gloomy predictions of the protectionist lobby, agriculture settled down to two decades of relatively stable prosperity from the early 1850s to the early 1870s. The countryside was fortunate to participate in the great mid-Victorian economic boom, and the free traders were vindicated – at least for the time being.

The increase in prosperity affected all sections of the rural population, even though the effects among particular groupings and in particular regions were variable. Partly as a result, rural society took on an altogether more orderly and ordered appearance. This was the rural England of Loamshire and Barchester, a rural England that was not, as will become apparent, without its tensions, but which was nevertheless 'settled'. Neither Eliot nor Trollope were unaware of the broader historical sweep of social and economic change, but each could, with only the gentlest of ironic touches, present an idyllic version of rural society which seemed plausible to their readers. Eliot's stage-coach observer could see little to disturb such a lulling vision:

The passenger on the box could see that this was the district of protuberant optimists, sure that old England was the best of all possible countries, and that if there were any facts which had not fallen under their own observation, they were facts not worth observing: the district of clean little market-towns without manufacturers, of fat livings, an aristocratic clergy, and low poor-rates.

Trollope, too, could describe the condition of rural England in terms of:

Its green pastures, its waving wheat, its deep and shady and – let us add – dirty lanes, its paths and stiles, its tawny-coloured, well-built rural churches, its avenues of beeches, and frequent Tudor mansions, its constant county hunt, its social graces and the air of clanship which pervades it. . . .

As literal descriptions of mid-Victorian rural England these are quite false, but they could not plausibly have been written during the turmoil of the first half of the century.

Nevertheless, the countryside prospered. It was not a *simple* increase in prosperity, in the sense that living standards were rising within the context of an unchanging society, for the *basis* of this prosperity shifted during these two decades. The population census of 1851 clearly demonstrated the underlying trends of work. On the one hand agriculture appeared to be at its peak of activity and influence, with the numbers employed being the highest ever recorded. Yet the census also disclosed that for the first time Britain contained a predominantly urban industrial population who, as the repeal of the Corn Laws had indicated, were likely to make a very different range of demands on agriculture and the countryside. As the census made clear, the most direct demand was for labour and thenceforward the industrial and commercial boom was to continue to draw labouring families out of agriculture, with first a relative and then (after 1871) an absolute drop in the population of rural areas.

Agriculture also had to accustom itself to the improving living standards of the urban population and the consequent changing pattern of demand for food. James Caird, who was to chronicle agricultural change in this period in much the same way as Arthur Young half a century before him, shrewdly underlined the significance of this as early as 1852:

With the great mass of consumers, bread still forms the chief article of consumption. But in the manufacturing districts where wages are good, the use of butcher's meat and cheese is enormously on the increase; and even in the agricultural districts the labourer does now occasionally indulge himself in a meat dinner, or seasons his dry bread with a morsel of cheese . . . the great mass of the consumers, as their circumstances improve, will follow the same rule. . . .

Every intelligent farmer ought to keep this steadily in view. Let him produce as much as he can of the articles which show a gradual tendency to increase in value.

The best way of ensuring that the articles produced did indeed show a tendency to increase in value was to diversify away from agriculture and participate directly in industrial and commercial enterprise. Farm workers voted with their feet and were to do so in great numbers, but farmers proved to be most reluctant either to leave agriculture altogether or to adapt their operations to the new conditions. Landowners, too, showed themselves willing to forgo the higher rates of return available for investing their capital elsewhere for the cachet of owning land. They, indeed, gained least from the general prosperity, caught up in the persistent tendency for returns to agriculture to decline as a proportion of returns to the economy as a whole. Once Britain embarked upon full-scale industrialization, landowners thus began to face difficult problems over capital accumulation. The historian F. M. L. Thompson has summarized their position:

In this way the landowners bore a good part of the cost of the ascendancy of commerce and industry and the secondary position to which agriculture was being relegated. Behind the facade of the 'Golden Age of English Agriculture' which is said to have lasted for the twenty years after the outbreak of the Crimean War, a distinct weakening in the economic position of agricultural landowners can be detected. . . . They were accepting financial sacrifices, in the sense that much greater returns could have been secured by putting their money elsewhere. . . . The economic distinction was certainly becoming more marked year by year between landowners who were purely agricultural and landowners who were guaranteed a share in the wealth generated by industry and commerce.

For the time being the generally prosperous conditions of the 1850s and 1860s papered over these fissiparous tendencies, but they were to be exposed more vividly when adverse economic circumstances returned.

In the meantime, agriculture flourished on the basis of 'high' farming. The term was used loosely to denote a high input, high output system of intensive farming assisted by another round of estate improvements. Progressive landowners and their more entrepreneurial tenants were prepared to make large outlays of capital in order to achieve higher output per acre. This was achieved through the application of recently-developed techniques of drainage, fertilizing, feeding and mechanization. Whole estates were once more reorganized in order to provide the necessary infrastructure – convenient farm roads, newly designed buildings, new field boundaries and drainage schemes, etc. 'High farming' was also used in a more technical sense to refer to the intensification of crop rotations, with a succession of new fodder and grain crops being used to fatten stock. As these literally fed their way through the system they produced an all-round intensification: high quality stock, lavishly fed on home-produced grains supplemented with imported proteins, produced more meat and manure, while the ploughed land, now enriched by more manure and new artificial fertilizers, produced higher yields of grain for the market and fodder for the stock. For as long as prices for both grain and stock remained high, a virtuous circle of innovation and improvement was created.

'High farming' was thus profitable farming – at least for those in a position to take advantage of the opportunities offered. It followed that high farming was also high-status farming, that farmers had now decisively separated themselves from the social standing of their workers, a product of the decline of farm service and the growing significance of working, as well as fixed, capital under the increasingly capital-intensive high farming regime. High farming therefore also marked the watershed of the landlord–tenant system in English agriculture, and on this system there was erected the characteristically tripartite class structure which 'ordered' the Victorian countryside. The three classes of landowner, tenant farmer and landless farm labourer became regarded as the natural hierarchy of rural society. While there was considerable internal differentiation (as Trollope, for one, was only too well aware), one's 'place' within these broad categories was unambiguously clear. Caird, writing at the end of this period, described how economic, social and political roles overlapped:

The landowners are the capitalists to whom the land belongs. Their property comprises the soil and all that is beneath it, and the buildings and other permanent works upon it. . . . In nearly all permanent improvements arising from the progress of agriculture the landowner is also expected to share the cost. And he is necessarily concerned in the general prosperity and good management of his estate, and in the welfare of those who live upon it, with which his own is so closely involved. He takes a lead in the business of his parish and from his class the magistrates who administer the criminal affairs of the country, and superintend its roads, the public buildings and charitable institutions are selected. Nor do his duties end here, for the landowner, from his position, is expected to be at the head of all objects of public utility, to subscribe to, and, if so inclined, to ride with the hounds, showing at one an example to the farmers and tradesmen, and meeting them on terms of neighbourly friendship and acquaintance. The same example is carried out in his intercourse with the clergy and schoolmaster, and his influence, where wisely exercised, is felt in the church, the farm and the cottage. . . . There is no other body of men who administer so large a capital on their own account, and whose influence is so widely extended and universally present.

This 'influence' was, indeed, so widely extensive as to render them an easily identifiable rural ruling class, presiding over virtually all the institutions within their local spheres of influence (see chapter 4). In this they were assisted by tenant adjutants:

The tenant farmers are the second class, and a much more numerous one. Their business is the cultivation of the land, with a capital quite independent of that of the owner. . . . A spirit of emulation exists among them, elicited by county, provincial and national exhibitions of agricultural stock, and by a natural desire, in a country where everything is open to comment, not to be behind their neighbours in the neatness, style, and success of their cultivation, or in the symmetry and condition of their livestock. They are brought into the closest relation with their labourers, and, although, occasionally, feelings of keen antagonism have arisen, there is generally a very friendly understanding between them. The farmer knows that it is for his interest that the labourers should find their position made so comfortable as to value it.

To the farmer is committed the management of the details of the parish, as those of the county to the landowner. His intimate knowledge of the condition of the labourer, and constant residence in the parish, fit him best for the duty of Overseer of the Poor, member of the Board of Guardians, Churchwarden and Surveyor of the Roads. He is frank and hospitable to strangers as a rule; in favour of the established political institutions of the country; loyal as a subject; often available in case of need as mounted yeoman; and constantly in requisition as a juryman in the courts of law.

Caird's portrait is, of course, an idealized one, representing an official credo of rural society as much as the less harmonious reality (see chapter 4 for further discussion of this). Yet the general classificatory scheme was one which was widely recognized. Several decades of resistance to the social consequences of agrarian capitalist development had at best affected only the timing rather than the content of the eventual outcome. After a lengthy period of social and political conflict a kind of accommodation had been reached, and to that extent overt resistance was held in abeyance. Respectful deference could be reciprocated by benevolent paternalism at each level of the class structure. At last, it seemed, everyone 'knew his place'. Rural society having thus been contained, those at the aristocratic apex were able to consolidate their positions of authority.

ARISTOCRACY, GENTRY, SQUIREARCHY

As Caird's comments on the nature of landownership indicate, the possession of a landed estate continued to provide the wherewithal to control the major institutions of Victorian rural society. From this point of view the landowner could fairly be considered to be a member of a rural ruling class. For as long as rural England was predominantly agricultural then the ownership of land was always going to provide the key to political power and a prestigious life-style. During the early part of the nineteenth century this supremacy had been threatened, first from without by the growth of urban industrialism and the rising middle-class entrepreneurs who profited from it, and secondly from within during the persistent social unrest in the countryside up to the Captain Swing uprisings. Following the traumas of the Reform Act in 1832 and the repeal of the Corn Laws in 1846, however, the landowning interest succeeded in restoring much of its influence, both locally and nationally. Within the 'natural order' of rural society their dominance was not to be seriously questioned or threatened until the final quarter of the century.

A complicating feature of this rural elite was that considerations of landownership were intertwined with considerations of nobility. During the mid-Victorian period it was still essential for a nobleman to be a landowner. The very fact that newly garnered wealth required a landed estate before it could be immortalized through ennoblement was a great source of strength to a landowning class in an increasingly industrial age. As long as the ownership of land and a country house were acknowledged as an essential part of achieving noble status, then the landed interest remained in the powerful position of determining the entrance qualifications to a national, as opposed to an agricultural, elite. The admission fee was generally acknowledged to be around 1,000 acres, an inconvenient, but not entirely discouraging, obstacle. National heroes who had the misfortune to be born commoners had, necessarily, to be fitted out with an appropriate estate upon their elevation to the peerage by a grateful monarch (as in the case of Nelson, Wellington and Disraeli), while those blighted by wealth accumulated through trade or manufacture similarly searched for a country seat to set the seal upon their aristocratic aspirations. Land, then, possessed a symbolic importance that stretched far beyond its economic or political significance, a factor which muted the attacks on the privileges which landownership conferred. It also enabled a social and political order based upon aristocratic values and landed interests to remain dominant long after the purely economic significance of agriculture had declined. This clearly assisted in the restoration of confidence which accompanied the era of high farming.

Although until the end of the nineteenth century it was

necessary for a nobleman to be a landowner, it was certainly not necessary for a landowner to be a nobleman. There were plenty of examples of landowners, including some large landowners, who were commoners, many of them descendants of medieval yeomen. Moreover the hierarchy of nobility – duke, marquess, earl, viscount, baron – was only a loose indicator of the amount of land owned. Since, after the passage of the Reform Act in 1832, the nobility retained few legal or constitutional privileges, landownership, rather than nobility *per se*, determined economic and political influence. Social status was, however, another matter: here nobility, rather than landownership, could be decisive. Whatever the outcome the relationship between landownership and nobility was complex and opaque to even the closest outside observer. In this respect the editor of the *Spectator* was quite wrong to suggest in 1865 that

The English 'aristocracy' is . . . only another word for the greater owners of land. It has little to do with office. . . . Still less . . . with pedigree. . . . Historical associations convey influence, but they cling to the property rather than the race, and the 'aristocratic element' of the English constitution is, in fact, simply the class which owns the soil.

The point is that it was never *simply* the class which owned the soil. Had it been so, England would probably have experienced a revolution during the nineteenth century like many of its continental neighbours. However, this quotation does reflect a shift in emphasis in the role of the aristocracy from a position whereby they enjoyed constitutional privileges to one which conferred more narrowly-defined economic privileges vested in the ownership of land.

THE NEW DOMESDAY SURVEY

In 1873, towards the end of the mid-century period of prosperity, a rare factual glimpse of the structure of land-ownership was given in a study which has come to be known as the New Domesday Survey. It consisted of a Return to Owners of Land, a survey of landownership which remains unique in modern times and which was initially promoted by

Lord Derby in the confident expectation that it would rebutt the allegations of Liberal reformists that Britain was in the hands of an elite of 30,000 landowners. In the event, this confidence was misplaced for the survey showed that the 'notorious 30,000' was an embarrassing understatement of the degree of concentration of landownership. Instead less than 7,000 men were revealed to own more than four-fifths of the land between them. However, the survey also revealed the extent to which this group was itself internally differentiated, and how the relationship between landownership and nobility was more complicated than the 'orderly' character of this 'golden era' of mid-Victorian high farming might have led some observers to believe. Here it is possible to follow the categorizations of Bateman (who compiled the survey), and divide landowners into three groups: aristocracy, gentry and yeomen.

The New Domesday Survey defined an aristocrat as the owner of an estate of over 10,000 acres (producing an income of approximately £10,000 per year or more). The survey showed that the aristocracy overlapped, but certainly was not coincident with, the nobility. Of the 363 aristocrats defined by the survey, 117 were not titled and, conversely, there were many peers (over 350) whose estates were not sufficiently large to qualify them as aristocrats. Some of these estates were very large indeed – forty-four were over 100,000 acres – and in each case they were much more than a mere collection of farms and cottages: in fact, they resembled a semi-autonomous federation of 'little kingdoms', each with its omnipotent aristocratic potentate. A large estate was, in other words, a functioning centre of political and social influence across the territory which it comprised, often extending into the sur-rounding area and sometimes, as in the case of the most powerful aristocratic grandees, across a whole county. This involved a complex set of proprietorial rights, not only over the agriculture of the estate, but over its minerals, its game, its Members of Parliament, its clergy – in short over the entire locality and its inhabitants. At its centre lay the 'Big House' with its imposing architecture and eighteenth-century parkland now brought to maturity and, in many cases, modernized to accommodate Victorian tastes. Its retinue of servants and other domestic workers provided the most direct link with the nearby villages, but the inhabitants of the Big House always remained outside the village community, both geographically and socially, cultivating an ideal of community rather than participating in the reality (see chapter 4).

These great estates occupied one-quarter of the land surface of England, so that even as late as the mid-nineteenth century it was still possible to regard rural English society, culturally and geographically, as a patchwork of great country houses exerting influence across their respective shires. The estates were, however, somewhat unevenly distributed, with a tendency to be situated in the more pastoral north and west, a factor which influenced the politics of land reform in the final quarter of the century (see chapter 7). Rutland emerged from the New Domesday Survey as the most aristocratic county with 53 per cent of its surface area covered by great estates, closely followed by Northumberland (50 per cent) and then Nottinghamshire (38 per cent), Dorset, Wiltshire (each 36 per cent) and Cheshire (35 per cent). The least aristocratic counties on this reckoning were Middlesex (4 per cent), Essex (9 per cent) and Surrey (10 per cent). There was, however, an aristocratic presence in all counties so that in only a very few localities was the influence of aristocratic values completely absent.

The aristocracy not only ran their estates. They also ran the nation. Indeed the aristocracy was primarily a metropolitan, if not cosmopolitan group who left much of the day-to-day management of their estates in the hands of agents while they busied themselves with the affairs of state and metropolis. While Parliament was in session and the Season in full swing they resided in London. F. M. L. Thompson has described their enthusiastic participation in a world consisting of

. . . politics and high society, of attendance at the House and gaming in the club, the place where wagers were laid and race meetings arranged, the source of fashion in dress and taste in art, the place where portraits were painted and galleries visited, as well as being the world of drawing rooms and levees, glittering entertainments and extravaganzas, soirées, balls and operas.

The aristocracy found no difficulty in moving to and fro between this glittering social whirl and the more measured parochialism of rural life. At least once a year the aristocrat and his family retinue would migrate to their country seat to settle the estate's affairs, conduct a tour of inspection, keep the local populace up to scratch by a visible presence – and, not least, indulge in a little sporting activity. The purpose of such visits was also to replenish the aristocrat's social and political capital by entertaining the local gentry, administering justice via the local magistracy and attending to territorial affairs involving the estate, the Church, local schools and local charities.

It was the exercise of such direct, personal authority which proved to be an enduring attraction of the aristocratic life-style. The ownership of other forms of capital could not be converted into personal social control in quite the same way. To the aspiring commercial or industrial entrepreneur the combination of title and personal power provided a heady attraction which few would want to refuse. It is intriguing to speculate on how this might have influenced the decline of Britain's entrepreneurial spirit. As the historian D. C. Moore has observed:

Presumably, the strong preferences which many landowners expressed for their agricultural as compared with their non-agricultural properties were neither testimonies to their dislike of money nor simple bucolic affectations, but measures of their realization that relationships having to do with agricultural property could be the source of power in ways in which relationships having to do with non-agricultural property could never be. . . .

Authority was the principal adjunct of wealth and, during the middle years of the century, land was the principal symbol of authority. Presumably it was this rather than any anticipation of significant increments of rent which explains why both the prices of rural land and the number of great houses being built or remodelled rose into the early 1870s.

Below the aristocracy in the hierarchy of landownership came the gentry, over 3,000 strong, and defined in Bateman's

Survey as owners of estates between 1,000 and 10,000 acres. If the aristocracy controlled the agricultural interest, then it was the gentry who ran it. They formed a more socially fluid class, but one which was also more provincial and more conservative. Replenished by judicious marriage and the odd shrewd purchase, they ensured that landownership never moved beyond the realistic aspirations of those whose wealth was founded elsewhere, and that landowners did not thereby become an enclosed caste. According to Bateman they accounted for 30 per cent of the land surface of England, but in a widely diffused manner which tended not to cramp the territorial imperatives of the aristocracy. The strength of the gentry lay in eastern England as well as in the west in Shropshire, Herefordshire and Oxfordshire. By the mid-nineteenth century the gentry was regarded as an essential pillar of county, as opposed to metropolitan, society. However, they were a very varied group, ranging from village squires to landowners verging on aristocratic grandees. In some counties their influence could be decisive. Relatively unencumbered by national political responsibilities, or by industrial and commercial business interests, they exemplified the close historical relationship between land and power. And on their own estates their power was virtually absolute, rendered all the more conclusive by their continual, year-round presence. As Tsar Alexander was to remark, the next best thing to being Tsar of Russia was to be an English country gentleman.

Denied the glitter of the London Season, the gentry organized the more modest social round of county society. There they complemented the activities of the aristocracy, assisting in the administration of justice, providing the officer corps for the county's military force and engaging from time to time in political life. They, or their wives, took a leading part in local village philanthropy and, after 1834, the gentry also administered the Poor Law. Their abiding pastime was, however, sport. In some respects, especially gamekeeping, this threatened to be socially divisive. Tenant farmers did not welcome the restrictions and disturbance attached to game preservation, while poaching was regarded by the working population of the village as partly a sport and partly a form of covert class warfare. On the other hand the gentry's particular delight was foxhunting and this also developed into more than a mere sport to become almost a celebration of the gentry's ideal of the rural community, binding all classes together in the thrill of the chase. Foxhunting embraced all levels of the rural social hierarchy while also providing the aristocracy, gentry and squirearchy with an excuse to socialize and share the same consuming passion. In so doing the hunt served a similar function to the London Season, even offering a parallel set of rituals and taboos in the intricacies of foxhunting etiquette.

The gentry's role in the re-establishment by the landowning class of an orderly countryside was considerable. During the mid-Victorian period, the gentry acted as the loyal subalterns of aristocratic rule, and there was little of the divisiveness which had marked the crisis of the 1830s, and which could be exploited, either locally or nationally, to bring about major structural changes. A shared code of conduct and morality therefore stretched all the way from the aristocratic magnates of national significance, down to the 2,000 or so squires – the lesser gentry with estates of 1,000 to 3,000 acres – and who together comprised the 4,000 or so entries in Burke's *Landed Gentry and Baronetage*. What bound them together was not merely the recognition of a common economic interest in landed property, but a set of values, an ethical code, which – very self-consciously – set them aside from the rest of the rural population. For they were not only landowners but *gentlemen*. Standards of gentlemanly conduct enabled a geographically scattered and economically diffuse aristocracy, gentry and squirearchy to retain its stability, its coherence and its pre-eminent role in defining cultural values. Social stability and agricultural prosperity during this period allowed both a restoration of aristocratic authority but, equally important, a revival of the gentlemanly ethic.

THE GENTLEMANLY ETHIC

The origins of the gentlemanly ethic lie in the medieval code of chivalry, initially a code of conduct evolved for the knights of the Middle Ages, a warrior class which nevertheless sought high standards of personal behaviour to accompany the necessary barbarities of violent conflict. The chivalrous code of the ideal knight was concerned with bravery, loyalty, fidelity, courteous behaviour, generosity and mercy; failure to accept such standards implied dishonour, to which death was preferable. Such a militaristic code had metamorphosed into the ethic of gentility in a more peaceful Tudor England. By the beginning of the nineteenth century, military prowess and a chivalrous sense of honour had been replaced by other attributes: a landed estate, a family tree, a certain degree of wealth, but most of all a set of rules concerning personal conduct and behaviour, of what was 'done' and 'not done'. This was accompanied, from the early nineteenth century onwards, by a remarkable revival of interest in all the trappings of the medieval ideal: in Mark Girouard's gently ironic phrase, a 'Return to Camelot'.

In a post-Enlightenment world, governed by the principle of reason, chivalry seemed faintly silly; in the Romantic reaction to an age of burgeoning industrialism it seemed less so. Malory's *Morte d'Arthur*, which had been out of print since 1634, was published once more in 1816 and again in 1817, but it was the novels of Sir Walter Scott which captured the interest of a broad reading public in the ideal of the gentleman, and it was he, more than any other single figure, who popularized and modernized the medieval code. Scott attempted to absorb the best elements of what he called 'the wild and overstrained courtesies of Chivalry' into a contemporary system of etiquette and manners. His achievement was to demonstrate the contemporary relevance of what had hitherto been regarded as an anachronism. In fact, Scott's ideal of a gentleman was largely of his own making, but it struck an immediate chord in the public mind. As Girouard comments:

Scott gave his thousands of readers a Walter-Scott version of the

Middle Ages that captured their imagination because it was presented so vividly, was so different from the life they themselves lived, and yet seemed to express certain virtues and characteristics which they felt their own age was in need of.

Scott's fictional popularization of an age of chivalry was consolidated by Sir Kenelm Digby's *The Broad Stone of Honour*, a non-fictional history of chivalry, which strongly advocated such a code to its readers. Its original sub-title was 'Rules for the Gentlemen of England'. For Digby, chivalry was a permanently valid code. He vehemently attacked prevailing notions of utilitarianism as 'refined selfishness' and, far from placing his trust in a belief in rationality, he attacked 'that principle, the curse of modern times, which leads men to idolise the reason and understanding, and to neglect and even despise the virtues of the heart'. Digby's arguments were to have considerable subsequent influence. In particular his belief that character was more important than intellect was to inform a lengthy tradition of the gentlemanly amateur in the conduct of public life. He also popularized a number of other aspects of the gentlemanly ethic – for example, the belief that gentlemanly virtue was a natural gift and could not be learned or acquired; that a true gentleman should not be interested in money; and that a real gentleman enjoyed a natural affinity with the lower classes in contradistinction to the much-despised middle classes:

So far from intending any reproach upon the lower classes of society, I pronounce that there is even a peculiar connection, a sympathy of feeling and affection, a kind of fellowship, which is instantly felt and recognised by both, between those and the highest order, that of gentlemen. In society, as in the atmosphere of the world, it is the middle which is the region of disorder and confusion and tempest.

It followed that

. . . the lower orders of people in England are generally, if not always, desirous of serving gentlemen instead of persons of inferior rank.

The natural gift of gentility should not be confused with the accident of birth. It was certainly easier, according to Digby, for men of good birth to be chivalrous, by virtue of their upbringing and because public opinion expected it of them, but 'that general spirit or state of mind which disposes men to heroic and generous actions' could be found anywhere. The problem for the aspirant Victorian gentleman was therefore a tantalizing one: how could one be sure of possessing something so vaguely defined as a 'general spirit or state of mind'? At times it seemed that nothing so exercised the collective mind of the mid-Victorian propertied classes than whether or not they were regarded as 'real gentlemen' among the particular social echelon with which they wished to identify themselves. By the 1850s chivalric metaphors came naturally to the lips of any educated man with aspirations for gentlemanly status. But still the assured conferment of gentility proved to be elusive. A rash of castle-building ensued; public schools were created to educate real-life Tom Browns in the values of gentility; organized team games became non-militaristic examples of fellowship, discipline, physical prowess and other knightly attributes. Nevertheless, the inner doubts remained. Rather like the seventeenth-century Puritan who could never be assured of eternal grace, the merely monied could never conclusively confirm their gentlemanly statues. The characters of Trollope's novels, for example, were riddled with doubt on this score.

A major problem, as scores of writers of manuals on manners and etiquette testified, was that admission to the coterie of those who were unassailably 'gentlemen' depended upon an effortless command of the bewildering and intricate nuances of gentlemanly demeanour and behaviour. These ultimately decisive aspects of the gentlemanly ethic were both unwritten and unspoken, and could be abruptly changed or modified without warning. As countless aspirants found to their chagrin, the taste and fashion of the immediate past were no guide to the correct gentlemanly conduct of the present. 'Real' gentlemen understood these changes instinctively; those insensitive enough to be unaware of them were defined as 'other people'. Gentility was thus a matter of social acceptance. By such means a highly status-conscious, but never entirely exclusive, 'inner circle' could both ration admission and control its members. The gentlemanly ethic was thus a device for perpetuating distinctions of status, and an agency of social discipline, ensuring that attitudes and values conformed to a readily identifiable pattern. The notion of gentility both conferred legitimate authority on those who held power in rural society and defended the rituals of social intercourse which accompanied the exercise of this power.

The gentlemanly ethic thus underpinned the principle of hereditary landownership which continued to shape nineteenth-century rural England. By his acceptance as a 'real gentleman' in the rural community the landowner hoped to ensure the deference of farmers and farm workers which, he believed, was essential to the continuing harmony and stability of class relationships. It also enabled the landowner to claim an unimpeachable moral superiority over the other inhabitants of the rural world, so that the other 'natural orders' would instinctively acknowledge the landowner as one of their 'betters' as well as one of their rulers. The gentleman landowner would thus be granted a legitimate right to rule, but would also accrue certain obligations and duties. Those further down the social scale would expect a paternalistic concern for their own welfare, that their interests would be protected from the vagaries of the outside world. The landowner was protector of the local community and its plenipotentiary on the regional or national stage. A gentlemanly sense of duty demanded a sense of service to the community; the realities of power demanded that he directed and controlled it. During a period of agricultural prosperity this contradictory character of gentlemanly authority could, for the time being, be contained.

THE BUSINESS OF FARMING

Many landowners took advantage of the prosperity of the period to embark upon another round of agricultural improvement. A number of large investment programmes were introduced on many estates, and many landowners also made systematic revaluations of their farms, linking rents to prices.

High farming both demanded and created the conditions for new items of capital investment, but the returns to landowners through increasing rents were not to be as spectacular as those which accompanied the agricultural revolution of the eighteenth century. In this respect high farming turned out to be for the landowner a strategic miscalculation and a misdirection of resources. The very heavy capital expenditure on buildings and drainage, which was a hallmark of this period, could only be recouped as long as rents were high, and although they did rise, the increase brought only minimal returns (compared with prevailing industrial and commercial investment), thus leaving estates vulnerable to any later decline. As I have already noted, landlords were thus subsidizing agriculture as well as contributing to its over-capitalization. Not for the last time agriculture entered into a love affair with technological innovation which could not be justified on purely hard-headed financial grounds.

High farming demanded new investment because the intensification of production, particularly on the heavier clay soils, was not feasible without it. The most essential improvement was drainage. It enabled farmers on heavy and poorly-drained soils to cut their costs of cultivation, speed up their operations, introduce new machinery and take advantage of new artificial fertilizers. But drainage was expensive to carry out and often difficult to organize, given the patchwork quilt of landholding which took little account of watersheds and watercourses. It was not such a straightforward business, therefore, as enclosure had been a century or more earlier. Where successful, however, the increase in yields could be spectacular, launching husbandry methods onto a far more intensive round of crop and stock rotations than could have been contemplated beforehand. Such was the interrelated character of high farming, though, that rising crop yields enabled higher stocking ratios, so that new drainage schemes also provoked heavy investment in farm buidlings – dairy parlours, cattle houses, pig-sties, barns, etc. Status considerations played their part here: there was a renewed passion for Victorian model farms. During the eighteenth century quite modest innovations had produced massive financial returns, but now the reverse was frequently the case. F. M. L. Thompson has described this effort as

a last, expensive, homage to king corn, and largely because subsequent developments showed that it was misdirected the returns to landowners were on the whole disappointingly small. In these low returns, and in the higher levels of estate expenditure in general, we can see a weakening in the position of many landowners springing from the context of agriculture itself. It was not accidental that this was happening at the same time as a decline in the wealth and status of the landowners relative to the middle classes, and the conjunction of the two developments must be accounted an important factor in the weakening of the landed interest. . . .

Farmers, however, did markedly better. Many were those listed as 'yeomen' in the New Domesday Survey, with holdings of between 100 and 1,000 acres. Each county could claim its share of yeoman farmers descended from the Middle Ages, and during the mid-Victorian period they prospered. They and the small proprietors on less than 100 acres assumed local importance in areas like the Fens, Cumbria, the Home Counties and Worcestershire. Ancient yeoman families were, however, leavened with *arriviste* manufacturers and full-time tradesmen, many of whom had little direct interest in the land and were frequently petty rural landlords. The great majority of farmers, of course, did not own their land, but were tenants, accounting in most regions for 85–90 per cent of the cultivable land. In the districts in which high farming predominated after 1850 – principally the arable south and east – tenant farmers prospered and their social prospects flourished. Their fortunes were, however, intimately bound up with those of their landlords, particularly when high farming, in order to produce favourable results, demanded an improving landlord prepared to undertake the necessary heavy investment. Tenant farmers were thus dependent upon the wealth of their landlords and the security, together with the freedom to make the best of their farms, that this gave them. The landlord who kept to his side of the bargain could reasonably expect the social deference and political support of his tenants in return.

Tenancy agreements varied considerably, but during the Victorian period there was a persistent tendency to replace leases with annual tenancies or tenancies-at-will. This reflected the fact that progressive tenants with entrepreneurial flair and technological know-how were far from easy to find, although such arrangements could also be advantageous to the landowner. Encouraged by rising prosperity, such tenants were willing to invest their own working capital in improving soil fertility and purchasing machinery. If necessary they could be compensated on departure by amounts which depended upon local custom but which acknowledged a *de facto* tenant right to share in the costs and benefits of capital improvement. Conversely landlords rarely enforced eviction over rent arrears or similar misdemeanours, and would subsidize their tenants through loans, rent remissions, rent reductions, etc., during lean years. The exact arrangements, and the ways in which they were implemented, were bound up in the highly personalized context of rural social relationships, with landlords (and their agents) exercising a benevolent concern for their tenants which derived from the wider obligations of paternalistic authority. A verbal agreement was often sufficient and while the relationship was not without its stresses they could be easily contained within the affluence of the high farming era. Thus the formal distinction between landlord's and tenant's capital was rarely adhered to in practice. Some landlords left most of the improvements to their tenants and acknowledged this by charging low rents; others shared the costs with their tenants; some invested heavily and increased rents accordingly, especially after 1850. Flexibility could be maintained for as long as each party stood to gain from the overall improvement in conditions.

Many tenant farmers were therefore fully participating partners in the improvements associated with high farming – a considerable contrast with the earlier age of improvement in the eighteenth century. Nowhere was this more apparent than in the application of new technology, especially in mechanization, a point not lost on the Frenchman, Hippolyte Taine, when he visited England in the 1860s:

. . . We stopped at a model farm. No central farmyard: the farm is a collection of fifteen or twenty low buildings, in brick, economically designed and built. Since the object was to put up a model, it would not have done to set the example of a costly edifice. Bullocks, pigs, sheep, each in a well-aired, well-cleaned stall. We were shown a system of byres in which the floor is a grating; beasts being fattened remain there for six weeks without moving. Pedigree stock, all very valuable. . . . Steam engines for all the work of the arable land. A narrow-gauge railway to carry their food to the animals; they eat chopped turnips, crushed beans, and 'oil cakes'. Farming in these terms is a complicated industry based on theory and experiment, constantly being perfected and equipped with cleverly designed tools. But I am not a competent judge of such matters, and amused myself by watching the farmer's face: he had red hair, a clear complexion but marbled with scarlet like a vine leaf baked by the Autumn sun; the expression was cold and thoughtful. He stood in the middle of a yard in a black hat and black frock-coat, issuing orders in a flat tone of voice and few words, without a single gesture or change of expression. The most remarkable thing is, the place *makes money*, and the nobleman who started it in the public interest now finds it profitable. I thought I could see, in the farmer's attitude, in his obviously positive, attentive, well-balanced and readily concentrated mind, the explanation of this miracle.

Farmers themselves were frequently enthusiastic for mechanization, and the demand for manufactured implements and machines of all kinds picked up with the onset of high farming. There were two main stages in the development of farm mechanization during this period. The first, from 1835 to 1850, involved the adoption of more sophisticated tools, particularly those associated with arable husbandry – seed drills, mechanical threshers, iron-frame ploughs, lined cultivators, modern zigzag harrows, etc. Simple machines were also available such as corn-dressers, chaff-cutters, oat-crushers, etc. The introduction of these implements reflected dramatic improvements in machine technology which were a by-product of the railway boom of the 1840s. The nascent agricultural engineering industry was itself heavily involved in the manufacture of railway equipment, and the scale of its growth was readily visible at the Great Exhibition at Crystal

Palace in 1851, where over 300 firms were represented. The pace of mechanization had been held back in the aftermath of the Captain Swing riots, but in the more settled circumstances after 1850 it quickened appreciably. The second stage of mechanization was dominated by two particular items, the steam thresher and the mechanical harvester, both of which were adopted on a wide scale across southern England. By the late nineteenth century, virtually all harvesting and barn work was performed by machine; steam traction was widely applied for threshing and, on heavy clay lands, for ploughing. The absence of mechanization was noticeable only on small farms and allotments, and – across a broader range of holdings – in the uplands.

The pace of mechanization clearly varied considerably from one locality – and even one farm – to another. It was influenced not merely by availability, but by a host of economic, topographical and social factors. Mechanization was an integral feature of the reorganization of farm management which accompanied the move to high farming. The adoption of the new technology frequently demanded changes in the physical layout of the farm and its buildings. The steam plough, for example, required large rectangular fields, and hedges were grabbed up and new roads laid down in order to accommodate it. Wholesale mechanization could be afforded only by the larger farms, which were in any case better placed to take advantage of the economies of scale offered by the new technology. This added to the growing economic differentiation between large and small farms, a factor reflected socially in the contrast between the prosperous and socially-aspiring large tenant farmer and his economically and socially marginalized 'two horse' neighbour.

In embracing the new technology, however, agriculture was becoming more closely linked to a complex of manufacturing industries which were providing many of the inputs which supported high farming. The agricultural engineering industry grew rapidly during these years, simultaneously becoming concentrated around major manufacturers with a national, indeed international market, who gradually displaced small-scale, local workshops. The increasing use of artificial fertilizers also provided the basis for a growing agro-chemical industry. Later, during the final two decades of the century, food processing was also to be reorganized and consolidated around 'brand name' manufacturers. In these ways, not only were significant elements in the chain of food production being displaced from farms, but agriculture itself was becoming, slowly and unevenly, transformed into a capital-intensive system of production which in the twentieth century was to be termed 'agribusiness'.

The full flowering of agribusiness awaited a further round of technological innovation associated with the internal combustion engine. For the time being, however, it was steam, that great symbol of Victorian progress and confidence, which captured the imagination of the agricultural innovator. In the prevailing climate of optimism which characterized the mid-Victorian period of high farming it seemed that the harnessing of steam power to agriculture could guarantee the prosperity of farming in the same way as it had assisted in creating the wealth of the manufacturing districts. This optimism was to prove misplaced.

CHAPTER 4

VILLAGE LIFE AND LABOUR

Mid-Victorian high farming marked the culmination of more than a century of self-confident, aggressively commercial, agricultural 'improvement'. Not surprisingly it also consolidated a distinctive form of social life in the countryside by shaping and fashioning the structure of the village community. Indeed it was between 1846 and 1873 that the social and ecological pattern of what is now regarded as 'the traditional English village' became firmly established, particularly in the lowland areas in the south and east where high farming was in such prosperous ascendency. This should act as a cautionary note to what is customarily regarded as the immemorial antiquity of the English village, whose timelessness is often falsely assumed. As historians such as W. G. Hoskins and W. E. Tate have demonstrated, the nucleated settlement that is regarded as characteristic of the English village is a comparatively recent development, initiated by the enclosure movement and the agricultural revolution of the eighteenth century, and consolidated by the movement of farmers out of the village during the nineteenth century. Over much of lowland England, then, previously scattered agricultural dwellings gravitated towards a definable parish centre around the church or manor house. The continuity of settlement pattern is more apparent in the upland areas of the north and west – where scattered farmsteads and dwellings have remained more of the norm – but even here colonization of the remoter areas, such as Cumbria, was still proceeding as late as the eighteenth century. So the English village is neither as ancient nor as unchanging as is commonly thought.

It was during this mid-Victorian period, moreover, that many of the villages which we now regard as quintessentially rural assumed a predominantly agricultural function. The industrial and commercial development of the British economy during the nineteenth century produced a pattern of urban and industrial concentration that succeeded in 'ruralizing' the countryside – that is, much of the small-scale manufacture and domestic handicraft which had previously been located in villages was rendered obsolete by the new system of factory production that was taking place in the new industrial towns and cities. Many of what are now regarded as the most spectacular examples of the traditional English village were in fact medieval textile 'towns' which reverted to an agricultural status following the transfer of textile production to the industrial North during the nineteenth century. This was a pattern repeated in many areas. Thus, although the countryside did not become completely agricultural, because of the continuing importance of mining and quarrying in many localities and the tenacious existence of some manufacture in the agricultural ancillary trades, farming became increasingly the mainstay of the rural economy. The population of the majority of rural villages was therefore dependent upon agriculture for a living. Even if those in the village were not working directly on the land as farm workers, they were involved in occupations closely associated with farming such as blacksmiths, wheelwrights, millers and other craftsmen and ancillary workers. Because of this dependence on agriculture the village was becoming an 'occupational community', one whose whole existence was intimately bound up with the fortunes of a single industry – farming.

It is this occupational community that is today regarded as 'traditional'; but in the mid-nineteenth century it was quite novel: villagers then looked back to a quite different kind of traditional village community, one which had existed prior to enclosure and the onset of a fully commercialized agrarian society. It was *this* community whose loss dismayed and angered so many rural observers in the late eighteenth and early nineteenth centuries, among them Goldsmith, Crabbe,

Cowper, Clare and, most famously, Cobbett, whose *Rural Rides* was the most influential polemic against the new social and economic order. Writers such as these looked back – in a fashion not altogether untainted by nostalgia – to a lost village community whose inhabitants were more independent and self-sufficient, less afflicted by the privileges of property and the exploitation of class. As we have seen (in chapter 2), it was the transition from this kind of village community to the occupational community of the mid-nineteenth century which provoked the widespread social unrest of the 1820s and 1830s. The 'traditional village community', then, does not exist, except as a folk memory. The village was constantly changing and evolving throughout the nineteenth century. Similarly what constituted 'community' (or, if one prefers, 'a *real* community') was always a subjective assessment: the preferences and values of the observer, as much as the social reality of a particular locality, were decisive.

The relevance of these comments to the appraisal of village life between 1846 and 1873 becomes more apparent when one considers how this period is to be characterized. It is customary to regard it as a period of social tranquility, a succession of peaceful and prosperous decades between the upheavals of Captain Swing and the later conflicts surrounding the Revolt of the Field led by Joseph Arch. The village is portrayed as an 'organic community', wherein a benevolent squirearchy, a respectful tenantry and deferential farm workers worked and lived together in mutual harmony and affection, each stratum knowing its place in an ordered and orderly world. There is certainly some evidence to support such a view if one cares to look for it. During this period there was a decline in overt class conflict; village life did become more settled and the country-side was, within reasonable limits, pacified. But such a view takes account only of the tranquil surface of rural society: it represents very much an official credo, a 'view from above'. Beneath this superficially harmonious exterior there was a very different kind of village existence, a rural underworld of resistance, resentment and quasi-criminal activity, hidden from public gaze, where covert conflict between classes remained and was pursued. This was the village of 'us' and 'them' – of religious dissent, secret societies, poaching gangs and the veiled intimacy of the four-ale bar. The 'official' and the 'unofficial' village constantly vied for predominance, not merely in the everyday activities of rural affairs, but also in the hearts and minds of the inhabitants.

THE OCCUPATIONAL COMMUNITY

As with any isolated and largely self-contained community, the agricultural village was often the object of a fierce loyalty among its inhabitants. From its own customs and traditions the villagers could draw upon a strong sense of identity and morality which probably represented the greatest sources of strength in the face of the material adversity which affected all of the rural working population. Inevitably the boundaries of what was and was not considered socially acceptable and permissible were more clearly defined in nineteenth-century village life than is frequently the case today, as indeed they were in Victorian society generally. This in itself conferred a sense of order on village life, a sense of 'place', in both a geographical and a social sense, which could be recognized and accepted as a natural and unchanging fact of life. For those villagers who accepted their 'place', this created a sense of psychological certainty and with it a not altogether un-welcome sense of security. For those who found this social order irksome – the rebellious, the ambitious or simply the single-minded – village society was unduly narrow and restrictive, a dispiriting and mean-spirited place, shackling the individualist by the vicious purveyance of gossip and innuendo.

In her autobiographical account of village life in Oxford-shire, *Lark Rise to Candleford*, Flora Thompson, though writing of a somewhat later period towards the end of the nineteenth century, captures this double-edged quality of village society as both a safe haven and a harsh prison. She also suggests that the narrow intimacy of social affairs in Lark Rise provided a means of accommodating to the otherwise harsh circumstances of rural life:

The discussion of their own and their neighbours' affairs took the place occupied by books and films in the modern outlook. Nothing of outside importance ever happened there and their lives were as unlike as possible the modern conception of country life, for Lark Rise was neither a little hotbed of vice nor a garden of Arcadian virtues. But the lives of all human beings, however narrow, have room for complications for themselves and entertainment for the onlooker, and many a satisfying little drama was played out on that ten-foot stage.

In their daily life they had none of the conveniences now looked upon as necessities: no water nearer than the communal well, no sanitation beyond the garden closet and no light but candles and paraffin lamps. It was a hard life, but the hamlet folks did not pity themselves.

The hardness of this life stemmed from the chronic poverty and occasionally cruel exploitation to which the nineteenth-century farm worker – or 'farm labourer' as he was more customarily referred to – was subjected. Wages remained stubbornly and appallingly low. Farm workers worked longer hours for less than half of the average weekly industrial wage. Many lived permanently on the verge of starvation, a population which existed both literally and metaphorically on the bread line. However, the conditions of the farm worker, and with them the everyday life of the village community, could vary considerably across the country according to the distribution of landholding, the nature of agricultural pro-duction and the pattern of settlement. Here it is useful to refer once more to the distinction drawn by Caird between the predominantly pastoral north and west of England and the mainly arable south and east, a division which affected the organization and conditions of village life in the two regions. The greater use of hired labour on the arable farms created a clear-cut social division in rural society between farmers and farm workers, whereas in the pastoral areas little hired labour was employed, and the most significant division was between landowners and tenants. Although this is somewhat over-simplified, it is nevertheless significant that, during the nineteenth century, rural unrest persistently took the form of trade union conflict in the arable areas and of tenants' rights in the pastoral areas. The socially significant class boundary was therefore drawn at a different point in each case and this in itself points to the danger of conflating the two types of society. For this reason I will refer here mostly to the lowland zone; the upland areas will be analysed more fully in chapter 7.

In eastern and southern England, then, where the bulk of hired farm workers were concentrated, there was for the most part a distinct and recognizable class division between farmers and their employees. The rural village was correspondingly divided socially between the workers who inhabited the village itself and the farmers and landowners who increasingly lived outside on their own holdings of land. Both geographically and socially, therefore, agricultural employers and landlords were not part of the rural village community as far as the agricultural worker was concerned. Although there was an 'official' village community within which landowners, farmers and clergy were included, and which was occasionally celebrated in traditional (and public) rituals and ceremonies, there was another community, a locally-based, working-class subculture, which excluded 'them' in authority. This subculture represented the core of the occupational community. It was basically a neighbourly community of kin and workmates, not dissimilar to that which existed in many urban working-class neighbourhoods, but which the outsider could find virtually impenetrable. It was sustained by the isolation of the rural village, by the strong kinship links between the village inhabitants and by the need for co-operation in times of family crisis. Most importantly it was forged out of the common experience of both work and leisure activities, which meant that a code of behaviour was reinforced both at work and in the village community. The nature of arable farming, which required a large labour force to tend the crop, conferred upon rural society a rigid social hierarchy: whatever the internal relationships within the village few were ever in any doubt that they lived under the shadow of the local employing class.

These conditions made the nineteenth-century rural village

a very close-knit society. The circle of friends and acquaintances with which the farm worker surrounded himself consisted predominantly of other farm workers, both at work and in the village. Consequently ostracism and gossip were powerful ways of enforcing the values and standards of village life. In addition the status and prestige of an individual or family within the village was often derived from the world of work, where certain skills were highly prized. Whatever its source, however, the village generated a strong sense of group identity. It represented a 'mutuality of the oppressed', as Raymond Williams has called it, in the sense that co-operation in times of family crisis – childbirth, illness, death, unemployment – was an accepted code of behaviour, reinforcing a communal identity among a population which lived in continual poverty.

Relationships with farmers and landowners were clearly different from those between fellow workers. For relationships with farmers and landowners across most of lowland England were, almost by definition, relationships with authority. Although the precise configuration of landowners and farmers could vary considerably from village to village, there is little doubt that they formed, from the point of view of the farm worker, a coherent and easily identifiable rural ruling class against which the farm worker, either individually or collectively, was relatively powerless. Within the village, therefore, the world was divided into two distinct and separate groups: 'them' and 'us', master and man. The locally powerful were acknowledged rather than accepted; in Flora Thompson's words, they 'flitted across the scene like kingfishers crossing a flock of hedgerow sparrows'. They attended the church, patronized the local tradesmen and supervised the affairs of the village. They felt entitled to, and duly received, the customary genuflections that were accorded their rank, but they belonged to the 'district' or the local 'house' rather than to the village. Their power was easily visible and universally comprehended. In a rural area farmers and landowners not only possessed a near monopoly over employment opportunities, but they also controlled most of the other major institutions of rural society: housing, education, the Church, charity, poor law administration and the law. Any farm worker could therefore easily anticipate the consequences of 'going against' the local farmers and for the most part they resigned themselves to the situation, bit their tongues rather than spoke out and kept themselves very much to themselves.

In this way the mid-Victorian village was placid – in contrast to the upheavals of the early part of the century. In some areas placidity no doubt went with a genuine affection and respect for a benevolent squire or a generous employer. Elsewhere it could be no more than the necessary pose of the powerless, a less-than-genuine adherence to expected behaviour. In most areas there were probably elements of both. Such was the level of personalized authority, and thus idiosyncrasy, that it is impossible to generalize. But in view of events during the 1870s it is important not to mistake the placid and relatively undisturbed surface of these relationships as implying any deeper sense of social harmony and commitment. There remained a thriving rural underworld in which a whole range of activities, such as arson, poaching and the propagation of usually inconsequential subversive talk in the taproom of the local alehouse, bore witness to a continuing, if covert, sense of deprivation and class antagonism. None of this amounted to any collective and overt form of resistance, such as had occurred in the 1820s and 1830s, but neither did it amount to a wholesale endorsement of the locally powerful elite. Indeed the most demonstrative verdict was given by the thousands who, individually and quietly, turned their backs on rural society and sought to improve their lives by moving to the towns.

THE VILLAGE IDYLL?

Wages and living conditions in rural areas certainly gave good cause to perpetuate a festering resentment. Wages were not only low, but a large proportion of the agricultural labour force was casualized and underemployed. The threat of the workhouse was constant. In addition housing conditions remained a scandal, as a succession of government inquiries in the 1850s and 1860s vividly demonstrated. Housing was, of course, a crucial resource in its own right, but housing provision had connotations which went far beyond the mere availability of shelter. The pattern of housing clearly affected the social composition of the village, but the decision to build new cottages also had far-reaching consequences for the local labour market and therefore for the potential level of wages and, most importantly, Poor Law provision. The most important regulator of rural housing was the pattern of local landownership. In the so-called 'closed' villages, the resident squire had little or no incentive to build, for fear that the attraction of additional labourers' families might later become a charge on the poor rates. In the 'open' villages, petty landlords erected ramshackle accommodation for rent, but given the low level of wages they were by no means a profitable investment. Rents were low and the accommodation frequently damp, insanitary and semi-derelict. Thus those who could afford to build – the richer landowners – had least incentive to do so, while in the open villages surplus labour depressed wage levels, making it impossible for rents to rise to a level that would render improvements profitable. A few large landowners were stirred by their social conscience to construct 'model' cottages and villages, but for the most part the farm worker was consigned to an overcrowded hovel.

During the middle of the century rural housing conditions became a matter of deep concern to many liberal-minded onlookers. There was a clear contrast between the prosperity of farming and the abject poverty of the farm labourer. Health inspectors worried about sanitation risks; clergymen were concerned about the moral consequences of overcrowding; and many employers began to view with alarm the potential which open villages offered as hotbeds of political agitation. Each had some cause for complaint. The government 'Blue Books' which reported on the 'Sanitary Condition of the Labouring Population of England' presented a vivid, if not lurid, account of conditions. Overcrowding was endemic and actually became worse between 1851 and 1861. Only 250 out of more than 5,000 cottages inspected had more than two bedrooms, even though the average number of persons per house was 4.87. Roofs were often warped and the interiors damp and badly aired; floors were frequently rotten or full of holes and the living rooms were dark, damp, cold and smoky. As late as 1874 a reporter from *The Times* described conditions in the Suffolk village of Exning as follows:

Many cottages have but one bedroom. I visited one such cottage in which father, mother and six children were compelled to herd together – one a grown-up daughter. . . . In another case the woman said they had put the children upstairs, and she and her husband had slept in a bed on the brick floor below until the bottom board of the bed had fallen to pieces from damp, and then they had to go among the children again. The sanitary inspector visits these dwellings occasionally to prevent overcrowding, but the difficulty is for the poor to find other cottages, even when they are inclined to pay more rent. Some of the worst of these cottages belong to small occupiers; some are mortaged up to the hilt, and the owners often can afford neither to rebuild nor repair. It is a hard thing, again, for the sanitary inspector to pronounce a cottage unfit for human habitation, when no better – perhaps literally no other – can be had for the family.

Changes in the administration of the Poor Law following the Union Chargeability Act of 1865 removed some of the disincentives to build in the 'closed' parishes. Further changes were brought about by the demise of the gang system of labour, following the Gang Act of 1867. The employment of gangs had been regarded as the cheapest means of overcoming labour shortages at periods of peak demand, such as harvest. However the system fell into disrepute during the 1860s, following a number of scandals over the exploitation of women and children. The Act introduced a licensing system and restricted the employment of females and minors, thereby eliminating many of the economic advantages of employing a semi-permanent 'casual' labour force. Farmers, especially in the 'closed' villages, then sought to secure their supply of labour by building cottages near their own farms. These were known as 'tied' cottages, as opposed to the 'free' cottages which were rented directly from the landowner. Tied cottages could be held only for the duration of employment on the farm; if the worker ceased employment for any reason he could be required to seek housing elsewhere. In the final quarter of the nineteenth century the significance of tied housing was to grow. It was to provide an important source of reserved housing for farm workers – particularly after the break-up of the landed estates when many former estate cottages fell into the hands of farmers – but it was also to increase the degree of dependence upon farming employers and was to render farm workers even more vulnerable to petty harassment and oppressive threats.

The only cushion which lay between the poverty of wages and living conditions on the one hand, and the feared alternative of the workhouse on the other, was the incidence of private charity. The Poor Law had always coexisted in rural areas with a more informal, unofficial and personal form of poor relief – the charitable activity which formed an integral part of the relationship between agricultural workers and their social superiors. Indeed charity provided a substitute for the deficiencies of the Poor Law at the local level. Charity also complemented the Poor Law as a means of social control: charity was the carrot while the Poor Law was the stick which was to engender harmonious relationships between the social classes. Thus for several centuries the upper echelons of English rural society had cultivated a tradition of what the historian Geoffrey Best has called 'prudential charity', using repeated doles of food, clothing, almshouses, hospitals, schools and other worthwhile donations as a social sedative to tide the poor – especially the 'deserving' poor – over periods of temporary distress. Ulterior social, as well as generously Christian, motives were certainly recognized in the tradition of Lady Bountiful. During a notorious exchange of correspondence in *The Times* in 1874 (see chapter 6), Lady Stradbroke, looking back to the placid harmony of the previous decades, enumerated the farm labourers'

. . . many Benefit Clubs, clothing, coal and shoe clubs, etc. subscribed to unanimously and chiefly supported by their employers; their cottage garden shows and prizes; their dinners and treats at Christmas and harvest, schools for their children, which until the passing of the late Act, were kept up entirely, and many are still, by their employers and landlords. All these are benefits and comforts which are not thought of, and would not be feasible in large manufacturing districts, but which add materially to the happiness and unity of the two classes – employers and labourers.

Charity, then, was not only a kind of social analgesic applied to deaden the pain of poverty and powerlessness; it was also an attempt to cement together the potentially conflicting classes in the nineteenth-century rural village. It enabled landowners and employers to exercise a central core of benevolence, which, whatever the vicissitudes, was successful in binding rural society together as a recognizably functioning entity up until the First World War. Local landowners and farmers acted out their self-assigned roles as benefactors and protectors of their communities. A paternalistic concern for the village's welfare, generosity in the endowment of local institutions and societies and frequent visits to the sick and needy could produce feelings of deference and gratitude which allowed the poor to identify with what was otherwise a very arbitrary and oppressive society. As Flora Thompson put it: 'If the squire and his lady were charitable to the poor, affable to the tradesmen, and generous when writing out a cheque for some local improvement, they were supposed to have justified the existence of their class.'

Rural philanthropy was, however, a very patchy affair. By no means all villages were in receipt of the patronage of a local 'Big House'. Nor were the effects of charity always those that were intended. Undue condescension and unnecessary interference in private lives could produce results that were entirely contrary to those that were desired. As one nineteenth-century adviser on these matters wrote: 'Let it never be forgotten that the lower classes are extremely sensitive to the *spirit* in which they are treated, and that the moral influence of charity depends infinitely more upon the manner of the donor than upon the value of the gift.' It was always possible for the rural poor to be servile rather than grateful, to become professional mendicants, or to accept charity cynically while withholding their goodwill. Thus charity offered without the proper 'spirit' could become a meaningless ritual, as was the case in rural Northamptonshire in the 1860s, described by W. L. Burn in his *The Age of Equipoise*:

Women and girls dropped low curtsies, men and boys touched their caps and pulled their forelocks at the sight of any of the quality. Doles of warm clothing, boots and shoes, flannel and calico, sheets and blankets were distributed in the great hall every Christmas. A fat ox was killed and joints of beef were given to labourers and tenants. But of the real existence of their poorer neighbours and dependants, of their habits and thoughts and ways of living, the inmates of the big house knew nothing.

There were many villagers who held themselves at arm's length from the circle of benevolence, dependence and obedience, just as there were others who held the local squire and his lady in the deepest affection. In these matters, the experience of one village could be wildly – and notoriously – at variance with the next. Burn sums up this situation:

The shadow of the Big House loomed over a society which was becoming more and more hierarchical; yet it was, almost certainly, a misfortune for the labouring man if there was no Big House in the parish, if there was no one, squire or parson or maiden lady, to cushion him in time of need. One can only guess at the proportion of cases in which benevolence demanded the reward of obedience or conformity.

THE COMMUNITY IDEAL

There was, then, always a shifting boundary between the expectations of the village community as perceived by those in authority over it, and a more intractable and impenetrable village subculture of which those in authority were only dimly aware. The notion of 'community' as a stable and harmonious social order expressed the former conception of the village;

that of 'community' as a local neighbourhood bound together by the common historical experience of family, work, and place expressed the latter. Each conception of the village community emphasized different aspects, which is not to say that they did not correspond at times, but they should not be regarded as completely coincidental. Those in authority certainly tried to cultivate a sense of identity with the local community – as opposed to, say, other villages in the area or the more impersonal ties of class. Charity was, as we have seen, a key factor in this. The parish also represented a *spatial* framework within which these orderly and harmonious relationships could be played out – ideally a self-contained little enclave, cut off from the potentially subversive trends and ideas of the outside world. 'Limited horizons', 'knowing your place': the clichés applied to this kind of attitude, like all clichés, express a kernel of truth. In addition, as indicated in chapter 1, this sense of community was also to be expressed visually and aesthetically in a landscape which conferred a sense of place. Ideally (and this was no doubt statistically not altogether typical) all three aspects should run together: the village should consist of clearly-defined 'natural orders' who rarely ventured beyond the parish boundaries – apart from their upper- and middle-class emissaries who were the representatives of the village to the outside world – and who lived in a picturesque setting of parkland, manor house, church tower and quaint cottages.

There were many English landowners who tried assiduously to cultivate this idealized 'community' in their own locality; some were brought up in the midst of it, and, safely cocooned by wealth and residence, actually believed in it without realizing the less congenial reality that lay behind it. They may even have been reasonably successful in transmitting their ideal from time to time to those who found some sense of personal security in it. Such people visualized, in Geoffrey Best's words, '. . . a beautiful and profitable contrivance, fashioned and kept in smooth working order by that happily undoubting class to whom the way of life it made possible seemed the best the world could offer.' The solidarity of 'community' in this representation was very different to the unavoidable communality of the poor referred to earlier in this chapter. The 'organic community' expressed in the ideal existed almost entirely at the level of symbolism – in such rituals as 'beating the bounds', in village fairs and festivals, in the pursuit of sports as diverse as foxhunting and cricket. In each case it could be pointed out how all the village came together as equals and how a profound and authentic sense of community reigned. In many cases, no doubt, this symbolism could override the more mundane, everyday exploitation involved in work on the land which continued to underpin this idealized view. More frequently, however, the villagers translated such events, including the festivities associated with family affairs at the Big House, into an excuse for communal celebrations of a rather different kind, which sometimes threatened, as much as reinforced, social order. This will be taken further in the following section of this chapter.

Throughout the nineteenth century there continued the tradition of altering the physical layout of estate and village in order to reflect the idealization of community life. Perhaps the most celebrated of the mid-nineteenth century architects and designers who engaged in such work was John Loudon, who was particularly sought after by the *nouveaux riches* of the countryside. The underlying social assumptions of his designs are apparent in the following passage taken from his, *An Encyclopaedia of Cottage, Farm and Villa Architecture . . .* (1853):

To me nothing is more cheerless than that exclusive solitary grandeur so much affected in the present day, which forbids the poor even to set foot within the precincts of greatness. As the most beautiful landscape is incomplete without figures, so the general effect of a park is always lovely, unless it have a footpath frequented by the picturesque figures of the labouring classes, and giving life and interest to the scene.

This landscape with figures was itself something of a departure from the eighteenth-century convention, from which the 'labouring classes' had been banished altogether (except for purely ornamental purposes, such as newly-employed hermits). Loudon was, however, concerned to strike a balance between lofty seclusion and involvement in parish affairs. Thus the residence

. . . should always form part of a village, and be placed, if possible, on rather higher ground, that it may appear to be a sort of head and protector of the surrounding dwellings of the poor. . . . Supposing, then, that the estate is bounded on one side by the great public road, about a mile from the house; I would form a good parish road from the most convenient point in the public road, through a pretty enclosed country, watered by the stream from the park, which I should cross by a bridge of one or two arches, near the parish mill, and thence ascent to the village, passing among the scattered farm houses and cottages, with their pretty gardens and orchards, crossing the village green, on which should stand the school-house shaded by lofty trees, to the other extremity of the village, where a handsome arched gateway should form the entrance to the park. Passing through the gateway into an open glade of oaks, the church will be seen at a little distance through the trees, through which the road is continued with a gentle ascent, till the house suddenly presents itself, stables and offices, backed by a woody eminence; and sweeping across the plain in front, through some scattered trees and hollies, you at length reach the steps of the porch.

Thus Loudon conjures up a powerful vision of the ideal English village community, in which various aesthetic, social, moral and even agricultural factors are woven together in order to produce a hierarchically-ordered, but organic unity. What member of the 'picturesque labouring classes' could fail to be impressed and overawed by such a prospect?

Where conditions allowed, this vision of a happy and harmonious community could be acted upon. The locally powerful assumed the responsibilities of leadership, transforming their often arbitrary control into an ethic of 'service' to the community. Through charity and patronage they sought amity and affection, but the achievement of these elusive aims was at best patchy and sporadic. Beyond the official credo of the village community a more intractable social reality remained, one that was much more impervious to the seductive version offered by even the most socially-conscious landowner and farmer. This does not mean that conflict was always and everywhere endemic, but it does mean that complete acceptance was generally withheld in the 'alternative' village centred on the pub and tackle shed.

COMMUNITY AND LEISURE

Although the organization of work was the major function of the nineteenth-century agricultural village, leisure activities of various kinds occupied most villagers on Sundays and at other times in the week when work permitted. During the mid-Victorian period, patterns of rural leisure, particularly for the labouring population, were in a transitional phase. From the latter part of the eighteenth century onwards, and especially during the early Victorian period, concerted efforts were made by the propertied classes to diminish the significance of popular customs and traditions and to render them more civilized, sober and law-abiding where they were not made defunct. This meant that the traditional round of festivals, ceremonies and celebrations was in decline and it had not yet been supplanted by modern forms of mass, commercialized leisure which emerged during the final quarter of the nineteenth century and developed further in the twentieth century. Thus patterns of leisure in the mid-Victorian countryside were restricted, and, by our standards, probably dull. Once again the popular image hides a less than idyllic reality.

Between 1780 and 1850 many traditional sporting occasions and other forms of festivities had disappeared or were on the wane. Cock-fighting and bull-baiting offended Victorian principles of civilized behaviour; many festivals, fairs and holiday celebrations were considered to be too much of a risk to public order and were discouraged or even suppressed. Recognized holidays thus became rare: perhaps Christmas Day and the day of the village feast in lowland areas, with the addition of the annual Hiring Fairs in the North. Such was the decline in festivities, indeed, that it became a talking-point. One defender of popular calendar festivals observed in 1849:

The utility of festivals to nations and society in general is a question of considerable controversy: the opposing arguments are founded chiefly on the interruptions they occasion in public business, the facilities they afford to improvidence and idleness, and the abuses by which they have been too frequently disgraced among the working classes, to the injury of both their means and morals. There is a sad truth in the last objection; but, on the other hand, it is contended that the institution of festivals is natural to humanity, and one of the distinguishing traits of our species; that they serve great moral purposes, in reviving the pious or elevating recollections connected with those events which they generally commemorate, and apt to be forgotten in the dusty bustle of business, or the dull routine of mechanical employment. It is also maintained that they contribute to the cultivation of social virtues, and refresh, with needful relaxations and amusement, the toil-worn lives of the labouring population, which without them would be 'all work and no play', with the proverbial consequence – that all human privileges and arrangements are liable to abuses, and those to which they have been subjected, are no arguments against festivals.

In 1859 another observer commented that:

In most agricultural districts it is wonderful how little play there is in the life of the labouring class. Well may the agricultural labourer be called a 'working-man', for truly he does little else than work.

And it was said of farm workers in Yorkshire around 1870 that:

. . . their amusements were few. . . . The labourer's life . . . was work and rest; of honest, healthy, whole-hearted play he had none . . . his only amusements were the drinking of a pint of beer at the inn, and the enlivenments of the village feast, which was celebrated once a year.

The sense of decline was the more acute because traditionally an annual calendar of ceremonies and festivities had provided a framework for the passage of events in the village community. As J. Arthur Gibb, writing in 1898, put it:

Fifty years ago 'twere all mirth and jollity. . . . There was four feasts in the year for us folk. First of all there was the savers' feast – that would be about the end of April; then came the sheep-shearer's feast – there'd be about fifteen of us would sit down after sheep shearing, and we'd be singing best part of the night, and plenty to eat and drink; next came the feast for the reapers, when the corn was cut about August; and last of all, the harvest-home in September.

This annual calendar, reflecting the structure and rhythm of the agricultural year, provided an important element of continuity in the daily lives of most villagers and bound them together through the shared experience of common work, leisure, religious participation and acknowledgement of the importance of the local landed family. In short, it gave them a sense of place, both socially and geographically. Through this cycle of traditional ceremony the established hierarchy of the village was reaffirmed and the sense of localism – most obvious in 'beating the bounds' of the parish in Rogation week – was reinforced. In this way traditions, customs and ceremonies interlocked to give a sense of importance to the local village community.

By the middle of the nineteenth century, however, this traditional popular calendar was rapidly becoming outmoded. The moral perceptions of the Victorian middle class demanded that they should be transformed into somewhat empty rituals more in keeping with prevailing notions of proper behaviour. The emphasis upon thrift, sobriety and hard work was summarized by William Howitt, who observed in 1840 that: 'England is no longer merry England, but busy England.' Despite resistance from the rural working population, by the second half of the nineteenth century village life had lost many of its festivals and ceremonies. Those that remained were rarely popular in any socially meaningful sense, but reflected attempts by the local establishment to construct an idyllic representation of village life in which relations between the classes consisted of benevolent paternalism and grateful deference and avoided the damaging conflicts inherent in the pursuit of profitable agriculture. The fact that this 'merrie England' – the 'return to Camelot' – was wholly mythical, was neither here nor there. What mattered was that the vulgar and even riotous elements of traditional customs were replaced by an appropriate respect for person and property which did not interfere with the important business of commercial farming. Numerous examples of this change could be given – for instance, the concerted attempts to suppress Shrovetide football, Whitsun ales and even Guy Fawkes night celebrations – but a particularly instructive example concerns one of the central elements of the rural calendar, harvest, and how the traditional harvest-home was transformed into a tame and sanitized harvest festival.

The changes wrought in harvest-home represented an alternative to outright suppression: the incorporation of a formerly popular custom by respectable, middle-class values. Harvest-home was traditionally the great climatic celebration of the farming year. Once the last load had been drawn into the farmyard the excuse was seized to engage in a round of feasting and drinking which celebrated the successful completion of the hard and exhausting work associated with harvest. It was the one occasion in the year when a degree of equality was allowed: farmers and workers ate at the same table; employers not only provided ample quantities of food and ale, but they frequently served at table. Singing, dancing and a good deal of drunken horseplay and semi-serious chafing were the norm. Harvest-home was regarded as a right by the workers in return for their co-operation in the long and often difficult business of harvest. Farmers were expected to be unstinting in their provision of food and drink, and to tolerate, for once, the familiarity of their workers. It was a classic ritual involving the temporary reversal of the usual roles of employer and employee – thereby reaffirming the normal state of affairs for the other 364 days of the year. In the North and West, sheep-shearing suppers frequently performed a similar function. By the middle of the nineteenth century, however, the old harvest-home had been replaced in many areas by a thanksgiving or harvest supper in which all the farms in the parish combined together under the auspices of the local clergyman. A religious service was often involved. Gradually the church service gained the ascendancy over the supper and its associated revelries. By 1889 one approving clergyman, the Revd. Sabine Baring-Gould, could write:

The harvest home is no more. We have instead harvest festivals, tea and cake at sixpence a head in the school-room, and a choral service and a sermon in the church. . . . There are no more shearing feasts; what remain are shorn of all their festive character. Instead we have cottage garden produce shows. The old village 'revels' linger on in the most emaciated and expiring semblance of the old feast.

Thus was a popular custom purged of its disagreeable qualities and granted a patina of respectability more in keeping with the public observance of Victorian middle-class morality. Respectable behaviour was thereby encouraged and the ideal of the village as an 'organic community' reinforced.

Of course, success could never be guaranteed. Some traditions were merely forced underground. And the old subterranean 'dark village' subculture continued. Moreover the rural village could never be hermetically sealed from the potentially subversive influences of the wider world outside. Throughout the nineteenth century the countryside was increasingly infiltrated by the culture of the towns and cities. Urban ways and urban tastes were becoming part of the fabric of rural leisure activities. First the railways and then the bicycle, and – later – the bus and motor car, broke down the isolation of the rural village. Urban pastimes and urban facilities became increasingly accessible to every rural labourer. And a distinctively *rural* culture became absorbed into the growing mass culture of the English working class in the latter decades of the nineteenth century. This process was not, however, limited to leisure activities. External influences were at work on rural society as a whole which were eventually to undermine the localism that supported a separate rural culture.

EXTERNAL INFLUENCES

It is not altogether helpful to regard the rural village as a static and traditional society fighting a rearguard action against the encroaching influence of the urban world. Such a view ignores the extensive internal transformation that was occurring in rural society, brought about by continuing developments in agriculture. These were as much responsible for the manifest social changes in nineteenth-century rural England as its increasing exposure to external influences (see chapters 3 and 5). Nevertheless these external influences did exist and there were changes in the character of rural life which can be attributed to them. If rural society cannot be considered as the passive receptacle of urban innovations, neither can it be considered in isolation from them. And there is little doubt that by the third quarter of the nineteenth century the integration of rural and urban society was proceeding apace.

Changes in the technology of transport were the most obvious agency involved. The railway boom of the 1840s established a national network of trunk routes which passed through, rather than specifically served, rural areas. But the fundamentals of steam railway technology (horizontal rather than vertical boilers, superheated steam, etc.) had been developed; all that remained was to extend the network and to make further improvements in safety and efficiency. Rural branch lines were in general constructed rather later – in the late 1860s and 1870s – and it was not until the 1880s that they were generally accessible, for reasons of cost as much as geography, to the rural working population. It was not only Dickens who viewed the railways as a great symbol of modernity. Such was the popular perception of the day. Hence the arrival of the railway in rural areas was generally greeted with great enthusiasm: a village, or more likely a small country town, could pride itself on being progressive. There were also material benefits – cheaper coal and manufactured goods coming in; agricultural produce, now with access to a wider market, going out. The landed upper classes were more suspicious, partly on what would now be called environmental grounds (many lines were forced into tunnels or cuttings in order not to despoil the view from the Big House), and partly because the railway's role as the harbinger of modernity was feared: could the authority of the squire over the village ever be the same again? In a number of cases – Stamford and Northampton being the most notorious – the railway companies were originally forced to make wide detours, such was the opposition of local landowners to allowing so subversive an influence to cross their land.

In some respects these fears were justified. The railways did enable the rural population to become more aware of, and to some degree to participate in, the world beyond the parish boundary. The availability and choice of domestic goods improved. Newspapers could be distributed across a much wider area, their dissemination also helped by the abolition of stamp duty in 1855 and paper duty in 1861. The national penny post, introduced in 1840, rapidly became dependent upon the railways for speedy and comprehensive coverage. As a farmer announced to a large gathering at the opening of the Mid-Wales line into Llanidloes: 'It would no longer be said of us (as it had been said) that darkness covered their land and gross darkness their people.' The railways also brought one further indirect effect: the introduction of the electric telegraph, which sprang from the need to transmit information on train movements, but which by 1870 had developed into a national system.

The reduction in rural isolation was not merely a matter of transportation, however. It also involved a much less tangible set of cultural influences. Two examples illustrate this most clearly during the mid-Victorian period – education and religious dissent.

RURAL EDUCATION

At the beginning of the Victorian era, many rural villages had no schools at all, while the remainder were funded by a variety of means but always on the basis of local initiative. The nature and extent of provision was then extremely variable and typically attenuated by the demand for child labour on farms. From 1839 onwards, however, the government increasingly intervened, at first by aiding local funds, then by establishing a national inspectorate, certification of teachers and, by 1853, a capitation grant based on average attendance. This culminated in 1870 in the introduction of the first Education Act, which introduced the entirely new element of compulsory attendance. This pattern was typical of the history of government intervention in the whole area of social welfare in so far as it affected rural areas during the nineteenth and twentieth centuries. Rural inhabitants received the benefits of increasing participation and citizenship which were established first at a national level and which trickled down into rural areas. This process was accompanied by growing state intervention and by changes from permissive to mandatory legislation.

As the parliamentary debates on the Education Act made clear, the impact of universal, compulsory education up to the age of twelve was feared by many farmers and landowners. It was seen to 'raise a man above his work' and Lord Onslow, in the debate on the Bill, trusted that '. . . there would be no attempt to establish a very high class of education in our rural schools, as over-education would have the effect of driving away manual labour from the country.' As far as the quality of education in most rural areas was concerned, he need not have worried. Even after the enforcement machinery was established in 1876, many rural parishes dragged their feet over providing a school and ensuring attendance. The withdrawal of children from school in order to help on farms when required remained a common practice – and of course the peculiar timing of the academic year was designed in order to allow harvest operations to be completed before education recommenced. Nevertheless Lord Onslow's fears were also well-founded. The spread of new ideas, tastes and manners via the incipient mass media of the newspapers and journals was not dependent only upon the railways but upon the growth of literacy. As compulsory education spread, not only did a wider world become accessible but, because of the increasingly centralized control over education, the content of the curriculum became less definably rural. In this way, too, a new generation of schoolchildren were inducted into a mass culture.

NONCONFORMITY

If education presented the rural population with the possibility of an alternative in the secular realm, then the startling growth of religious nonconformity in the countryside between 1830 and 1870 marked a parallel development in the realm of religious adherence. The growth of religious dissent, indeed, marked the vitality of the 'alternative' rural community to the local establishment of squire and parson. The relationship between the Church of England and Victorian landed society was universally acknowledged as an intimate one, even before the soubriquet 'The Tory Party at Prayer' became familiar. They were joined by ties of family, social background, outlook and expectations. The Church retained its historic commitment to a rural society presided over by the great landed families, and the parson himself remained an influential figure in propagating and reinforcing the values associated with the preservation of the orderly hierarchy. Religious nonconformity was therefore ineluctably bound up with social dissent. It symbolized a form of protest at the prevailing social order, nonetheless channelling it into a form which did not directly threaten the status quo. It is necessary to emphasize, however, that the struggle between Church and Chapel represented an important theme of Victorian political conflict in the countryside. In the debates over compulsory Church rates and tithes, the funding of education and over disestablishment itself, deep social tensions in rural society were made manifest through the idiom of religious controversy. Once again the apparent tranquility of rural life during this period is belied by a closer examination of the underlying changes.

In the immediate aftermath of the Captain Swing disturbances, rural noncomformity underwent a rapid expansion, especially in the Eastern Counties. Primitive Methodism in particular captured the imagination of thousands of agricultural workers, who sought in it some future compensation for their current deprivation. Between 1829 and 1835 the number of adherents multiplied four times and although after this membership levelled off, the 1860s saw a further rapid expansion prior to the onset of a further round of rural trade unionism (see chapter 7). Because nonconformity – of whatever kind – expressed an alienation from the established social and religious order of the countryside, it flourished most in those villages which, for one reason or another, were least under the influence of the traditional authority of squire and parson – for example, 'open' villages, nucleated settlements or villages situated well away from the nearest parish church or manor house. With the rebellion of the 1830s crushed and active trade unionism nullified, religious nonconformity offered the only major organized means of retaining the rural traditions of class antagonism which had characterized the transition to the new commercial farming economy.

Religious nonconformity was not, however, merely a passive vehicle for transmitting such traditions. It also moulded these traditions in its own image. Nonconformity, for example, contributed to a new sobriety in rural working-class behaviour. It is, as Hobsbawm and Rudé point out,

. . . quite incredible that the newly saved village Baptist or Primitive Methodist, with his hatred of liquor, pubs and sports, should have taken part in the rick-burning and cattle-maiming so patently associated with the bold, hard-drinking and hard-playing poachers and their circles.

Their respectability was at first to split the unanimity of rural working-class culture – into 'roughs' and 'respectables' – and must also have contributed to the plausibility of the settled and harmonious characterization of rural England which gained ground after 1850. Other aspects of nonconformity were rather more subversive, however. It was a powerful educative force which, through the institution of day and Sunday schools and by providing opportunities for villagers to meet, discuss and organize in a formal and systematic manner, made farm workers more articulate and socially aware. In many respects the organization of nonconformist religion, par-ticularly Methodism, was to provide a model for the future structure of trade unionism in the countryside, and it is therefore not surprising that so many union leaders and officials were to be supplied by the Methodist Movement. The presence in a village of a Methodist chapel was often to be a decisive influence in the founding of a local union branch – if only by providing a safe haven for union meetings.

Perhaps the most subversive aspect of Methodism and other forms of religious dissent, however, was that they furnished the rural worker with a sense of justice – or more precisely, in respect of his wordly lot, injustice – through the prevailing tenets of nonconformist biblicism. An important, though largely intangible, trend during the mid-Victorian period concerned the growing impatience of the rural poor with charity and paternalism and an emergent alternative demand for social justice. Such a claim was based not upon the quality of paternalistic concern evinced by a personally known guardian of the landed interest, but by appeal to an impersonal and universal set of moral principles introduced from beyond the world of the parish. Religious dissent offered a profound threat to the legitimacy of squirearchical rule by generating alternative ideas of what was right and proper and what was fair and just in the exercise of secular authority. It also fired a somewhat cowed and dispirited rural working population, following their experiences in the 1830s, with a new passion and zeal for improvement. Thus, when overt class conflict returned to the countryside in the 1870s, it was to be extensively influenced by the culture of nonconformity. Meetings of the newly-formed trade unions were to bear many of the characteristics of a religious revival, with prayers and hymns adopted as an integral part of the proceedings. The appeal to divine blessing, which had begun as an attempt to escape from the deprivations of the present world, had become an essential buttress against attempts to undermine the new collective form of resistance to injustice in the countryside.

In the face of these external influences in the fields of transport and communications, secular education and religious nonconformity, it became apparent that the ideal of the benevolent rural community was increasingly at variance with the reality. In an increasingly urban, industrial and pluralistic society it would be unrealistic to suppose that the legitimacy of the squire and parson's authority could remain unquestioned. Nor could the village remain as self-contained and isolated as idyllic preconceptions demanded. Nevertheless, much as always depended upon the precise nature of local circumstances and most of the developments described in this chapter were extremely variable in timing and extent. But slowly, hesitantly and with many vicissitudes, the village community was being drawn into the embrace of the wider society and the important changes in the last quarter of the nineteenth century were, for the most part, externally generated. For change, when it came, was to be sudden and cataclysmic and owed little to the social and cultural factors described in this chapter. For the whole artifice of the Victorian 'organic community' rested upon the prosperity of Victorian high farming. In the quarter of a century after 1846 few participants thought to question this prosperity. Yet within a remarkably short time few were to have any confidence that these conditions could ever be regained.

CHAPTER 5

AGRICULTURAL CRISIS

The last quarter of the nineteenth century was a period of agricultural crisis. From 1875 until 1939, with only a brief respite during and immediately after the First World War, British agriculture was in a state of chronic depression, characterized by falling commodity prices, lower rents, increasing bankruptcies and an unkempt rural landscape. The transition from the generally prosperous decades of 'high farming' in the 1850s and 1860s was stark indeed. The latter quickly came to be regarded as a 'golden age' of British agriculture, in contrast to the generally unexpected and bewilderingly abrupt onset of depression and ruin. Contemporary observers were struck most of all by the suddenness of this change and for some time put it down to the appallingly bad weather of the late 1870s – a temporary misfortune that would presently correct itself. With the benefit of hindsight, however, it is possible to recognize the 1870s as a turning-point in British rural history, when the agricultural implications of the Industrial Revolution and the expansion of international trade finally became clear. It was a period in which farming in Britain ceased to be either a major industry or even a major source of the nation's food supply.

More recent interpretations of this period have therefore emphasized the inevitability of structural change which culminated in the final quarter of the nineteenth century in a transitional period rendered more prolonged and more difficult by the failure to perceive it as such at the time. For agriculture was not uniformly depressed: some branches of production actually expanded, and in those areas where they were concentrated, a modicum of prosperity was maintained. Consequently, the agricultural depression has to be regarded as a period of structural change in the rural economy and society, rather than one of uniform decay. This, however, in no way detracts from the significance – social and political, as well as economic – of the events during these decades.

AGRICULTURE IN A FREE TRADE ECONOMY

Paradoxically the prosperity of the 1850s and 1860s saw the development of many of the salient features responsible for depression in the 1870s. The commercial success of high farming was dependent upon high prices for both sheep and wheat. The continued existence of such high prices appeared to vindicate the adherents of free trade principles and to eliminate the objections made at the time of the repeal of the Corn Laws in 1846. Unfortunately, however, Britain was a high-cost producer of both sheep and wheat. In the subsequent two decades this mattered little, since international competition was negligible, but in the 1870s competition from low-cost producers in the Americas, Australasia and Eastern Europe became a reality. There was also competition from within Western Europe, where some countries, notably Denmark and the Netherlands, began to specialize in the production for export of high-value foods such as dairy products and bacon.

As other countries in Western Europe industrialized during the latter half of the nineteenth century, so they moved to protect their agricultures by introducing tariffs, particularly after the onset of depression. Britain remained unique in its commitment to free trade principles and the consistency with which they were applied. From 1842, when import duties were reintroduced to prevent large-scale dumping, successive governments strictly adhered to free trade principles in agricultural commodities. To Britain's urban majority, 'free trade' meant 'cheap food', and successive proposals for tariff reform consistently failed to win electoral support. Only during the First World War, in what were generally recognized as wholly exceptional circumstances, were the principles of *laissez-faire* to be set aside. Otherwise agriculture was forced to assume a new and subsidiary role in the British economy. Since the key to Britain's prosperity was assumed to lie in her capacity to export manufactured goods, it was believed to be in Britain's interest to obtain food from the cheapest possible sources and thereby reduce the real cost of industrial wages. The immiseration of British agriculture was, in the context of a mature industrial economy of this kind, regarded as a small price to pay.

The full force of the depression fell on one of the key commodities of mid-Victorian high farming: wheat. In 1870–4 wheat was selling at an average of 55 shillings (£2.75) per quarter; by 1895–9 it was 28 shillings (£1.40). Because of the integrated, rotational character of high farming, such a collapse in the price of one commodity produced a crisis in the whole system. Arable agriculture in the south and east of England could not remain profitable at these prices. Corn growers faced ruin, but could only impotently observe their own threatened extinction as imports flooded in. Once the railroads had opened up the prairies and pampas of Canada, the United States and Argentina, the continuous import of cheap grain was assured, and these regions duly quadrupled their exports of grain to Britain between 1870 and 1900. As a result the arable areas of Britain were devastated, East Anglia notoriously so. This epicentre of the depression has provided the most vivid images of agricultural decline: 'dog-and-stick' farming, overgrown hedgerows, broken-down fences, dilapidated farm buildings, empty, depopulated villages. As a result the differential impact upon other producers has frequently been overlooked. Livestock producers, for example, suffered to a lesser degree while certain branches of farming, such as horticulture, poultry production and dairying actually expanded. But there were few cereal farmers willing to undertake the changes required: such was the social cachet of corn and the belief that depressed prices were temporary that the precepts of high farming continued to mesmerize them.

Such misperceptions were not assisted by a succession of perniciously difficult seasons: at first it was the weather which appeared to be the major culprit. There was a succession of wet summers in 1875, 1877, 1878 and 1879. The quality of the grain harvested was poor and, because of the difficult conditions, the cost of obtaining it was high. There was no compensation to be had in the form of higher market prices, however, since the arrival of massive imports took up the slack. Capriciously these wet summers were later to be followed by a succession of droughts – especially in 1892, 1893, 1895 and 1896 – which were to hit livestock producers at a time when they might have expected some benefit from reduced feed prices that had resulted from the lower cost of grain. Farmers in the pastoral counties thus found it difficult to sustain their recovery from the ravages of disease – rinderpest and pleuro-pneumonia among cattle, liver-rot among sheep – bequeathed by the earlier wet weather. The adverse seasons of the late 1870s were significant because for a while they diverted attention from the true causes of depression and delayed the adjustments that were required. By the time that the underlying changes in the market had been more fully appreciated, the bad weather had wrought a more insidious, but less quantifiable effect: it had so lowered morale within the farming community that there was less inclination to undertake the necessary measures in what was still going to be a most difficult struggle.

It was R. E. Prothero, later Lord Ernle, who, in his magisterial *English Farming Past and Present* (1912), succinctly summarized the new situation in which farmers found themselves:

English farmers were, in fact, confronted with a new problem. How were they to hold their own in a treacherous climate on highly rented land, whose fertility required constant renewal, against produce raised under more genial skies on cheaply rented soils, whose virgin richness needed no fertilizers?

To a generation which had grown accustomed to both unprecedented prosperity and ineffable technical superiority, these changed conditions were at first unintelligible, but they soon produced results that were clear to everyone – a series of bankruptcies, departures and liquidations in the 1880s. Falling rents provided some relief. But as the depression continued, numerous farms were left unlet and unsold; some were simply abandoned. Landowners were forced to grant rent reductions and even complete abatements, but even so arrears continued to accumulate. By the end of the century, rents were back to the level of the 1840s, a reduction of over 25 per cent, although the impact was very variable, with some areas exceeding 50 per cent while others, especially in the pastoral counties, barely touched 10 per cent. The decline in rents allowed the burden of depression to be shared between landlords and tenants, but in neither case was it sufficient to restore good fortune. Landlords encountered major difficulties in keeping their existing tenants and in finding new ones. In some cases falling rental income produced absolute losses. In all cases the depression was sowing the seeds of the break-up of the landed estates which was to occur after the First World War. Tenant farmers, meanwhile, found lower rents to be only a mild palliative. A few departed while they still had some capital; but most hung on, acting with no great alacrity to change their old ways, to await the gloomy inevitability of their own demise.

A depression, any depression, is not merely a period of economic difficulty and decline, however. It also presents new opportunities for innovation and renewed growth. So it was with the agricultural depression at the end of the nineteenth century. The significance of entrepreneurial dexterity in circumventing the worst ravages of the depression is well illustrated by the examples of those farmers who did adapt, and did so with sufficient speed and acumen to remain reasonably prosperous. For example in Essex, the notorious heartland of the depression, Edward Strutt introduced cost-accounting methods on the Terling estate. These demonstrated that feeding cattle along traditional lines – mixed high farming – did not pay. He promptly gave it up. The response of many other farmers was sluggish because they did not know – due to their rudimentary system of accounting – the relative costs of different aspects of their farming enterprise. As far as they were concerned, accounting meant keeping an eye on the bank balance. Very few farmers could therefore acquire the knowledge to follow Strutt's example.

A less easily demonstrable accusation directed at farmers in the cereals counties was that they had gone soft and were unable to apply themselves with the necessary thrift and diligence to the business of working for a living in these more difficult times. This allegation was given some plausibility by the large-scale migration of farmers from the less-depressed North and West to take advantage of the cheap land and cheap tenancies in the South and East. The best-known of these migrations was that of Ayrshire dairy farmers to East Anglia, where, by dint of their frugality, hard work, family labour and abandonment of outdated farming methods, they made at first a reasonable, and later a prosperous, living. Successive migrations from Scotland occurred between the 1870s and the 1930s. Those who were able to take advantage of cheap rents and, later, extremely cheap land prices, were actually capable of expanding. Their descendants were particularly well-placed when agriculture was placed on a sounder economic footing after the Second World War.

Innovation also took place in husbandry methods, albeit slowly at first. Dairy farming, particularly where access to the urban market could be guaranteed, could be modestly successful. Butter and cheese-making were removed from the realms of household economy and produced by standardized methods in centrifugal separators established in new 'creameries' along Danish lines. Market gardening, also with access to the urban market, innovated with new products. In West Yorkshire rhubarb was grown commercially on farms abandoned during the early 1880s. Later in the same decade bulb-growing expanded rapidly around Spalding in Lincolnshire. Potato-growing also prospered close to urban centres – in the Lothians, Yorkshire, West Lancashire and Cheshire, for example. Cornwall developed as a centre for early flowers and vegetables. The Vale of Evesham also became a major market-gardening area – even asparagus was found to flourish in its clay soil. The depression also saw the development of glasshouse cultivation in areas like the Lea Valley and Worthing. Tomatoes ceased to be a rare and exotic import; cucumbers were often grown alongside them. The glasshouse cultivation of cut flowers also began in earnest. These innovations meant that the demand for smallholdings and small farmers remained surprisingly buoyant in many areas, fuelling the demand for land reform and providing opportunities for entry into agriculture for the young and the energetic with little inherited capital.

These new developments contributed to the geographically uneven character of the depression. Even in the most depressed localities, individual examples of initiative could, and did, provide an equitable standard of living. Recovery, when it came, was similarly patchy, but from 1896 a slow and sporadic improvement was discernible. It was not, however, a return to the halcyon days of the mid-Victorian period, but rather a re-establishment of some sort of equilibrium at a much lower level of economic activity. From then until the First World War the agrarian economy bumped along the bottom of the trade cycle which seemed unwilling and unable to sustain any substantial up-turn. After a brief interlude produced by wartime conditions, the depression returned and was to remain until the end of the 1930s. Low farming, it seemed, was here to stay.

AGRICULTURAL CRISIS AND THE INDUSTRIAL STATE

The agricultural depression represented not merely a change in the international trading position of British agriculture, but a fundamental realignment of the role of agriculture in the mature industrial society which Britain had now become. On the eve of the depression it was still possible to conceive of Britain as a mixed economy in which agriculture represented a significant part of the nation's productive activity. The swiftness of the decay of agriculture was a spectacular feature of Britain's 'Second Industrial Revolution' in the final quarter of the nineteenth century. Agriculture, which had been a vibrant sector for investment and profit, became an economic backwater. The population of the countryside began to undergo an absolute decline, its surplus population exported to the burgeoning conurbations and their newly-developing large-scale industries. The countryside itself, deprived of its productive importance, became more and more an 'amenity', something to be appreciated and consumed. The National Trust was founded in 1895 with a view to conserving such 'heritage'; later, in 1926, the Council for the Protection of Rural England was also established in order to maintain the countryside as a picturesque recreational attraction. Decay, and even ruin, became the hallmarks of a desirable rustic aesthetic.

The precise role of agriculture in this industrial society, or even within the countryside itself, was not entirely clear. Comparisons with other societies in Europe which were similarly placed were either unhelpful or depressing. Most Western European countries had managed to expand both agriculture and industry in the last quarter of the nineteenth century, but they had achieved this, for the most part, with the aid of tariff protection for their agricultural products. The free-trade exceptions – Denmark and the Netherlands – had flourished even more spectacularly, undermining the arguments of those who favoured tariff reform in Britain. But they had done so partly on the basis of penetrating the urban British market with poultry, pig and dairy products. The key to their success lay less in adherence to the principles of free trade than in reorganizing their agricultural production around an export market geared specifically to meeting the growing demand for high-value foods in the urban, industrial centres. This was where the structural inertia of British agriculture took its toll. Even the much-vaunted technological superiority of British agriculture was to disappear as the depression wore on. The familiar nineteenth-century spectacle of continental observers marvelling at the technological wonders of British agriculture became reversed; not one of the plethora of commissions of inquiry into the state of agriculture during the depression was complete without despatching some of its members to investigate developments on the Continent.

The spectacular transformation, which the depression manifested, in the role of agriculture in the overall British economy is exemplified in its declining contribution to agricultural self-sufficiency. In the early 1870s Britain was more than 85 per cent self-sufficient in temperate foodstuffs. The penetration of imports exceeded 20 per cent only in wheat, and in animal products it was less than 10 per cent. By the early 1900s, however, imports provided more than 75 per cent of wheat and cheese, two-thirds of bacon and hams and one-third of fresh meat. Canned food was almost entirely imported. These trends continued after the First World War, driving up Britain's dependence on imported temperate foods to more than 50 per cent. Ironically it was on the basis of what is today known as an 'English breakfast' – bacon and eggs – that the prosperity of Danish and Dutch agriculture was founded. The English producers themselves were, however, slow to perceive the possibilities.

According to the theory of comparative advantage associated with free trade doctrine, it was quite in order for Britain to surrender the production of those agricultural staples – cereals was the most pertinent example – to those parts of the world where natural conditions were more suitable. What was more difficult to explain was British agriculture's lamentable performance in products where it had natural advantages of its own. This was all the more puzzling in view of the fact that in the past British agriculture had shown a remarkable capacity for structural and technological change – as the afore-mentioned succession of admiring foreign visitors had testi-fied from the early eighteenth century onwards. Moreover, British agriculture was organized along thoroughly com-mercial lines. It ought to have been less resistant to the developments required – a resistance which might have been expected among the still predominantly peasant agricultures of continental Europe. Britain also possessed a rapidly expanding urban population, rising real incomes and thus an expanding market for foods like meat and dairy products. By virtue of its soil and climate Britain was well placed to produce these and fend off foreign competition. Furthermore, farmers had every incentive. In contrast to the dramatic collapse in wheat prices, those of milk and fresh fruit and vegetables remained high and relatively stable. In the light of all these factors the performance of British agriculture was, to say the least, disappointing. Was overseas competition so irresistible? Or is it necessary to look for deeper causes?

THE CAUSES OF DECLINE

Historians are themselves divided in their interpretations. The initial response, exemplified by Prothero, was to emphasize the adverse effects of falling prices, profits and rents. Such an explanation does not completely convince, partly because it is tautological – depression is caused by depression – notwithstanding the fact that depressed economic conditions undoubtedly create a vicious circle of decline. More recent interpretations emphasize structural change and the uneven incidence of depression between sectors. Although an important corrective to the earlier, more simplistic view, this is not entirely satisfactory since both structural change *and* absolute decline were involved. The higher output in livestock and horticultural production did not compensate fully for the decline in cereals. Indeed, according to the best estimates available, overall agricultural output grew little if at all during the last quarter of the nineteenth century and was actually lower in the 1920s than in the early 1870s. Sectoral shifts undoubtedly occurred, so that the contribution of the livestock sector to the national agricultural product increased from 60 per cent to over 75 per cent during this period, while within the arable sector the share of fruit and vegetable production rose from 25 to 47 per cent. Yet, compared with what was required, these changes were neither radical nor extensive. The major shift – into fruit, vegetables and poultry – still only accounted for 16 per cent of total production by the 1920s.

The first place to seek an explanation for this lack of adaptability is in the economic structure of the agricultural industry itself. Victorian high farming was simultaneously land, labour and capital intensive. It was a highly integrated and finely-tuned system – 'high' in the sense that it was both high cost *and* high output – but because it was based on 'mixed' farming, with a variety of outputs, it was also believed to be highly flexible. This, sadly, was a conventional wisdom that was to be cruelly exposed by the depression. Because high farming was so integrated – indeed it possessed a symmetry which, since the eighteenth century, had become a source of almost aesthetic pride – it could only be tinkered with at the margins, rather than radically restructured, without a major leap of entrepreneurial imagination, not to mention capital restructuring. The response to falling prices was not so much to abandon the system, therefore, as an attempt to run it on a low-cost basis. Land was substituted for labour and, to a lesser extent, for capital. Thus the area under arable cultivation declined from 18.3 million acres in 1870 to 13 million acres in 1930, while permanent pasture increased over the same period from 12.1 to 17.1 million acres. Nevertheless this still represented a considerable proportion of land under plough by the 1920s. It is apparent that attempts were made to shift the emphasis of commodities within the classic mixed farming system, rather than change the system. The major adaptation wrought by depression was thus from a highly intensive to a semi-intensive form of mixed farming.

This was not enough. Even at reduced levels of input – cheap imported feedstuffs, lower stocking densities – mixed farming proved to be a very expensive method of agricultural production. Lower costs simply produced lower fertility, lower crop yields, lower maturity rates for livestock – and lower incomes for farmers. When semi-intensive 'low farming' failed to revive profits, the last resort was 'tumbledown' farming – essentially an extensive form of ranching on semi-permanent pasture (the latter frequently a euphemism for weeds). Even this was of little use. In the hardest-hit eastern counties the climate was often too dry to permit useful permanent pasture. Poor grassland was frequently over-grazed. A diet of thistles and dock was incapable of carrying any but a few stock, let alone fattening them.

The answer to this vicious circle of decline and deterioration lay in British agriculture developing more specialized systems of crop and animal production, lowering costs by taking advantage of economies of scale but maintaining high output. High-value, processed products for the urban market were the sectors ripe for specialization. This was not a fanciful suggestion: the examples were there in Denmark, the Netherlands and even among the few shrewd British farmers who made the necessary changes. It is difficult to avoid the conclusion that a deeper cause of depression was not merely the economic structures which constrained agrarian change, but an absence of entrepreneurial spirit. British farming failed because, despite the superficial evidence of the 1850s and 1860s, British farmers were, on average, poor businessmen. Indeed the depression, contrary to economic theory, often released the most efficient farmers, who were quick to spot what was happening and baled out while they could still take some capital with them. Inertia was thus reinforced by selective out-migration. Farmers stuck to the old ways, even to the point of obstinacy. By the end of the depression, wheat – a crop widely recognized as unprofitable and whose price had fallen furthest – still occupied nearly 1.5 million acres. Farmers' attachment to cereals production – 'the besetting temptation of English agriculture', as one contemporary critic observed – was so great that even where wheat was abandoned, barley was often substituted. How can such apparent irrationality be explained?

FARMERS AND THE SOCIOLOGY OF RISK

If the failure of British farming during the depression was a failure of entrepreneurship then this suggests that the causes were as much social as narrowly economic. This is not to deny that some farmers were restricted by tenancies which demanded outdated rotations, or by a lack of capital to undertake the new investment required. But the success of the few provided an eloquent commentary on the poverty of the majority. Most farmers were poor entrepreneurs: they were the unfortunate harbingers of a parallel failure in industrial entrepreneurship later in the twentieth century.

Farming in the nineteenth century was a commercial business but, as we have already seen (in chapter 3), it was also a way of life with its own attendant hierarchy of status and prestige. Tenant farmers were by no means untainted by the aristocratic values of gentility. Their rising good fortune in the 1850s and 1860s allowed their aspirations to be modestly realized. It was Richard Jeffries, the journalist and critic, who was most vitriolic in his assessment of this. The prosperity of the mid-Victorian, high-farming period, he noted, had made farmers less inclined to work – or at least engage in manual labour. Their role in agriculture had been reduced to the provision of capital and the supervision of the labour of others. This released the farmer and his family to indulge in a life-style which their newly-found prosperity had brought for the first time within their reach. Jeffries, with thinly-disguised disapproval, could only wonder at this:

The polished spokes of the wheels glitter in the sun, the hoofs of the high-stepping pair beat the firm road in regular cadence, and smoothly the carriage rolls on till the brown beech at the corner hides it. But a sense of wealth, of social station, and refinement – strange and in contrast to the rustic scene – lingers behind like a faint odour of perfume. There are the slow teams pulling stolidly at the ploughs – they were stopped, of course, for the carters to stare at the equipage; there are the wheat ricks; yonder a lone farmstead, and black cattle grazing in the pasture. Surely the costly bays, whose hoofs may even now be heard, must belong to the lordly owner of these broad acres – this undulating landscape of grass and stubble, which is not beautiful, but evidently fertile!

A very brief inquiry at the adjacent market town disposes of this natural conclusion. It is the carriage of a tenant farmer – but what a tenant! ['The Fine Lady Farmer – Country Girls' in *Hodge and his Masters*]

The pursuit of this life-style was accompanied by a growing sense of social separation from those who now performed the bulk of the manual labour on the farm – the stockmen, horsemen and day-labourers. This increasing social distance was reflected in the new vogue for physical separation: by the mid-nineteenth century it had become fashionable to build a new and substantial farmhouse away from the village (where most tenant farmers had previously resided) and out on the farmer's own holding of land. In these new residences the farmer and his family could act out their own pretentions to gentility. Again Jeffries is gently mocking:

The Grange people, indeed, are so conspicuous, that there is little secrecy about them or their affairs. The house they reside in – it cannot be called a farmstead – is a large villa-like mansion of recent erection, and fitted with every modern convenience. The real farmstead which it supplanted lies in a hollow at some distance, and is occupied by the head bailiff, for there are several employed. As the architecture of the villa is consonant with modern 'taste', so too the interior is furnished in the 'best style', of course under the supervision of the mistress. Mrs ⎯ has filled it with rosewood and ormulu, with chairs completely gilt, legs, back, seat and all, with luxurious ottomans, 'occasional' tables inlaid with mother-o'-pearl, soft carpets, polished brazen grate-fittings, semi-ecclesiastical, semi-medieval, and so forth.

Jeffries draws a sharp, and doubtless somewhat exaggerated, distinction between the rough-hewn hospitality and uneducated, boorish joviality of the past with the more genteel and cultivated world of the contemporary tenant farmer. He is particularly hard on the 'airs' which farmers' wives and daughters have acquired. Yet his concern is not merely a puritan distate for easy living, or an anti-intellectual defence of what others might regard as a bigoted, provincial mode of thought. He is concerned that in enjoying the intellectual and economic progress of their time, they should not forfeit the hard work and thrift of their predecessors:

A moderate-sized farm, of from 200 to 300 acres, will no more enable the mistress and the misses to play the fine lady today than it would two generations ago. It requires work now the same as then –

steady, persevering work – and, what is more important, prudence, economy, parsimony if you like; nor do these necessarily mean the coarse manners of a former age. Manners may be good, education may be good, the intellect and even the artistic sense may be cultivated, and yet extravagance avoided. The proverb is true still: 'You cannot have your hare and cook him too.'

Jeffries's paramount concern is, then, with the erosion of the work ethic of farmers and with the dilution of their entrepreneurial spirit. The prosperity of the mid-Victorian 'golden age' induced the failure of agricultural entrepreneurship in the final quarter of the nineteenth century. In Jeffries's view the fundamental values embodied in the capitalistic ethos had been usurped by those of other-wordly gentility. This left the farmer peculiarly ill-equipped to adapt in the face of adversity. The commitment to a particular way of life created its own reluctance to change. A deep attachment to a cherished and cultural way of life was easily resistant to the exigencies of 'mere' economics. Under these circumstances apparent economic irrationality becomes more understandable. For *making* a living has become a means rather than an end – and it is the end which must be preserved at all costs.

This account in itself provides a number of clues to the reasons for entrepreneurial failure when agricultural prices took a turn for the worse in the 1870s. It can be applied to the apparently obstinate attachment to the production of cereals at a time when market conditions demanded otherwise. For cereals production was, *par excellence*, the branch of agriculture which could be comfortably combined with gentlemanly pursuits. It embodied a seasonality of effort which allowed a good deal of free time outside seed-time and harvest. It involved the employment and management of a large labour force – thereby confirming a sense of authority. It also avoided the daily grind and socially stigmatizing contact with animal excrement which attended dairy farming and intensive livestock production. In other words, cereals growing fitted into a particular life-style in a way in which alternative sectors of agriculture did not. A movement out of cereals production was a threat to status to be set against any likely improvement in profitability. Far better, so many farmers believed, to hope that something would turn up, than to attract the inevitable social stigma attaching to other branches of agricultural production and to abandon the life-style to which they had become accustomed. Change, under these circumstances, could occur only reluctantly, grudgingly and, above all, slowly.

The result was that the depression was unduly prolonged. Ironically this eventually produced changes in the structure of British agriculture that were far more widespread than might have been the case, had farming proved more adaptable at an earlier stage. For the British agriculture which emerged from depression in the late 1930s possessed a very different social aspect from the British agriculture which entered depression in the mid-1870s. As we shall see in the following two chapters, the experience of depression had a profound effect upon the social structure of rural England during this period.

CHAPTER 6

NEW JERUSALEMS

Between 1850 and 1870 the rising prosperity of tenant farmers created a growing sense of social distance from their workers. Across lowland England, for example, where the bulk of hired farm workers were employed, the practice of employing 'farm servants' – workers who 'lived in' with their employers and even shared their meals – declined dramatically. In the pastoral areas of the north and west the practice continued, encouraged by the annual hiring fairs at which employers and employees sealed their annual contract, but in the lowland counties relationships between farmers and their workers became more impersonal and limited more narrowly to the conditions of their employment. As many farmers moved out of the village into their newly-erected farmhouses, so they tended to leave their farm servants behind. The latter became 'outdoor servants', or orthodox labourers, many of whom were hired on a casual basis by the day. Thereafter the relationship between farmer and farm worker conformed more closely to its counterpart in urban industry, although farm workers could never match the achievements of the urban, industrial working class in such matters as wages and conditions, trade union representation and citizenship rights, as I shall show in this chapter.

Until the 1860s farm workers shared little of the prosperity of their employers, but then their standard of living began to improve – a slow and sporadic, but nevertheless discernible alleviation of the worst aspects of their chronic poverty. This improvement owed less to the generosity of their employers than it did to the gradual tightening of the rural labour market, aided by the steady flow of workers to the towns in search of higher wages and greater opportunities for personal advancement. For the first time since the Napoleonic wars, farmers began to compete for better quality labour, but this competition was circumscribed by the threat of imprisonment which hung over farm workers for breach of employment contract if they left their current work. The Master and Servant Act of 1867 removed these restrictions on labour mobility – and inadvertently provided new opportunities for farm workers to improve their conditions by resort to collective, as well as individual, action. By the early 1870s the combination of agricultural prosperity, the widening social and economic gulf between employers and employees and the removal of archaic restrictions on farm workers' conditions of employment provided fertile conditions for an outburst of rural labour protest which exceeded the unrest of the 1830s.

The signs of increasing tension had been present since the late 1860s, when sporadic outbreaks of unionization occurred in the Midlands and southern counties. An attempt was made to form a national union in 1868, under the aegis of Canon William Girdlestone, who had been active in organizing the migration to the north of hundreds of his parishoners at Halberton in Devon. Despite support from other middle-class radicals and urban trade union leaders, the campaign failed to establish itself at grass-roots level. In 1871 a more spontaneous union movement manifested itself, most notably in Herefordshire, where Thomas Strange, a Primitive Methodist schoolteacher, formed a union designed to promote emigration, but which disavowed strikes. At its height it spread across six counties and achieved an estimated membership of 30,000. Similar organizations also emerged in Lincolnshire and Leicestershire, but they all failed to cohere on a national basis. The signs, nevertheless, were there. Abetted by the agitation for parliamentary reform and a renewed burst of urban unionization, farm workers seemed poised to emerge from the apparently quiescent acceptance of their conditions which had characterized the mid-Victorian countryside.

JOSEPH ARCH AND THE NATIONAL AGRICULTURAL LABOURERS' UNION

In 1872 the villages finally took the flame. The first sparks flew in Warwickshire, where a meeting of farm workers was held at Harbury on 29 January, and a further one at Charlecote a week later. The Charlecote workers – eleven in all – formed a club and enlisted the help of a local champion hedgecutter and Primitive Methodist lay preacher, Joseph Arch. Within a week Arch was addressing over a thousand workers at Wellesbourne, where it was agreed to form a union. Two weeks later this fledgeling union handled its first strike after the Wellesbourne men had demanded a wage of sixteen shillings a week. Press publicity rapidly followed and the union's reserves were swelled by a rapid influx of cash from a sympathetic public. Eventually the strike was successful, an increase in pay was obtained and the strike was called off in the middle of April.

By now, however, the Wellesbourne strike had been overtaken by events. At the end of March the union had 5,000 members in sixty-four branches, and a meeting in Leamington established the Warwickshire Agricultural Labourers' Union. Within two months Arch was back at Leamington, this time presiding over the first National Congress of Agricultural Labourers at which was founded the National Agricultural Labourers Union. The NALU rapidly went from strength to strength. Indeed such was the 'explosion' of trade unionism across the counties of central, southern and eastern England, that the NALU had difficulty in keeping abreast of local developments. Arch was swamped by appeals for help and requests to make speeches. Farmers found themselves besieged by demands for higher wages and a shorter working week under threat of strike action. Here and there anti-union farmers' associations hit back with lock-outs, cottage evictions and petty repressive measures, but the union's exhilarating advance seemed unstoppable. By 1873 the NALU had attracted over 71,000 members and this rose further to over 86,000 in 1874. Wages also rose rapidly – in some areas by as much as 25 per cent between 1870 and 1872 – often without resort to strike action.

Arch's union was by no means the only organization involved. Indeed the characteristic pattern of the movement was the spontaneous formation of local unions which only later either appealed to, or came to the notice of, the national organizations, with whom they then frequently merged. This was truly a grass-roots 'Revolt of the Field', as it became known, rather than a movement which was nationally initiated and organized. Most counties south of the Trent experienced this sudden explosion of unrest from which innumerable little local unions emerged, eventually to coalesce around three more general ones: the NALU; the Eastern Counties Union, led by James Flaxman, a Primitive Methodist schoolteacher, which had its headquarters at Fakenham and was particularly strong in Norfolk; and the Amalgamated Labour League, led by William Banks (a radical journalist), with a membership drawn mainly from Lincolnshire. A meeting called in March 1873 in London to promote the formation of a single union broke down owing to the intransigence of Arch, and thereafter the movement remained split between the NALU, which in Arch's hands was a highly centralized union based still in Leamington, and the much looser Federal Union of Labourers, which allowed local unions a fair degree of autonomy. Despite this setback the year 1873 was one of heady triumph for agricultural trade unionism. Between them the unions could muster 120,000 members. Wages were raised all round. Little wonder that Arch could create the motto 'Press forward, push onward, rise upward without ceasing.'

Although the impetus came from the rank-and-file union members in villages up and down the country, this degree of success could not have been achieved entirely from the unions' own resources. Unlike the Swing uprising in the 1830s, the Revolt of the Field was communicated to a wider national audience through the medium of the national press, with the help of two relatively recent Victorian innovations: the railways and the penny post. This was therefore a movement in which wider influences – soon to be perceived and denounced by employers – were at work. Arch's union achieved national notoriety through the reporting of the *Royal Leamington Chronicle*; its sympathetic editor, J. E. Matthew Vincent, was to become the treasurer of the NALU and editor of the union's own newspaper, the *Labourers' Union Chronicle*. The *Daily News*, perhaps appropriately, sent its distinguished war correspondent, Archibald Forbes, to cover the Welles-bourne strike and later, in 1874, Frederick Clifford's reports in *The Times* fomented a wide-ranging national discussion on the plight of the agricultural worker. It was through the press that Arch was able to appeal for national support, particularly in the early days, when he was a shrewd exponent of publicity, and during the first rash of strikes the union was rescued from virtual penury by appeals to urban trade unions and radical MPs, which produced a flood of donations.

The unionism of the 1870s was thus typical of rural protest movements, in that it was dependent upon external sources of support. Arch was indeed fortunate in being so close to the geographical centre of radical Liberalism in Birmingham. Chamberlainite MPs were not slow to seize the opportunity of making political capital out of unrest in the Tory heartlands of rural England, and the NALU, including Arch personally, were vulnerable to political manipulation. Liberal MPs were heavily represented on the platform of the inaugural National Congress in Leamington. The demands of the unions for land, principally smallholdings and allotments, fitted in well with the much wider pursuit of land reform by the Liberals in the 1880s (see chapter 7) – but the more embarrassing demands, such as land nationalization and disestablishmentarianism, were ignored, and the conduct of a number of strikes owed as much to political considerations as to the interests of the members. In addition to the Liberal Party, urban trade unions also took a hand, hoping to stem the flow of cheap labour to the towns by improving conditions in the countryside.

The fact remains, however, that despite the increasingly national character of the movement's formal organization and political aspirations, its centre of gravity remained stubbornly local. The distribution of union membership was extremely patchy, with enormous fluctuations across very small geographical areas. This was an aspect of the movement which perplexed contemporary observers and mortified the early union pioneers. One village could be a hotbed of union agitation and the next could remain virtually untouched. Much depended upon the strength of personal – and therefore local – ties between farm workers and their employers. This was best illustrated by the almost complete inability of trade unionism to penetrate the pastoral areas of the north and west where farm service was still the norm and where annual hiring fairs regulated the labour market. On the other hand, trade unionism was most likely to flourish on large farms with 'outdoor' labour. The movement also drew its strength from those nucleated villages – many of them former 'open' villages – where the influence of the 'big house' was less than all-embracing. It was a common observation of more enlightened commentators that the unrest was directly attributable to the decline of attentive paternalism, manifested by the lapsing of charities and benefit clubs, the decrease in payments in kind and perquisites and the discontinuation of many club feasts and harvest dinners. The newly-developed self-consciousness of status among farmers had, so it seemed to a later Royal Commission, led to the demise of 'occasions for local conviviality'.

The Duke of Rutland, in a circular to the workers on his Cheveley estate, accepted the view that perhaps farmers had been abrogating their social responsibilities in the pursuit of profit maximization, and that some degree of rectification was perhaps overdue:

The relation of the farmer to the labourer must rest on one of two principles – either on that of the mercantile or the confidential. Hitherto it has been on the latter, and I hope you will allow it to remain so. The one treats the labourer as a man whose family and children are to be cared for and protected; the other treats him as a machine out of whom the greatest amount of work is to be obtained at the lowest cost. It may be that the mercantile would be the best principle for the farmer's pocket, thought I doubt it; but I am sure no paltry saving of money could compensate for the loss of kindly feelings and friendly relations existing between the different classes here.

The very personal exercise of such 'confidential' principles probably accounts for the movement's bewilderingly variable distribution from village to village. Apparently trivial differences could be decisive in influencing the outcome. For example, the Duke of Rutland who *wrote* to his workers, failed to stem the unrest; but Sir Edward Kerrison, a Suffolk landowner who *attended* a labourers' meeting, was entirely successful.

In general, the initial reaction of farmers and landlords to the growth of trade unionism in the countryside was one of complete surprise. The village community, hitherto regarded as serenely stable and harmonious (see chapter 4), had suddenly erupted into a maelstrom of bitterness, hatred and class antagonism. The suddenness of the union's growth led to a widespread belief in the existence of a small band of outside agitators stirring up trouble among gullible farm workers, a suspicion given a modicum of plausibility by the involvement of Liberal MPs, radical politicians and urban trade unionists. Appeals were made to ignore these mischievous 'outsiders' and to remember the benevolence of those who had their best interests at heart. Such paternalism infuriated Arch and the other leaders – if only because it could be so effective in neutralizing the appeal of trade unionism where it was properly directed. However, where paternalism and benevolence failed, then crude oppression was quickly resorted to. The Duke of Marlborough deliberately made over the cottages and allotments of his estate to his tenants so that they could evict union members. At Ascot-under-Wychwood in Oxfordshire, six women were sentenced to between seven and ten days' hard labour for giving blackleg labour 'rough music' – a case which attracted the wrath of *The Times*. All over the south of England union members were threatened with eviction from their cottages and from their allotments. Elsewhere charity was withheld. In Hampshire a union member was refused a coffin for his child. In north Oxford-

shire a farmer flogged his middle-aged labourer for daring to
join a union.

The bitterness with which the farm workers' mainly
modest and politely-worded requests were met indicates that
more was at stake than an improvement in their material
conditions. In many cases what was perceived to be at issue
was none other than the continued existence of the paternalistic social structure of the English countryside. The rise of
rural trade unionism threatened the principle of inherited
authority upon which the whole class structure of rural
England was based. The preservation of social stability
demanded that the 'natural orders' should 'know their place':
that an orderly chain of paternalism and deference should
accompany the exercise of power and authority down the
social scale. For the labourers, what was at stake was the
possibility of changing an unjust society, and this seemed
infinitely more worthwhile fighting for than the concession of
another few pence a week, or a Saturday half-day.

THE GREAT LOCK-OUT

The sweeping success of rural unionism in 1873 tended to
obscure some of its inherent weaknesses. Despite the substantial dissatisfaction which the Revolt of the Field reflected,
the obstacles to collective action among farm workers remained as formidable as they had always been. Scattered in
small numbers across the length and breadth of the countryside, often in isolated or inaccessible farms and communities,
they were extremely difficult to organize in any effective
fashion. Strikes were frequently rendered ineffective by a
combination of the ability of farmers to keep going with
family labour and the capacity of crops to keep growing and
animals to keep fattening – even when labour was withdrawn.
In the open spaces of the countryside it was also difficult for
the unions to police disputes and prevent the importation of
non-union labour. For a time the agricultural trade unions
could disguise these crucial limitations by the rapidity of their

growth and the sheer enthusiasm and commitment of their members, but at no time was more than one farm worker in eight a union member, and even in the highly unionized counties, more than two out of three remained outside the movement. At first farmers were willing to concede wage demands rather than fight back, if only because agricultural prosperity had granted them sufficient profits to do so. But, by a cruel irony, the growth of trade unionism in the countryside coincided with the onset of agricultural depression. It was not long before the resistance of the employers was stiffened, and the vulnerability of the union movement clearly exposed.

The organized opposition to unionization, which effectively broke the movement, began in East Anglia. The village of Exning, near Newmarket, had a long history of opposition to the traditional rural hierarchy. Like many such centres it was an 'open' village, removed from the direct social and economic influences of a local estate. In September 1872 local farmers had received a petition signed by seventeen men asking for an extra shilling a week. In response the farmers formed a defensive alliance, the Newmarket Agricultural Association, and decided to ignore the letter. The request was repeated in February 1874, whereupon, having given one week's notice, the farm workers proceeded to strike. This time the farmers' reply was to decide that 'all union men be locked out after given one week's notice' and they later resolved that 'the members of this association shall not in future employ any men to work for them who are members of the union'. On 21 March 1874, 1,600 men were locked out for refusing to leave the union. The lock-out quickly spread into the surrounding counties, so that at its height 10,000 men were thrown out of their jobs across most of East Anglia and even as far afield as Dorset and Gloucestershire.

It was immediately apparent that the dispute was over something much more significant than an extra shilling a week. For participating farmers and landowners the issue was: who rules the countryside? The chairman of the Newmarket Agricultural Association set the tone of the dispute at the

Association's first public meeting: 'This is not a struggle for a paltry rise of one shilling in wages', he stated, 'It is not a question of wages at all. The question is, Are these delegates to rule over us?' Frederick Clifford, the *Times* correspondent sent to cover the dispute, offered a similar judgement:

I rarely heard a farmer utter an unkind word against his labourers, except, perhaps, in the way of complaint that some among them did not work up to the proper standard. It was the interference of an executive sitting in Leamington, Lincoln or London, which the farmers dreaded and could not bring themselves to brook.

In Clifford's view, the farmers would have readily conceded the wage demand, had it come solely from the Exning men themselves. It was the idea of the men owing allegiance to a union leadership outside the village, rather than the 'natural' leadership of local society, which seemed to them to under-mine the whole basis of social order in the countryside. If this were condoned, there was no telling where it might lead. Once farm workers were no longer amenable to the definitions of their betters over what was natural, right, proper and equitable, then social stability would be irrevoc-ably undermined. Farmers and landowners therefore set about defending their local spheres of influence with every weapon – coercive, economic and ideological – that was available to them.

The lock-out thus provides a fascinating insight into the assumptions, usually unstated but here perforce articulated, which guided class relations in Victorian rural society. Thus the Duke of Rutland, in the circular to his estate workers (referred to above), admonished:

Now, with respect to the union, the question is, not whether it is lawful to belong to it, of which I think there can be no doubt, but whether it is a good thing, in the interests of the employed and the employer, that you should do so. I am strongly of the opinion that it is not a good thing, as those who advocate it are generally entire strangers, who do not live among you, and who know little of your position, or wants, or necessities.

Referring to the influence of Radical, Liberal MPs, Lord Walsingham believed that

. . . it was as ridiculous that disputes between farmers and labourers should be settled by Mr Morley or Mr Dixon, as it would be if any farmers . . . interposed between the Manchester cotton-spinners and their 'hands' to decide upon the hours of labour.

Farmers from around Woodbridge in Suffolk confided in Clifford that:

We could not forget that the union had destroyed the peace of our villages, and we determined not to recognise in any way a combination so conducted. If our men had anything to say to us on their own account we were ready to hear them, but we were also determined to ignore concerted demands made by an anonymous committee, and showing the cloven hoof of the Union.

Arguments like these were, according to Clifford, 'the farmers' *tu quoque*, and in some form or other you heard it wherever you went'. It was 'interference' by strangers, whether philanthropists or paid delegates, which the farmers so violently resented.

The bitterness which characterized the lock-out, and which to the outsider seemed so out of proportion to the ostensibly mundane issues involved, attracted the attention of just that wider audience whose intervention farmers and landowners so detested. The Bishop of Manchester initiated a remarkable correspondence in *The Times* by asking:

Are the farmers of England going mad? Can they suppose that this suicidal lock-out, which has already thrown 4,000 labourers on the fund of the Agricultural Union, will stave off for any appreciable time the solution of the inevitable question, what is the equitable wage to pay the men? The most frightful thing that could happen for English Society would be a peasant's war. Yet, that is what we are driving to, if insane counsels of mutual exasperation prevail.

An eloquent response from Lady Stradbroke made it clear what was at stake:

Our labourers have hitherto been a content, peaceable, honest set of men. Delegates have now been sent down from districts like your own, where class has been fighting class for a quarter of a century, and have sown the first seeds of unhappiness. . . . Come down and judge for yourself if the agricultural labourers in this east of England will act wisely in throwing themselves into antagonism with their employers and benefactors. Far from blaming the farmers and calling them mad for resisting the spread of the union, you would, I am sure, counsel the men to have nothing to do with it, to trust those who have supported them in sickness and distress, and who in self-interest, even putting aside all higher motives, will never trample upon a class whom they have been taught from their growth up to regard as fellow workmen.

The argument continued in the correspondence columns of *The Times*, but meanwhile the farmers were determined to win their war of attrition in the East Anglian countryside. Somewhat to their own surprise, they were able to cope with the essential tasks of the farming calendar, using imported blackleg labour, their own families, the help of neighbours and even resorting to a spell of long-unaccustomed work on the land themselves. For five months the workers also remained solid, drawing upon the strength of support from within their own village communities. What finally broke the men's resistance was the ability of the farmers to gather in the harvest without the help of the locked-out labour. By the end of July 1874 it was clear that the harvest was not being hindered, despite the absence of between six and seven thousand workers. Moreover, the financial support of the men was driving the unions into bankruptcy. On 27 July the NALU executive, meeting in Leamington, capitulated. It resolved to promote emigration in lieu of the wage claim. Payments from the strike fund ceased. Two days later the Federal Union followed suit. Seeking a return to work, many farm workers were only re-employed on the understanding that they should resign from the union; many others found that they had no job to return to. Whatever gloss union leaders and sympathetic observers could place on these events, the lock-out had defeated the unions. They found themselves broken, both financially and spiritually, by the experience.

Many union members looked upon the decision of their leadership as a betrayal. The membership departed in droves, provoked also by petty recriminations among the union leaders, divisive feuds and real or imagined financial scandals.

The membership of the NALU, for example, dropped precipitously from 86,000 in 1874, to 24,000 in 1878 and 15,000 in 1881. It struggled on as a benefit society, mainly in the eastern counties, while Arch was increasingly patronized by the Liberal Party, eventually to become a pathetic figure, prone to incipient alcoholism, devoutly respectful of royalty and unsympathetic to socialism. By 1889 the NALU contained only 4,000 members, but in 1890 a brief revival occurred under the influence of the New Unionism in the towns. For a time a rainbow series of missionary vans was to brighten the English countryside, as farm workers were being persuaded as to the veracity of trade unionism, socialism and land reform. The NALU improved sufficiently to attract 15,000 members, but even this brief revival was killed off by a poor harvest and severe winter in 1893. In 1896 the NALU was finally dissolved. To all intents and purposes, agricultural trade unionism was dead.

In the aftermath of the lock-out there was no shortage of post-mortems. The immediate blame was placed on the organization of the unions concerned: the overbearing character of Arch, the inability to join forces in a single union, financial mismanagement. The rapid disillusionment with unionization matched the rapid and enthusiastic growth of trade unionism in the countryside between 1872 and 1874. One was, indeed, the product of the other. Exaggerated expectations, fostered by the leadership's frequent references to the children of Israel and the Promised Land, merely enhanced the sense of failure and betrayal. The Revolt of the Field always contained this somewhat mercurial quality. It was likely therefore to be badly affected by a major defeat, such as was inflicted in 1874, and wither away. In retrospect it can be seen as a transitional phase in the development of rural trade unionism, containing elements of the earlier, more obviously pre-political, uprising of the Captain Swing era, but also the rudiments of modern, twentieth-century trade union organization. Swept along on a tide of millenial fervour, the unions could not afford, tactically or financially, to become embroiled in a long-drawn-out battle. Little less than instant success would suffice, and when this was not forthcoming the enthusiasm waned rapidly. As the prospects of success fast receded, the feasibility of collective action and then the utility of trade unionism itself were increasingly called into question. The Revolt of the Field thus tested the traditional patriarchalism of the English countryside, but it did not destroy it. In a paradoxical way this brief explosion of unrest demonstrated the continuing tenacity of the tradition of underground rural resistance and protest, while also attesting to the continued strength of rural patriarchal rule. The two continued to coexist side by side, as they had done for centuries previously, until the farm workers mounted a renewed challenge on the eve of the First World War.

The Farm Worker and the Depression

Bereft of an effective union, the farm worker was left to survive the agricultural depression through his own individual action. The most common reaction to agricultural decline was not, therefore, collective trade unionism, but individual migration. From the mid-nineteenth century onwards, the gap between industrial and agricultural wages, together with the apparently insatiable demands of industry for labour, had drawn the farm worker away from the land and propelled him towards the towns. This had always been the most prevalent, the most widespread and the most silent protest by agricultural workers over their living and working conditions. From a peak of just over one million farm workers in 1861, the number fell to 609,000 in 1901 – or, expressed another way, the percentage of the male labour force engaged in agriculture fell from over one in five to less than one in ten. This rural exodus was caused *both* by the 'push' of agricultural unemployment and the 'pull' of higher industrial wages and better employment prospects during the depression.

This persistent haemorrhage of the rural working population was widely believed to be seriously affecting the quality of rural life during the latter half of the nineteenth century.

However, the effects were difficult to evaluate precisely. The mechanization of the latter half of the nineteenth century – principally involving the mechanical reaper and the threshing machine – certainly reduced the demand for labour on farms, but the major impact fell upon casual labour, the significance of which was much reduced by the end of the century. As far as permanent full-time workers were concerned, the 'drift from the land' was on a scale which produced a slow, but measurable, squeeze on the rural labour market, which was to persist even after the onset of the agricultural depression. This was reflected in the movement in wage rates. Farm workers' wages held steady at between 13s and 14s a week until 1878. Then the depression and the succession of bad harvests took their toll, and wages slipped to below 13s. However, the upward movement was continued in 1889 and lasted until 1902, allowing the farm worker to improve his standard of living against the general agricultural trend. To that extent, as Peter Perry has noted in *British Agriculture 1810–1914*, it was a depression for capitalists rather than wage-earners.

Such a verdict needs to be qualified and placed in its context, however. It would be more valid to state that farm workers were less adversely affected by the depression than farmers and landowners. Moreover, their slow improvement in living standards needs to be assessed in relation to their chronic primary poverty. Even by the end of the century, farm workers remained among the lowest paid of all categories of workers, enjoying (if that is the appropriate term) an income which was only a little over half of the average wage. The standard of rural housing remained execrable, and in old age there was little alternative to the widely-feared workhouse. There also remained wide regional and local variations in wage rates and living conditions, so that averages for the country as a whole could easily mislead. Most capricious of all were payments in kind, although there was general agreement that these were in decline towards the end of the century with the exception of some 'potato ground' and beer at harvest. Thus, though wages rose, this was in relation to the appallingly low wages upon which, in part, the mid-Victorian agricultural prosperity had been based. But if farm workers could in no sense be regarded as prospering, then at least they avoided the worst ravages of the depression and were able to circumvent their share of the prevailing deterioration in agricultural conditions.

In the end, it was migration, rather than trade unionism, which was to prove a more influential factor in the farm worker's standard of living. There were a number of reasons for the rural exodus. It was certainly easier to become mobile following the extension of railways into rural areas, and even the role of the bicycle should not be entirely overlooked. More difficult to assess is the influence of the slow widening of the farm worker's 'limited horizons' – an increasing perception of, and impatience to participate in, a wider world beyond the farm gate and the parish boundary. The countryside was being opened up to a broader set of cultural and political influences, as the Revolt of the Field indicated. English rural society had never been a completely closed world and its cultural isolation should not be exaggerated. The necessary connections with the wider world of trade and commerce would always guarantee a set of linkages with the national society. However, there is ample evidence to show that by the end of the nineteenth century the countryside was being subject to a new round of cultural and political changes whose genesis was elsewhere. Slowly, haltingly, the farm worker was being granted the citizenship rights which were later to be taken for granted. Effective education after 1870 undoubtedly had a profound influence on the aspirations of farm workers – and the opposition of farmers and landowners to its introduction was based primarily upon this perception of its far-reaching consequences. The vote was also extended to most farm workers in 1884 – and elected local councils were introduced in 1888 and 1894. Innovations like these symbolized the growing incorporation of the farm worker into a national culture and a national society. The distinctiveness of local villages and regions began to decline. Local customs and ceremonies died out or were transformed into quaint rituals emptied of any real meaning. The farm worker, to adopt a phrase used by a trade union official in the twentieth century, was beginning to find his 'place in the sun'. Migration to the towns or overseas marked not merely a material dissatisfaction, but a cultural aspiration.

Until the Boer War – and the discovery, during recruitment, that large numbers of the population were underfed and physically debilitated – the migration from the countryside was not regarded as a threat to national vitality, either culturally or genetically. Thereafter concern was expressed that the drift from the land was responsible for a deterioration in the physique of the working man, while also reducing the 'genetic pool' in the countryside with disastrous results ranging from indolence to incest. It was certainly believed by most rural observers that those who left the land and migrated to the towns were the young, the energetic and the intelligent, leaving behind a residual sediment of the old, the indigent and the unskilled. By the end of the nineteenth century the age structure of rural and urban areas was indeed markedly different – and so was the balance between the sexes, with a preponderance of men in the countryside. However, it is not without significance that the conventional wisdom of the towns was the exact opposite: urban observers believed that they were receiving the drifters, the shiftless and the workshy, the unattached flotsam of agricultural change. In the absence of any decisive evidence, it is difficult to adjudicate on these mutual stereotypes.

The suspicion remains that it was the more intangible influences on the rural population that were the most influential. With increasing education and accessibility to the wider world came the recognition that the typical rural village was in fact a rather dull and unattractive place in which to eke out one's daily existence. Increasing knowledge brought rising expectations and growing dissatisfaction. The organized challenge of the 1870s had failed to transform the structure of rural society and improve the collective prospects of farm workers; they thus sought to assuage their continuing dissatisfaction in a more individual way – and voted with their feet. The absence of trade unionism around the turn of the century should not, therefore, be misinterpreted: it does not suggest any noticeable improvement in employer–employee relations. Indeed Wilson Fox's reports to the Board of Trade on the conditions of farm workers, which he presented in 1900 and 1905, suggested a marked deterioration. But by this time it was becoming apparent, even to the most loyal agricultural worker, that the 'organic community' extolled by their 'betters' was falling apart under the impact of the depression. Customary definitions of how rural society should be ordered were by now widely challenged. It was not the farm worker who was responsible for this, though in a modest way he had participated in it, and it was not at the division between employer and employee that rural society was to be pulled apart and reconstituted. Instead the rupture was to occur higher up the class structure, at the division between landlord and tenant. It was the tenant farmer who most successfuly challenged the 'natural order' of nineteenth-century rural society.

CHAPTER 7

THE LAND QUESTION

In the long run the depression was to affect most the section of rural society which seemed best placed to withstand it: landowners. As we have already seen (in chapter 3), the Victorian landowner was always more vulnerable to economic adversity than his eighteenth-century counterpart. It was one of the costs which landed society was forced to bear during an age of industrialization, and one which could only be fully mitigated by those prepared to be sufficiently adaptable to participate directly in the industrial and commercial world. The prosperity of the 'Golden Age' of high farming was not enough in itself to recompense the landowner for the considerable infrastructural outlays which high farming demanded. The mid-century improvements had, in many cases, been expensive. They required a sustained period of high rents to provide commensurate returns, and on the whole landlords were not to obtain them. Across most of the country, depression brought falling rents – by 25 per cent in real terms on average between 1873 and 1893 – and despite the previous two decades of prosperity landlords found it increasingly difficult to cope with these losses. The depression did not initiate the decline of the landowning class, but it did hasten it; thus, by the end of the nineteenth century, the position of landed capital was becoming increasingly fragile.

With the economic position of landowners undermined, their political power and social dominance were also called into question. Within the rural community the diligently forged chains of paternalism and deference began to pull apart – not, as the previous chapter showed, where employer met

employee so much as where landlord met tenant. It is in itself
an interesting comment on how far the customary acquiescence to the conventions of social authority rested in large
part upon an awareness of economic self-interest. The most
immediate cause of stress in this relationship was the prevailing level of rent. As agricultural prices fell and profitability
declined, so many tenant farmers began to demand rent
reductions. Landowners, now under some pressure themselves, were less capable of exercising their hitherto traditional
role of protecting their tenants from the full force of agricultural distress by their magnanimity over rent. Although rents
did fall this was frequently brought about more by force of
circumstance than by any charitable motivation. Farmers
found it necessary to press for rent reductions – to organize
and mobilize themselves – and in so doing they discovered
other grievances for which they demanded redress. Chief
among these was the legal right (as opposed to locally-
determined tradition) to claim compensation on termination
of the lease for any improvements they had carried out during
the period of their tenancy. As we have already seen (in
chapter 3), many of the improvements associated with high
farming were of a kind in which the tenant, as well as the
landowner, was involved. Depression sharpened the awareness of, and the necessity for, legislation over 'tenant right',
and the campaign by farmers for reform in this is reflected in
the view that landowners could no longer be relied upon to
exercise their traditional obligations and, tacitly, that a
gentlemanly agreement was no longer a substitute for a legally
enforceable contract.

What became known as the 'land question' in the final
quarter of the nineteenth century, was not simply a matter of
shifting the balance of the relationship between landlord and
tenant, however. It was also concerned with the distribution
of landownership and the social and political privileges which
accompanied it. Even at the time of the repeal of the Corn
Laws, there were demands for the 'aristocratic monopoly' of
the ownership of land to be broken up and for free trade in
corn to be accompanied by a 'free trade in land'. Attempts to

rally radical forces around such a campaign largely failed, however, mainly because an attack upon landed property raised the alarming prospect of its extension to other forms of property, and this was altogether too dangerous for the middle-class supporters of repeal to contemplate. The matter was revived in the 1870s when tenant right, the demand for smallholdings by the agricultural trade unions and land hunger in Ireland, Scotland and Wales, all conjoined to put the 'land question' firmly on the political agenda. It was Lord Derby's misguided attempt to quell the demands for a greater diffusion of landownership which produced the 'New Domesday Survey' of landowners in 1873 (see chapter 3). Its findings served to redouble the efforts of reformers, and the issue became an important plank of Chamberlainite Liberal reformist policies. This period produced significant items of legislative reform, but not the wholesale redistribution of land which many radical reformers had sought. With the succession of Conservative governments in power between 1886 and 1906 the issue subsided, but it was revived with a vengeance in the period between 1909 and 1914. This second phase was apparently more decisive, but in truth the political assaults on landed property were far less effective than the steady drip, drip of economic exigency which undermined the position of the landowner throughout this period.

THE GEOGRAPHY OF LAND REFORM

A readily observable feature of the movement for land reform in the late nineteenth century concerned its geographical pattern. Although the issue was taken up by a whole range of urban and metropolitan politicians and intellectuals, at the grass roots it was a movement firmly based in the pastoral districts of the British Isles. In geographical terms there was comparatively little overlap between the trade union movement of the arable areas of south and east England and the organization of tenants associations in the north and west. Of course, this was not simply a matter of geography. It also

concerned the very different farming systems in these two
regions and the different social structures which they supported. The experience of Arch and the other trade union leaders
during the 1870s is indicative here. Trade unionism made little
headway in the pastoral areas, partly because annual hiring
fairs provided a means of regulating the labour market which
circumvented the collective bargaining of trade unions. More
fundamentally the kind of rural society associated with
pastoral farming did not lend itself to trade union organization. Most farms used only family labour and hired workers
were relatively few and far between, hired in the main in only
ones and twos. Many workers came, in any case, from
farming families themselves, perhaps earning a living while
awaiting their succession to the family farm. Work with stock
often involved considerable isolation and there was relatively
little of the work in groups and gangs associated with arable
husbandry. Indeed many farmers in the pastoral areas remained 'working' (i.e., labouring) farmers in a way abandoned by many of their counterparts in the south and east.
These and other factors tended to reduce the social distance
between farmers and farm workers: many workers in pastoral
areas continued to 'live in' and in many other respects their
everyday lives were not unlike those of their employers.
Consequently the social divisions between employer and
employee, which the Revolt of the Field had highlighted in the
arable districts, tended not to arise, and labour relations
remained generally more settled.

Differences in the structure of agriculture also generated
differences in the pattern of rural settlement. Chapter 4
described certain aspects of settlement patterns among lowland villages and how, by the mid-nineteenth century, there
was a tendency towards nucleated villages consisting of the
dwellings of farm workers with their employers living in
farmhouses outside the village itself. In chapter 6 I suggested
that this pattern of settlement both reflected the growing social
cleavage between farmers and their employers and provided
fertile ground, especially in the so-called 'open' villages, for
trade union organization. The settlement pattern in the

pastoral areas was quite dissimilar. In Ireland, Wales, the upland areas of Scotland and in Northern England, nucleated villages were far less common; instead, small market towns were complemented by a hinterland of scattered farmsteads and hamlets. This further undermined the possibilities of collective trade union organization among farm workers, even if they felt disposed to engage in union agitation. On the other hand, regular trips to market formed an important social focus for farmers, one which could be readily exploited for the purposes of political mobilization.

The most salient social division in the pastoral areas was not, then, that between employers and employees, but between landlords and tenants. In chapter 3 we saw how there was a preponderance of landed estates in the pastoral areas. A working tenant farmer would recognize certain differences between himself and a 'hired man', but he would also recognize certain commonalities of accent, education, up-bringing, life-style and identification with the local area. A glance towards the Big House was, however, sufficient to convince him on all of these grounds – and more – that there was an insurmountable economic and social divide. It was a gulf which could override all other considerations in even the pastoral areas of England, but in Wales, Scotland and Ireland it was further reinforced by differences in language, religion, culture and nationality. Land reform in these areas was never solely an agricultural matter. It was a conduit for a whole range of national, cultural and political aspirations which inevitably demanded greater access to and control over land as a first step towards emancipation. Land reform thus began as a broadly-based political movement in these areas and only subsequently became a recognized issue in England. For this reason, it is impossible to understand fully the politics of land reform in England without reference to its genesis in Ireland, Scotland and Wales, and although this book is concerned with rural society in England, some consideration must first be given to these other notions.

IRELAND

Nowhere was the division between landlords and tenants more stark than in Ireland, where tenant farmers were much poorer than their English counterparts. Moreover, the potato famine of 1845–7 – and its terrible aftermath – was still well within the memory of many people when land agitation began once more in the late 1870s. The Irish remained primarily a subsistence farming population, more akin to the peasantry of many areas of continental Europe than to the infinitely more prosperous and commercially-orientated tenant farmers of, say, the eastern counties of England. Whatever the truth of benevolent landlordism in England, there was frequently little pretence made in Ireland, where many landlords were absentees, were Protestant adherents in a Catholic country and even spoke a different language. Arbitrary evictions were commonplace, rack-renting widespread and the incentive for tenants to undertake improvements thereby all but abolished. As a contemporary observer noted, their principal objective was, 'with the least possible expense, to raise a scanty crop, which would prove that they were unable to pay the rent'. One consequence was that rural Ireland was rapidly being depopulated at a time when the English rural population was still growing. By the early 1870s legislation passed at Westminster contained the implicit acceptance of the fact that amelioration of rural conditions in Ireland involved the conversion of the traditional landlord–tenant relationship into a system of peasant proprietorship. Land redistribution now became a realistic objective of the Irish rural population.

Although Irish agriculture shared some of the mid-century prosperity, it was hit hard by the depression. There followed a spate of evictions, the number rising from under one thousand in 1878 to over five thousand in 1882. These evictions were accompanied by a campaign of 'agrarian outrages', verging on rural guerilla warfare, which become known collectively as the Land War. The Irish National Land League, formed in 1879 with the long-term aim of restructuring the whole system of Irish landownership, became the principal vehicle for Irish aspirations, but its leaders were arrested in 1881 and the League banned. A second Irish Land Act, passed in 1881, went some way towards providing protection from arbitrary eviction and established a somewhat muddled judicial mechanism for fixing 'fair' rents. Although this produced a temporary abatement of rural violence, Irish land agitation continued, the proscribed Land League being replaced by the Irish National League, founded in 1882.

SCOTLAND

Under the conditions prevailing in the 1880s it would have been surprising if these events had not had some influence elsewhere. In the Highlands and Islands of Scotland, for example, there existed an agrarian structure which bore a strong resemblance to that of Ireland, in so far as it was similarly afflicted by absentee landlordism, cultural divisions and rural depopulation. Behind the Victorian romantic attachment to a Walter Scott version of Scotland lay the same reality of chronic impoverishment that was such a familiar feature of Irish history. There was not, however, the same tradition of revolt, and although a campaign for land reform had been established in the 1870s, it was not accompanied by any serious direct action. Nevertheless, in 1881, following some contact between fishermen in Skye and their Irish counterparts, a rent strike took place, and in the following year evictions were ordered. There followed a series of skirmishes – the 'Battle of the Braes' – when attempts were made to execute the evictions, culminating in the despatch of a gunboat in February 1883 and the arrest of four crofters. Meanwhile, the agitation had spread from Skye to other areas, and was only dampened down by the appointment of a Royal Commission – the Napier Commission – into the crofters' grievances. The publication of the Commission's report in 1884 was the signal for a further round of direct action in Skye and another resort to gunboat diplomacy. The Highland 'Land War' had meanwhile spread to other Hebridean islands, accompanied by rent strikes and land seizures.

The parliamentary response was the introduction of the Crofters Act of 1886, which provided for a Crofters Commission to set fair rents and to prevent arbitrary eviction.

It offered little immediate assistance, however, and land agitation continued. Skye remained the centre of revolt, and in 1886 it remained under virtual military occupation. A succession of harvest failures made matters even worse, and by the beginning of 1888 there were fears of a general uprising in the Highlands. Such a conflagration never occurred, however. Instead land agitation continued to take the form of localized action – principally rent strikes, land occupations and organized resistance to the authorities' attempts to enforce eviction notices and arrest lawbreakers. Slowly and sporadically the pursuit of the Highland Land War was undermined by some improvements in conditions, however meagre, prompted by the extension of the railway to Mallaig and Kyle of Lochalsh, and by the activities of the Crofters Commission in fixing rents and arbitrating over disputes. Rather than joining in an organized, collective response, many of the inhabitants chose emigration, assisted by a number of schemes promoted both privately and publicly. Some landlords made voluntary donations of land. As a public issue – rather than as a private grievance – Highland land agitation slid slowly into obscurity. Henceforth the reform of landlord–tenant relations in Scotland was to become as much an urban issue, with the Hebrides eventually returning to a melancholy peace.

WALES

As in Ireland and the Scottish Highlands, both language and religion were important factors in stimulating demands for land reform in Wales. Religious nonconformity and radical Liberal politics set the Welsh tenantry apart from both their Anglican, English-speaking landlords and the Conservative tenants across Offa's Dyke. Most parts of Wales were not badly affected by the early years of the depression, and the 1870s were largely consumed by festering resentment following the widespread eviction of tenants after the 1868 General Election, when many landlords despotically dismissed those who were believed to have voted against their wishes. After 1883, economic conditions deteriorated and a land reform movement soon emerged, although without the direct action symptomatic of the situation in Ireland and Scotland. In 1886, though, serious steps were taken to form a Welsh Land League along similar lines to the Scottish and Irish examples. A series of meetings took place among farmers in north and west Wales with a view to bringing together local bodies into a coherent national organization. Before this could take place, however, a simultaneous, though separate, dispute over the payment of tithes in North Wales led to the formation of an Anti-Tithe League, whose objectives included the 'Three Fs' – fair rent; fixity of tenure (i.e. freedom from arbitrary eviction); and free sale (i.e. legal recognition of tenant right) – advocated by the Land Leagues in Ireland and Scotland. Tithes were withheld, leading to the distraint of stock belonging to defaulting farmers. In the following year, 1887, matters became further inflamed and a full-scale riot took place at Mochdre in June, and further disturbances occurred in 1888 in various parts of North Wales. By 1889 the agitation had spread to the south and west, and a truly national organization had been formed, aided by a merger between the incipient Land League and the Anti-Tithe League which produced the Welsh Land, Commercial and Labour League. The agitation only subsided after 1890 when an Act provided that tithes should be paid by the owner, rather than the occupier, of land. Henceforth tithes were incorporated into the annual rent and although the issue was not finally settled until the disestablishment of the Anglican Church in Wales in 1920, overt opposition largely subsided.

The grievances of tenant farmers clearly did not disappear once the English border had been crossed. There were tenants in certain parts of England, particularly in the Northern Pennines and the Lake District, whose conditions were by no means superior to those in the Celtic areas. A notable difference, however, was the absence of linguistic, religious and cultural differences between English tenants and their landlords. Land reform in Ireland, Scotland and Wales could not be understood in isolation from the broader content of their colonial and quasi-colonial relationship with England and their consequent desire for greater self-determination.

Similarly, the land reform movement in England cannot be fully appreciated without the recognition that it was a central part of a much broader range of political conflicts which characterized the final quarter of the nineteenth century. Land reform in England lacked the nationalistic overtones of the Irish, Scottish and Welsh movements, but it constituted a rallying point for a much more broadly-based group of radical reformers and defined the terrain – both literally and figuratively – over which reformist politics was fought during this period.

THE LAND QUESTION IN ENGLAND, 1878–86

English tenant farmers were not without their grievances, but in general these were investigated without the necessity to resort to direct action outside the law. The Agriculture Holdings Act of 1875 created a legal prescription of tenant right and this became a statutory and inalienable right under a further Act passed in 1883. The Ground Game Act of 1880 allowed tenants to shoot ground game on their own land, whereas previously this had been the preserve of the landlord, even though it was the tenant's crops that were nourishing his sport. A Farmers Alliance was formed to pursue the 'Three Fs' in England, but lacking the cultural impetus of the Celtic areas, it soon ceased to be effective. The idea of peasant proprietorship was, in any case, by now wholly inappropriate under English conditions. English farmers were demanding equitable treatment *as tenants* and not the wholesale expropriation of their landlords' holdings. Similarly, while land redistribution was an aim of agricultural trade unionism during the 1870s, it was not pursued with the same zeal and determination as the demand for higher wages. The movement for land reform, while it encompassed the aspirations of both tenant farmers and landless farm workers, sprang as much from the political aims of a group of radical urban intellectuals, intent on destroying the power of landlordism wherever it was to be found. Land reform was thus part of a broader political programme with implications far more radical than the establishment of peasant proprietorship.

The intellectual focus of this programme was the work of the American land reformer, Henry George, whose book, *Progress and Poverty*, was published in England in 1880. George argued that land was a natural gift and 'belonged' to no one, in the sense that no one had the moral right to claim exclusive rights over it. The existing distribution of landownership was, according to George, the principal cause of human misery and injustice. Instead the land should belong to the community as a whole, with only the value of improvements of the land being retained by those individuals who introduced them. In 1881 the Land Nationalization Society was founded in order to promote the communal ownership of land. This was followed in 1883 by the establishment of the Land Reform Union, later to become the Land Restoration League, which developed into the leading organization promoting George's ideas, and was to prove an influential advocate of broader distribution of the benefits of landownership through taxation. The League argued that a tax on the value of land, irrespective of its use or improvement, would allow all other taxes to be abolished and would produce a more equitable distribution of wealth by allowing all ground rent to be used for public purposes. Throughout the 1880s George's ideas were constantly and energetically debated, arousing the interest not only of those concerned to promote agrarian reform, but also the reform of urban development and, indeed, a socialist transformation of society as a whole.

George's views found a voice in orthodox English politics through the publication of Chamberlain's *Radical Programme*. The sections dealing with land reform were composed by Jesse Collings, who was more influenced by the notion of peasant proprietorship than land nationalization. Collings advocated the creation of smallholdings by local authorities who would have the power to purchase compulsorily the necessary land, 'to be let at fair rents to all labourers who might desire them, in plots up to one acre of arable and three or four acres of pasture'. This doctrine of 'three acres and a cow', as it quickly became known, played a significant role in the General Election of 1885, and in 1887 an Allotments Act was passed which empowered local authorities to purchase land for allotments, mainly for farm workers, although this was not envisaged as a means of transforming such allotment holders into a class of peasant proprietors. Collings therefore continued to press for the introduction of local authority smallholdings, and in 1891 a Bill allowed County Councils to create smallholdings of up to fifty acres. In this way it was hoped 'to recreate the class of yeomen', but the Act remained remarkably ineffective, neither recreating a new class of yeomen nor producing benefits for the vast majority of the rural population.

A major difficulty was that, despite some initial enthusiasm for 'three acres and a cow' in 1884/5, most farm workers rapidly lost interest in the idea. By now few farm workers yearned for the restoration of whatever rights they had lost during the enclosure movement. They preferred higher wages in urban employment to the nominal independence of peasant drudgery. In the absence of a sustained grass-roots agitation for land reform in rural areas, the Land Restoration League attempted to encourage it in an evangelical fashion, sending lecturers into the countryside in a series of red vans to preach the teachings of Henry George and to convert farm workers to anti-landlordism. The invasion of red vans began in Suffolk in 1890, and soon spread to other districts. The Land Nationalization Society, not to be outdone, despatched a fleet of yellow vans into the countryside in 1891. For a time, somewhat bemused villagers were treated to the arrival of an apparently myriad series of vehicles in a rainbow succession of hues (the landlord interest also chipping in via the Liberty and Property Defence League), each attempting to persuade the inhabitants of the rationality and justice of their case. The results were negligible, and by the turn of the century they were disbanded. By this time it was clear that not only was there little spontaneous demand for land reform in rural England, but that neither could it be engineered.

After the turmoil of the early 1880s, land reform in England (but not in other parts of the British Isles) slid into the backwaters of the contemporary political agenda. The land question had by no means faded away completely, but the main focus of attention was in Ireland and, increasingly, in urban areas. In the pastoral districts there was some improvement in economic conditions after 1896, aided no doubt by the 50 per cent rate abatement on agricultural land granted as a straightforward relief measure in that year. Procedures relating to compensation for tenant right were also tidied up in 1900, but on the whole the steam had gone out of the issue. The campaign for the 'Three Fs' subsided, and the debate over landlordism moved on. Far more important in placing checks on the absolute power of landowners in rural areas was the introduction of local council administration in 1888 and 1894. Although in many areas the changes were at first more apparent than real, the replacement of personal benevolence by a system of professional administration marked a significant departure. The traditional functions of the local landowner were henceforward to be increasingly discharged by public authorities. This left landowners politically exposed. If they were no longer willing or able to undertake their role as benefactors and administrators of rural society, improvers of agriculture and protectors of their employees and dependants, then they became vulnerable to the charge of being little more than parasitical receivers of rent. In this context the campaign for tenant right was quickly overtaken by the demand for land value taxation.

Diaspora: 1909–23

With the election of a Liberal Government in 1906 the land question returned to the forefront of English politics. During the election campaign Campbell-Bannerman, the future Prime Minister, had served notice of his party's intentions:

We desire to develop our own undeveloped estate in this country – to colonise our own country – to give the farmer greater freedom and greater security. . . . We wish to make the land less of a pleasure-ground for the rich, and more of a treasure-house for the nation. . . .

There are fresh sources to be taxed. We may derive something from the land. . . . We can strengthen the hand of the municipalities by reforming the land system and the rating system, in which I include the imposition of a rate on ground values.

The Liberal Party's landslide victory gave it a clear mandate to act, and the new government introduced legislation further extending tenant right and strengthening the provision of allotments and smallholdings. These were, however, only preliminary manoeuvres. Proper battle was engaged in only after Asquith became Prime Minister in 1908. He selected as his Chancellor of the Exchequer David Lloyd George, who as a young Criccieth solicitor had been actively involved in the Welsh Land Movement of the late 1880s. The Government's overall legislative programme was turning out to be expensive. In addition to its proposals for national insurance and old-age pensions, it was committed to underwriting the cost of rearmament in the face of an increasingly belligerent Germany. The argument for some kind of new taxation was overwhelming and, for someone of Lloyd George's background, the possible source was obvious. His proposals were, in many respects, surprisingly modest – a very small tax on vacant land, ground rents and mining royalties, a Reversion Duty payable on termination of a lease, a tax on capital gains and increased estate duties. Nevertheless they provoked the constitutional crisis of 1909–11, thereby achieving a symbolic status well beyond their revenue-raising capacity.

Both the proponents of land reform and the defenders of the landed interest rapidly became victims of their own propaganda. Lloyd George's Budget became invested with a totemic significance which in reality it lacked. Hindsight is not altogether helpful here because other, arguably more pressing, events followed so hard upon Lloyd George's proposals that it is difficult to isolate their influence on the transformation in the structure of landownership which was to follow. It is perhaps significant that when the dust settled from the constitutional battles fought over the Budget, the land reformists remained far from satisfied, while the Conservative Party was moving towards some form of site value rating. In both cases the response hardly suggested that Lloyd George's proposals were revolutionary. The land reformists continued to press their case within the Liberal Party and succeeded in establishing a Land Enquiry Committee whose rural report was published in 1913. Its proposals were much more radical: a statutory minimum wage in agriculture; compulsory land purchase for allotments, smallholdings and housing; further compensation over tenant right, including rent protection; and the creation of a new Ministry of Lands to execute reform. A highly organized Land Campaign followed which pressed for immediate action, and by 1914 Lloyd George was formulating legislation which would have implemented many of the Land Enquiry Committee's proposals.

The outbreak of war pushed aside such considerations and in retrospect one can only speculate, with little profit, on what might have come of these legislative preparations. By the time the First World War had ended – and its aftermath had been dealt with – the pattern of landownership was radically different. As I shall show in chapter 8, the war brought about a considerable intervention of government in the control of rural affairs, not least in the organization of the agricultural industry. Such intervention was politically more acceptable under the peculiar conditions of the wartime economy, but once initiated it was difficult to reverse. Although this presented a number of opportunities for furthering land reform, they were not taken up, partly because the reform campaign had itself lost momentum in the face of other, more immediate, priorities. By the time the reformists were able to re-marshal their forces, not only was the party-political terrain completely transformed, but so also was the distribution of private landownership.

Between 1918 and 1922, one-quarter of the land surface of Great Britain changed hands – a sale of land unprecedented since the dissolution of the monasteries in the sixteenth century. It is conventional to regard this period as marking the breaking up of the landed estates, an aristocratic diaspora from the land provoked by Lloyd George's budget and the morale-sapping traumas of the First World War. There is certainly enough truth in the interpretation to render if plausible, but, as will be seen, it is by no means the whole truth. Many great estates were indeed broken up and something of a decisive shift in the class structure of rural society thus occurred. Since the land was sold primarily to sitting tenants there thus emerged a new breed of owner-occupying commercial farmers whose significance was to increase as the twentieth century progressed. Before the First World War only 10 per cent of farmland in England and Wales had been owner-occupied, but by 1927 that proportion had risen to 36 per cent and it was to continue to rise, albeit more slowly, during the remainder of the inter-war period. A curious feature of this transformation was that it was scarcely noticed at the time beyond the columns of the specialist farming press. In a predominantly urban industrial society the plight of the agricultural landowner seemed now to be of only marginal interest. Moreover, the degree of indifference with which this aristocratic abdication was greeted provided a telling comment on the extent to which the land reform movement had fizzled out since the heady days immediately before the outbreak of war. The fact that many landed estates were dismantled, virtually unnoticed, hardly suggests that land reformists were celebrating a triumph for democracy which they had successfully engineered. It also indicates that all was not quite what it seemed.

Such was the prevailing mood between 1909 and 1914 that it would have been inconceivable that an upheaval of this magnitude could have taken place without resort to public demonstrations and even physical violence. If the breaking up of the great estates occurred in a mood of private sorrow rather than public anger, it was perhaps because the great estates were no longer worth fighting for. Most of those who departed did so with as much dignity as they could muster, but without a fight and, in many cases, with scarcely a backward glance. In the wake of the First World War there were no doubt many landowners who were physically and emotionally exhausted. The carnage in Europe had robbed them of their heirs and reduced the attractions of holding on. In some cases also the sale acted as an emotional purgative and seemed an apt conclusion to what was widely regarded as the end of an era. The war had also brought more mundane, but scarcely less pressing, changes in life-style: higher income tax and death duties (the latter particularly important when two generations could be killed off in quick succession in Flanders); a shortage of domestic labour that was to prove chronic; rationing; and increasing state intervention in agriculture. In their various ways all these factors undermined the style of life to which the landowner had been traditionally accustomed, and thus weakened his resolve to continue. However, they account more for the timing of the departure than its inevitability. Increasing taxation and the tragedies of war provided the appropriate moment, and may even have precipitated a headlong rush rather than an ordered withdrawal, but the underlying causes were of a long-term economic nature whose roots lay deep in the nineteenth century.

The long agricultural depression had, in a significant number of cases, altered the character of landownership from that of attractive investment to economic encumbrance. Particularly in the corn-growing areas, mounting rent arrears, falling rent rolls and neglected capital investment were commonplace, and even in the pastoral areas the depression had reduced the attractions of landownership as an economic proposition. Socially and politically landownership was no longer, as has been indicated, the unequivocal passport to status and power that it had once been. The latter part of the nineteenth century witnessed a further erosion of aristocratic privilege and dominance, even in the heartlands of rural England, and this further reduced the attraction of owning land as opposed to other forms of capital. More fundamentally still, the development of Britain as an industrial and urban society had brought about a persistent trend for returns of agriculture to decline as a proportion of returns to the economy as a whole. Agricultural land, quite simply, had ceased to be a sound economic investment compared with other opportunities that were available. Those landowners who prospered did so on the basis of income accrued from elsewhere – from commerce, manufacturing, mineral rights and from urban development. For those less fortunately placed, economies in personal expenditure were enforced even before the depression set in, and by the eve of the First World War there were a number of landowners who had become reconciled to the inevitability of sale, if only someone, in the prevailing depressed market conditions, could be persuaded to buy. A trickle of land sales was thus discernible in the five years leading up to the outbreak of war.

War itself reinforced many of the inducements to sell. The costs of estate management and maintenance had risen appreciably. Moreover, the social and political influence of the landed families, which might have offered some compensation for economic adversity, seemed to have disappeared for ever. All that was required was a set of buoyant economic conditions to release a pent-up supply of land onto the market. Between 1918 and 1922 these conditions were present during a brief, euphoric and misleading post-war agricultural boom when, for a brief period, British agriculture was once more isolated from its major overseas competitors by the disruptions caused to international trade. Once normal trading patterns and shipments had been re-established then the resumption of large-scale meat and grain imports was to renew the downward pressure on prices, but the brief interlude of prosperity provided enough time for a rush of sales and for a decisive switch to occur in the balance between owned and tenanted land. It has been estimated that between six and eight million acres changed hands during the four years until the boom came to an abrupt halt and depression resumed. Those who bought, primarily sitting tenants, were thus faced with an immediate crisis of profitability, scraping along as best they could in an attempt to make a living and service the loan which they had used for purchase. For those who could hang on, however, their time would come again – although it would require another world war to provide the political will to guarantee their prosperity.

The significance of this period lies in the structural shift in rural society which occurred, rather than the decline of the aristocracy *per se*. Landed estates were indeed broken up, but the really large aristocratic estates were less affected than the smaller holdings of the gentry. The latter were less flexible, culturally as well as economically, in coping with the pressures they faced; aristocratic genders, on the other hand, possessed ample resources to act as a buffer against adversity and were also capable of greater diversification into other forms of economic activity. A surprisingly large proportion of aristocratic estates therefore survived and remained, albeit with rather more discretion, to form a key element in the structure of agricultural England. They were to survive, however, increasingly by becoming owner-occupiers themselves, so that the process of change which began in 1918–22 was less the decline of the aristocracy than the decline of the landlord–tenant system – and with it the tripartite class structure of rural society which had prevailed for the previous century or more. It is an irony of English rural history that those landowners who departed did so with as much relief as regret, happy to off-load an increasingly troublesome asset of doubtful value to those sufficiently optimistic to buy. After nearly half a century of demands for land reform, the reality of change was anti-climactic to a degree which few could ever have foreseen.

CHAPTER 8

BUST TO BOOM AND BACK AGAIN

The First World War, like the Second, was accompanied by a considerable extension of state control into all aspects of everyday life – agriculture among them. Indeed in some respects the degree of state intervention in agriculture was to become far greater than in the sphere of industrial production. Thus at the point at which the landlord–tenant system was to decline as the major vehicle of agricultural development and change, the state was to intervene, at first reluctantly and hesitantly, as the midwife of orderly progress in agricultural affairs. Since 1793 agriculture had been the only industry to have its own department of state, the Board of Agriculture, nominally a committee of the Privy Council (which never in fact met) and headed by a President who was, in effect, the Minister of Agriculture. This quaint arrangement ended at the beginning of 1920 when a ministry proper was created – itself an acknowledgement of the changes wrought by wartime conditions. The Board's role was an enabling rather than an interventionist one: it collected statistics, conducted investigations, sponsored research and disseminated information on good practice. It was hardly, though, an instrument for undertaking major structural change.

GOVERNMENT TAKES A HAND

Accordingly, when war broke out in 1914 the Government saw little need to disturb the essentially *laissez-faire* arrangements which prevailed. Lord Lucas, the President of the Board of Agriculture, announced that food supplies were plentiful and that there was no occasion for increases in prices. The Government's view, echoed in the farming press, was that agriculture, of all the industries, was least likely to be affected by the war. For at least two years this non-interventionist – and somewhat complacent – view remained, during which time the very extensive impact of the war on agriculture became all too apparent. The most immediate effect was a simple and direct one: the army enlisted or requisitioned large numbers of men and horses and huge quantities of fodder. Around 15 per cent of the agricultural labour force, self-selected from the young and fit, left in the first year alone, only partially compensated for by the employment of women and the early release of school children. Horses were also requisitioned by the army, which first purchased and then requisitioned the necessary fodder and litter. Other agricultural inputs were also severely affected. Overseas supplies of artificial fertilizers were virtually cut off and the supply of imported animal feeds severely disrupted. The prices of such raw materials inevitably rose. This, combined with the equally severe disruption to imported foods, led inevitably to steep rises in the price of food to the consumer. By the middle of 1915 it was clear that something had to be done. The Government consequently appointed the Milner Committee to report 'on what measures, if any, were desirable to increase the output of agriculture in England and Wales, assuming that the war would continue beyond the harvest of 1916'.

The Milner Committee advocated in outline form a structure of state intervention in agriculture which was to become a familiar one in succeeding decades. Faced with the need to expand production, especially arable production, the Committee concluded that this could only be achieved by giving farmers guarantees of assured prices for the years ahead, pitched at a level which would provide an incentive for bringing more land into cultivation. The Committee recommended that the guarantee should take the form of a 'deficiency payment' which would be paid when the market price fell below the guaranteed price. The Committee also argued that a guaranteed price for wheat would enable farmers to pay higher wages and attract back to the land those workers who had sought higher-paid employment elsewhere. These proposals were rejected by the Cabinet, although a further suggestion was taken up, namely that county councils should establish committees to organize food production in their areas – the forerunners of the War Agricultural Executive Committees. Nevertheless, for the time being, a policy of exhortation and advice was believed to be sufficient, and state intervention remained minimal.

Throughout 1916, and in the early months of 1917, the supply of food deteriorated markedly. Submarine warfare had intensified and the imports of cereals, sugar and meat were much less than requirements. The proposals of the Milner Committee were hastily resurrected, but still the Cabinet hesitated, apprehensive of granting an open-ended commitment, but caught between its desire to raise home food production and its wish to avoid the cost of guarantees. The Cabinet noted that:

. . . if they decided to give the guarantee to farmers, the country might, in view of a possible intensification of submarine warfare, find itself in a serious position owing to a decrease in home production of cereals due to the refusal of farmers to cultivate crops. If, on the contrary, the farmers were guaranteed the prices, it might result in a position after the war in which the State was paying for crops prices far in excess of what the state of the international market required.

In the event, the Government opted for guaranteed minimum prices for wheat and oats for six years, with a review after four, in 1920. The *quid pro quo* for guaranteed prices was the minimum wage for farm workers: £1 5s a week for all adult males, supplemented as required by newly-established wages boards. Controls over cropping and stocking were also introduced, with owners and tenants being liable to follow directions issued by local committees to ensure that land was used in the national interest. The Corn Production Act of 1917 embodied these proposals and therefore established, for the first time since the Corn Laws, the principle of a guaranteed price for corn. This was set at £3 per quarter in 1917, £2 15s in 1918 and 1919, and £2 5s in 1920–22 – compared to £1 13s as the average prevailing price from 1910 to 1914. When the market price fell below these levels the government guaranteed to make up the deficiency in a 'deficiency payment' to farmers, while allowing the consumer the advantage of the cheaper price. This was to form a model for price intervention in agriculture thirty years later when state intervention was to become a more permanent feature of agricultural affairs (see chapter 10).

Within its terms of reference, the Corn Production Act was undoubtedly a success. Both total production and yields of arable crops increased, although price guarantees were not the only factor. Labour shortages were alleviated by change in enlistment policy and the formation of a Women's Land Army which by 1917 had 25,000 members. The army was persuaded to return some of its horses, and tractors made their first appearance on many farms – although those workers with the skills to service them were unlikely to be employed in low-paid agriculture. The most controversial aspect of the new regime turned out to be the exercise of cropping and stocking controls. In some areas the heavy-handed application of directives led to considerable ill-feeling. There was also some suspicion that the Government was using the war as an excuse to establish an infrastructure of control which could be perpetuated in the post-war era. Whatever the truth of this, parliamentary concern was sufficient to render the enforcement of cropping orders virtually a dead letter by the end of the war. It was clear that, in so far as farmers were prepared to accept state intervention, then it was through the indirect manipulation of price signals, rather than via direct control over husbandry management and practice.

CLASS CONFLICT IN THE COUNTRYSIDE

The fact that the guaranteed minimum price for corn was so closely tied to a minimum wage for agricultural labour in the provisions of the Corn Production Act was a tribute to the renewed organization of farm workers into agricultural trade unions. The years immediately before the outbreak of war were characterized by turbulent industrial relations throughout Britain. For all its recent docility, agriculture was not immune to the whiff of class conflict drifting across from the industrial heartlands – indeed, for a time, class warfare in the countryside on a scale unparalleled since the 1870s appeared a distinct possibility. This was in pronounced contrast to the position at the beginning of the twentieth century when the agricultural worker was, to all intents and purposes, devoid of any trade union organization whatsoever. There was, therefore, no organization to protect the agricultural worker when, following the Liberal landslide victory in the General Election of 1906, many farmers took revenge on their employees for having voted against their wishes, evicting from tied cottages those suspected of radical views or simply of having voted for the Liberal Party. In Norfolk, which had been a centre of union activism in the 1870s, a number of farm workers turned for help to a local councillor and Liberal Party activist, George Edwards, who had been a union organizer in the 1870s and 1880s. After some hesitation, Edwards, at the age of fifty-six, agreed to establish a farm workers' union in Norfolk once more. He used his Liberal Party connections to appeal for money and help, and on 20 July 1906, a conference was held in North Walsham from which emerged the Eastern Counties Agricultural Labourers' and Small Holders' Union. By the end of the year, Edwards had set up fifty-seven branches, with a total membership of 1,600.

In the early years the Union was a creature of the Liberal Party, a practical alternative to the red and yellow vans as a means of organizing the rural vote. The first Executive Committee was therefore packed with prominent Liberals who viewed with some alarm any sign of militancy among the rank-and-file members. Edwards, a devout Primitive Methodist lay preacher, shared their belief in moderation and conciliation. 'I can't explain it,' he later wrote in his autobiography, 'but I always had, from the moment I took a leading part in the trade union movement, the greatest horror of a strike, and would go to almost any length to prevent it.' Within two years Edwards had built the membership up to 3,000, cycling over 6,000 miles a year around Norfolk in order to do so. In March 1910, a year of great industrial and political turmoil, there was a spontaneous strike for higher wages and better conditions in the village of Trunch, near North Walsham, and in May a more widespread stoppage based in the village of St Faith's. The St Faith's strike was a long and bitter one, settled in January, after seven months on terms which represented a defeat for the men. Many union members were victimized and this provoked the membership to sever the Union's links with the Liberal Party, which was suspected of devious political manoeuvering during the course of the strike. At the Union's annual conference in Fakenham in February 1911, the members voted for affiliation to the Labour Party and the TUC. This was a considerable contrast to the reaction to defeat in the Great Lock-Out of 1874. On that occasion a set-piece conflict which had resulted in defeat quickly led to the disintegration of the union. Now it resulted in a renewed determination to succeed. Indeed in 1912 it changed its name – somewhat pretentiously given that its membership hardly spread beyond the boundaries of Norfolk – to the National Agricultural Labourers and Rural Workers Union.

Edwards retired through ill-health in 1913 and was replaced by the more militant R. B. Walker. A strike in Lancashire during that year threatened the ascendency of Norfolk over the affairs of the Union, but a simmering dispute over the balance between local and national control was overtaken by a wave of spontaneous rural unrest in 1914 which compared with that of 1872 (see chapter 6). There were strikes in Essex at Helions Bumpstead, Steeple Bumpstead and other surrounding villages, and in several areas of Norfolk, including Trunch once more. At Flitcham on the Sandringham Estate a successful strike led to demands elsewhere for 'the King's money and the King's conditions'. At Burston, near Diss, a bizarre episode which included the sacking of the local schoolteacher for his support of the Union, led to a trade union-funded 'alternative' school being constructed. Other strikes took place in Wiltshire, Cheshire, Lancashire, Kent, Northamptonshire, Oxfordshire, Bedfordshire, Herefordshire, Gloucestershire and Somerset. Nearly all of them were successful, farmers generally being willing to concede demands on the basis of a tightening labour market and a slow return to agricultural prosperity. By the middle of 1914 membership was approximately 5,000, to which were added the agricultural members of the urban-based Workers Union, which had begun recruiting farm workers in 1912 and within two years had established 150 branches in fourteen counties.

This growth in collective organization among farm workers had been matched on the employers' side: indeed one tended to provoke the other. In 1908 Colin Campbell had formed the Lincolnshire Farmers' Union in response to growing trade union agitation in that county. It rapidly developed into a national organization with county branches and became the leading representative of practising farmers. The National Farmers' Union (as it soon became) opposed land nationalization, but supported greater security of tenure. It quickly became the leading employers' organization, even though most of its members were opposed to the notion of collective bargaining. The NFU also refused at first to admit landowners (though not owner-occupiers) to its membership since it was concerned to represent tenant farmers against landowners over such matters as tenant right. It was also hardly coincidental that it was in Lincolnshire in 1907 that a group of landowners had formed the Central Land Association to combat the Liberal Party's threat of land reform. By 1910 the CLA had 1,000 members, of whom over 100 were MPs. The NFU was thus formed to protect the interests of farmers against both the threat of trade union agitation among their employees and what they regarded as the undue political influence of their landlords.

This emerging collective mobilization of the competing class interests in agriculture threatened some kind of conflagration during the summer of 1914. Most counties which had

not already experienced a strike, for example, were preparing
for such a confrontation, and both sides seemed to be girding
themselves for the kind of winner-takes-all combat which had
occurred in 1874. The conflagration, of course, took place
elsewhere and was of a decidedly more deadly character.
Given a choice between class and country all the participants
chose the latter. The conduct of war not only set aside the
more parochial conflicts of employer and employee, but also,
through the instrument of state intervention, enabled each of
the emergent agricultural organizations vastly to increase their
membership and influence. In this sense the state not only
sponsored the growth of the NFU, CLA and the agricultural
trade unions by bringing them into the arena of policy
formulation and execution; it provided these organizations
with a *raison d'être* to their potential members. The war thus
stimulated an increase in the membership of all three organizations, even though class animosities were, for the time
being, held in abeyance. By 1918, approximately 200,000
farm workers were members of trade unions, while the NFU
could claim 80,000 members and the CLA approximately
8,000.

This state-sponsored collective organization was particularly apparent among farm workers. At first the general
industrial truce and the loss of nearly 250,000 farm workers to
the Armed Forces hit union membership hard. The National
Union lost nearly one-quarter of its members between 1914
and 1916 and the Workers' Union's losses were even more
excessive. It was the Corn Production Act that came to the
rescue of the unions, granting them the right to represent the
interests of farm workers on the new Agricultural Wages
Board and local District Wages Committees. Thus, more than
eighty years after the Tolpuddle Martyrs had been outlawed
for daring to form a union, agricultural trade unionism was
officially recognized and union leaders were granted a participating role, however modest, in determining the development of their industry. This represented a triumph for the
National Union's leadership, and a personal triumph for
Edwards, who had at an early stage recognized that, without

some legally-established form of collective bargaining, the chances of improving the conditions of an isolated and scattered labour force by unionization alone were extremely slender. Even the meagre initial wages award of twenty-five shillings (£1.25) a week could not dampen Edwards's satisfaction in achieving what he had been striving for, for over forty years.

The establishment of national negotiating machinery, complemented by local committees, suddenly made unionization relevant to the individual farm worker. The Corn Production Act succeeded in transforming what was, despite its title, a small regional trade union into a genuinely national organization. The Act also allowed the price of wheat, the wages of farm workers and the membership of agricultural trade unions to rise in unison. By 1920, when the Act came up for renewal, the membership of the National Union was approximately 93,000 (compared to 4,000 in 1916), while the agricultural membership of the Workers Union was estimated to have been as high as 120,000. These were, indeed, heady days for the agricultural trade unions. The end of the war in 1918 had not led to any immediate relief from labour shortages, and significant advantages were made in wages, together with a reduction of hours. Although the earlier awards were merely catching up lost ground, by 1920 wage rises had overtaken increases in the cost of living since 1914 and had also risen faster than average rates in industry. All this was achieved with little resort to the threat of strike action, since farmers were prospering, too. Furthermore, the Agriculture Act of 1920 continued the provisions of the Corn Production Act, including the guaranteed prices, wages boards and the minimum wage. In 1920 the National Union also changed its name and became the National Union of Agricultural Workers (NUAW).

Unfortunately at this highpoint in agricultural prosperity, when the prospects of a return to the depressed pre-war conditions appeared to have been finally banished, the political immaturity of all the farming organizations became devastingly apparent. In keeping with their new nationally-recognized status, leaders of both trade unions and the NFU found themselves increasingly drawn into wider issues of agricultural politics than merely minimum-wage legislation. Wartime conditions had led to a revival of political debate concerning the role of agriculture in the national economy. Both trade unions, on their own account and through the Labour Party, had become embroiled in policy discussions over such matters as smallholdings and allotments, the abolition of the tied cottage, the implementation of a rural public housing programme, free trade and the level and extent of state support for agriculture under post-war conditions. In July 1919 the Government announced a Royal Commission 'to inquire into the economic prospects of the agricultural industry in Great Britain'. The Commission included members from all of the farming organizations, including representatives of the English and Scottish trade unions. The Government demanded an interim report on guaranteed prices by the end of September, but the Commission was completely divided on the issue: twelve members signed a majority report recommending continuation; while the other eleven members favoured abandonment and signed a minority report accordingly. No final report was ever produced, the Government dissolving the Commission when it moved on to consider the politically sensitive issue of land tenure. Astonishingly, both the NFU and trade union representatives were signatories of the minority report. Indeed, they argued vehemently in favour of the abolition of price guarantees, and attacked the Government for accepting the majority report and pressing ahead with the 1920 Agriculture Act. The Workers Union journal referred to the Commission as the Government's 'tame creature', and the NUAW's President attacked the Agriculture Bill in Parliament. The NFU's opposition was based upon the adverse effect of high cereal prices on the costs of livestock farmers (who were much more numerous). That the trade union representatives supported this view is difficult to understand even in retrospect: it seems not to have occurred to them that the abolition of cereals guarantees might also involve the abolition of the minimum wage.

Within six months of having extended guarantees in the Agriculture Act, the Government took the NFU and trade union members at their word and and promptly repealed it. It did so because there was every sign that the Act would, for the first time, cost money: prices had fallen precipitously during the winter of 1920–1, partly as a result of the renewal of international trade in cereals from North America and elsewhere. The Corn Production Acts (Repeal) Act, which abolished price guarantees *and* minimum wage control, thus passed into farming folklore as the 'great betrayal' of British agriculture by conniving urban politicians. While it is true that farming support was abandoned without compunction once real resources were involved, the truth was, alas, rather more embarrassing. As a foretaste of what was to ensue, the employers' side of the Wages Board promptly moved an immediate reduction in minimum wage rates within a few days of the Government's announcement and before the Act was formally repealed. This reduction was carried and for the next two years all the gains that had accrued to farm workers from the conditions of wartime were to be quickly swept aside.

During 1921 and 1922 agricultural prices continued to fall rapidly. The price of what was halved in six months and farmers accordingly began to cut their costs, reducing the area under cultivation and shedding workers in their thousands. Under these circumstances the unions were powerless to prevent further cuts in wages, and by the end of 1922 they had been reduced by over 25 per cent on levels prevailing only two years previously – lower in real terms than the depressed level prevailing in 1914 or even that achieved by Joseph Arch in the 1870s. Rural unionization was once again threatened. The NUAW lost three-quarters of its members in three years and the impact on the Workers Union was worse still. Despite the movement of its headquarters from Fakenham to London in 1918, the NUAW became once more virtually a local union based in Norfolk, so that by the end of 1921, conditions had again been created whereby Norfolk had become a county in which bargaining between employers and employees was to achieve national significance. In 1922 the Union in Norfolk was itself riven by dissension, and a full-scale breakaway union was only narrowly averted, partly due to the personal intervention of the elderly George Edwards. In October the local farmers pressed their advantage. They proposed a further reduction in wages to twenty-five shillings for a fifty-hour week. Ironically this was the level of the original Wages Board settlement in 1914, but given the level of wartime inflation during the intervening period, it represented a cut in real terms of almost 50 per cent. Although the NUAW broke off negotiations, the Union was in no position to resist, and this rate was to prevail throughout Norfolk by the end of the year.

In February 1923, the employers returned to the offensive. They proposed a further reduction by threepence (1.25p) per week, an increase of four hours in the working week and, most alarmingly, an abandonment of the guaranteed weekly wage, with no payment for 'wet days' – in other words, a return to the casualization of farm labour which had prevailed before the war. This pushed the NUAW beyond endurance and a strike was called. It was recognized on both sides that Norfolk was being used as a test case and there is some evidence to suggest that it was a measure deliberately designed to provoke government intervention once more. However, this was to no avail and on Saturday 24 March the strike began in earnest. The NUAW Executive wisely decided to concentrate its effort in one area only, north and west Norfolk, where it possessed its greatest strength. Sympathy strikes elsewhere were discouraged in order not to dissipate organization and finances. The Union introduced a novel tactic – flying pickets. They cycled around the countryside attempting to prevent the use of non-union labour on seed-drilling. They were sufficiently effective to bring in a large number of police from surrounding counties, up to 600 on one occasion. This led to lurid newspaper stories about 'class war' in the Norfolk countryside, most of which were greatly exaggerated, but there is no doubt that in places the dispute was very bitterly fought indeed. At the 'Battle of Holly Heath Farm', for example, pickets were fired upon by an irate employer.

Luckily no one was injured and the pickets were able to march away singing the 'Red Flag' and 'Onward Christian Soldiers' – a typical admixture of bitter class conflict and a Christian sense of social injustice which characterized the strike.

Many employers were clearly taken aback by the strength of the workers' resistance, but behind the brave statements of the Union leaders, anxiety was spreading about the progress of the strike. At the beginning of March, 20,000 strike notices had been sent out, but by the end of the month the largest number of pre-strike members who had actually withdrawn their labour was less than 5,000 – and this was in the Union's national stronghold. Moreover, the Union was paying out nearly £4,000 per week in strike benefit and was heading fast for bankruptcy. As April progressed, the financial situation was becoming perilous and there was a slow but discernible drift back to work – more than 1,000 in the second week of April alone. On 9 April, NFU and NUAW leaders met in Norwich, but could reach no agreement. The NFU was still hoping to force government intervention, but in April the Government fell and, with a General Election in the offing, the Labour Party leader, Ramsay MacDonald, organized a settlement. The line was held at twenty-five shillings for a fifty-hour week and the guaranteed week was to be retained. A further clause pledged farmers to no victimization of striking farm workers. The NUAW interpreted this to mean that all strikers would have their jobs back; but the NFU's interpretation was that no such jobs would be given to outsiders. As a result there were further angry recriminations and by June 1,200 men remained unemployed. Exhausted and almost insolvent, there was little that the NUAW could do. In an atmosphere of hostility and betrayal the strike came to an embittered end.

For the NUAW the Norfolk strike was undoubtedly the most important in its history. Publicly, the settlement was presented as a victory, and in certain respects this was not untrue. In particular there was to be no return to the pre-1917 horrors of casualization, and to that extent it marked an important stage in the farm worker's struggle for better conditions of employment. Privately, however, the NUAW's leadership drew rather different conclusions. In the Union's strongest area only a maximum of 25 per cent of the membership had obeyed the strike call and the Union had been reduced to penury. The settlement meant that the farm worker had made no progress in real terms in forty years and, added to this, the Union leadership could only look on impotently, as many strikers were victimized and left homeless as well as jobless, as tied cottage evictions gathered pace. Moreover, all of this was in a dispute which the NFU had fought somewhat half-heartedly with a view to government intervention. In time the lesson which was drawn from the Norfolk strike, the last strike of national significance in British agriculture, was a simple one: the future of the NUAW lay in the re-establishment of a wages board and in working within its statutory framework; except in the most exceptional circumstances strike action could lead only to the demoralization of the membership and the speedy self-destruction of the Union.

The Return of Agricultural Depression

Without the benefit of price supports, agriculture was once more at the mercy of market forces and there could be little doubt, given prevailing experience since 1873, what this would mean. Depression returned once more and again it was the arable sector, which had been encouraged to expand cultivation during the war, which was particularly hard hit. Across East Anglia and the South-East 'dog-and-stick' farming returned. On this occasion, however, there was a much less fatalistic attitude towards the causes of depression, since the experience of the last years of the war had shown that a state-supported agriculture was technically feasible and could provide greater stability in prices. Lord Milner, chairman of the committee which had led to the introduction of the Corn Production Act, campaigned for the reintroduction of state support, suggesting that some measure of government assistance would be desirable in order to iron out the worst of the enormous fluctuations in agricultural prices. The Government's response, set out in a White Paper in 1926, was to reaffirm its commitment to free trade and to urge farmers once more to switch from cereals to livestock and dairy production, taking advantage of the cheaper foodstuffs now available because of low cereals prices. The Government would only assist farmers as a means of alleviating unemployment in rural areas, rather than as a broadly-based policy of agricultural support. Thus a series of measures introduced in the 1920s provided only minor amelioration and could not be regarded as a departure from the policy of *laissez-faire* which guided the Government's policy towards the farming industry. These measures included the provision of credits under the Agricultural Credits Act of 1923; a grant of one million pounds to be spent over five years on land drainage; grants for the improvement of roads in rural areas; and more support for rural district councils in order to enable them to construct more public housing. In order to relieve unemployment in the Eastern Counties, a restricted concession to price support was made through the British Sugar (Subsidy) Act of 1925, which provided a subsidy for sugar beet for ten years. By 1929 eighteen factories were operating and 230,000 acres were given over to sugar beet production, providing essential income for over 30,000 farms.

Following the 'Great Crash' of 1929, economic depression was to hit the whole of the Western world. In Britain agriculture was no longer the only industry to suffer massive unemployment and a down-turn in prices. Agriculture was, however, further affected by the sharp fall in industrial activity and the disruption to international trade. Agricultural prices declined by 20 per cent between 1929 and 1931, and then by a further 16 per cent between 1931 and 1933. This time the collapse of prices affected the livestock sector as well as the cereals growers. Large areas of land were now going to rack and ruin, while farmers and farm workers were rendered destitute in large numbers. Because agriculture was still not covered by unemployment insurance, unemployed farm workers and bankrupt farmers still had to apply for relief under the Poor Law. In the arable areas there was simply no market for the land, either to rent or sell. Thousands of acres became derelict. In a House of Commons debate one MP from Norfolk described the plight of that county:

Agricultural buildings are coming down, the farmers are despairing, and the labourers are losing their employment. . . . The waves of past depression have left their mark on Norfolk, where you can see the marks of the old fences reminding one that the land in the past has been cultivated.

Another, who had recently visited East Anglia, commented on

. . . the distress and hopeless outlook of every one connected with [agriculture] . . . I found that men had lost the wish to live and that the women were broken-hearted at the outlook and were without hope to cheer them in their dull monotonous existence. It seemed as though emigration or the dole were the only alternatives.

Under the circumstances the Government felt compelled to act, and after 1931 the principle of state intervention in the determination of agricultural returns was once more conceded, albeit slowly and very grudgingly. Price guarantees for wheat were reintroduced under the Wheat Act of 1932 which provided for price supports out of a levy on wheat flour. A Wheat Commission was set up to collect the levy and make payments to farmers, and in the following two years there was a large increase in the area planted with wheat. This was followed by the renewal of the sugar beet subsidy and the introduction of a subsidy to fat cattle under the Cattle Industry (Emergency Provisions) Act of 1934. Government assistance for agriculture was also granted indirectly through the imposition of tariffs and quotas on imported foods. Direct and indirect price supports were, however, only one strand of the Government's policy. The other was the control of production through Marketing Boards, essentially producer-controlled cartels, which were introduced in 1931, but which were only made effective after the passage of a second Agricultural Marketing Act in 1933. The scheme had begun with hops, but after 1933 it spread, with the assistance of the

NFU, to potatoes, pigs and milk. In addition to assisting with marketing and distribution (which, in the case of milk, brought the daily pint to urban doorsteps) the new Marketing Boards lightly controlled production and allocated quotas among producers in order to bring about higher and more stable prices. Farmers, who voted in the members of the boards, were generally willing to accept the restrictions on their freedom of action in order to reap the benefits of a controlled market. The Marketing Boards were largely successful in raising farm incomes. Controversy broke out from time to time over the details of administration, but their success can be measured by the fact that they have since become recognized fixtures of the British farming scene. Indeed it is the presence of such cartels which is largely responsible for the lack of progress in Britain, compared with most continental European countries, of agricultural co-operatives.

It required the renewed threat of war in Europe to persuade the Government to commit itself fully to intervention in agriculture. The Wheat Act and the Agricultural Marketing Acts were certainly important breakthroughs in government indifference towards agriculture. However, support had been given in a piecemeal fashion, reflecting the Government's reluctance to override the principle of *laissez-faire*. It was not until 1939, when strategic considerations began once more to become paramount, that a comprehensive measure of support was introduced. The Agriculture Act of 1937 paved the way by extending price guarantees to oats and barley and introducing a fertilizer subsidy. The Government continued to prevaricate, however, and throughout 1938 was expressing the view that even in the event of war there was no need to expand home production. It required the German invasion of Czechoslovakia to sweep aside all remaining doubts. Agriculture was again put on a war footing and a food production campaign was drawn up in order to ensure that the nation was not caught napping as it had been in 1914. As the harvest of 1939 was gathered in, it became clear that these plans would not be wasted.

'I'M HAPPY WHEN I'M HIKING' – THE OTHER RURAL ENGLAND

Although the 1930s was a decade of depression, the social effects were by no means evenly distributed. The old-established industrial areas of Scotland, Wales and the North of England suffered disproportionately from unemployment and poverty. The south-east of England, on the other hand, continued to experience economic growth, based largely on the expanding manufacture of consumer goods. Thanks to falling prices, those in employment tended to experience a growth in real income, a feature that was particularly pronounced in the more affluent and middle-class Home Counties region. Among the goods that this segment of the population began to 'consume' in increasing numbers was the countryside itself, rendered more accessible by suburban housing development and the more widespread purchase of the motor car. The idea that rural England was an urban playspace was not new in the 1930s, but the demand for various forms of countryside recreation increased considerably over this period. In sharp contrast to the bleak realities of agricultural England, a bucolic rural life was 'discovered' by the urban middle classes.

In many respects the hallmark of the 1930s Home Counties life-style was the suburban housing estate, a slightly *déclassé* version of the Garden City movement launched by Ebenezer Howard at Letchworth and Welwyn before the First World War. Scaled-down versions of John Loudon's country houses for the *nouveaux riches* (see chapter 4) were now within reach of the expanding army of white-collar workers. Job-lot developments of semi-detached suburbia, frequently promoted by the railway companies (the best-known being 'Metroland' along the Metropolitan Line to Amersham), offered a haven of domestic peace from an economically harsh urban environment. As the lower middle classes fulfilled their dream of suburban domesticity, those further up the social scale began to explore the surrounding rural hinterland. Not for the first time in English history, a step up the social ladder entailed a

move out into the countryside. As the historian John
Lowerson has put it:

The happiness of tennis club and herbaceous border stretched even
further with the more prosperous able to escape from suburban
dreariness, as they saw it, into the 'real' country. . . . Fresh air,
weekend walks and that most carefully contrived of all rural
environments, the golf course, gave the Home Counties' commuter
the illusion of minor gentility. . . .

Here the affluent urbanite constructed a rural England
almost totally at variance with the surrounding agricultural
realities which prevailed during this period. Knowledgeable
about the aesthetic appreciation of landscapes, the longevity of
rustic traditions and the value of the natural environment, they
were woefully ignorant about agriculture and the economic
basis of life in the countryside. In part this was because their
rural sensibilities were culled almost entirely from books: the
enjoyment of the countryside was a cultural and aesthetic
matter rather than something that was based upon personal
experience. In this the cultured urbanite was abetted by a
welter of popular 1930s literature. Today Stella Gibbon's
devastating satire of this literary genre, *Cold Comfort Farm*
(published in 1932) is better known than the work it was
attacking, but at the time the reverse was true, and works such
as Mary Webb's *Precious Bane* (the original butt of Gibbon's
parody) sold in their thousands. Lest anyone should be in any
doubt about what the respectful observer of the countryside
should 'see', a plethora of guide books, interpretative texts and
rural reminiscences flooded out from publishers to define this
other rural world for them. The countryside, in this perception, was a precious and cherished heritage of the 'real'
England, suffused with the picturesque and the quaint.
Accessibility by car reduced rural England to a series of
medieval churches and cream teas, or, as *The Morris Owner's
Road Book* put it: 'The pretty villages, the old farmsteads,
besides numberless quaint features to be found in our old
towns, all reach out from those bygone centuries and captivate
us with their reminiscences of ancient peace.' This was a far

cry from those aspects of rural life described earlier in this chapter.

As the popularity of living in and visiting the countryside grew, so did the alarm of those who wished to preserve its 'ancient peace'. The preservation movement was, again, not new: the Commons, Open Spaces and Footpaths Preservation Society had been founded as long ago as 1865 and the National Trust in 1895. Again, however, the 1930s saw a considerable extension of the activities of organizations devoted to the preservation of the countryside, prime amongst them being the Council for the Preservation of Rural England, founded in 1926. By the 1930s a recognizable 'environmental lobby' had emerged, committed to defending the countryside from the threat of urban sprawl and urban ways, symbolized by such modern accoutrements as bungalows, electricity pylons, filling stations and advertising hoardings. The dilemma which existed between promoting the spiritual pleasures of the countryside and preserving it from the 'madding crowds' of insensitive visitors was never far from the surface of the preservation movement's pronouncements: the countryside needed to be preserved for 'the nation', but *from* 'the public'. Cultural elitism was never entirely absent from these judgements. Only a self-appointed minority possessed the qualities to appreciate fully the cultural enlightenment which the experience of the countryside could bestow. As Lowerson points out, 'The attack on unsightly village garages and mock-Tudor tea shoppes often concealed a contempt for the economic opportunism which had prompted their owners. Few rural people were, or could afford to be, as concerned with trimness and neatness as those to whom their villages had become a solace.'

The preservation movement proved to be a strange political amalgam of patrician landowners, for whom the preservation of the countryside was closely linked to their conception of 'stewardship', and socially-concerned Fabians (Hampstead dwellers, but keen hikers of the Downs) who believed in the pursuit of social justice through national planning. It proved to be a powerful coalition, influencing legislation such as the

Restriction of Ribbon Development Act of 1935 and laying a basis for the development of a planned countryside which was to emerge in the late 1940s. A key figure in this movement was Patrick Abercrombie who was both a founder-member of the CPRE and a leading figure in the Town and Country Planning Association, which promoted the interests of the embryonic planning profession and campaigned for legislative containment of urban expansion. Abercrombie was an outspoken advocate of Green Belts around the major conurbations, *cordons sanitaires* intended to keep urbanism at bay. He spearheaded an articulate and influential body of opinion which ensured that rural preservationist sentiment and town and country planning policy were closely intertwined. At an early stage the CPRE had advocated the establishment of National Parks, on the American model, in order to preserve the most beautiful areas of the countryside. In 1931 the CPRE set up a Standing Committee on the National Parks in order to pursue this aim. The unifying conception of Green Belts, National Parks and other such designations was to ensure the preservation of rural landscapes and a rural way of life from the encroachment of urban sprawl and urban ways. The myopic reverence for this rural way of life ensured that precisely *what* it was that was being preserved was never examined too closely.

If the mock-Tudor bungalow or semi represents one powerful image of the 1930s countryside, then another was the bare-kneed and rucksacked hiker setting out to commune with Nature on downland or fell. In the south of England such a pursuit could take advantage of the dense network of ancient footpaths and bridleways which criss-crossed areas like the Downs and the Chilterns. In the North, however, access to open countryside was not so easy. For example, northern cities like Manchester and Sheffield were surrounded by the beautiful open moorland of the Peak District, but it was rendered virtually inaccessible by the restrictive property rights of local landowners, anxious to allow their grouse to remain undisturbed, and buttressed by a fearsome army of gamekeepers determined to keep urban denizens at bay. The

Ramblers Association, which had been founded in 1932, launched a campaign to open up the moors and hills to the public. The issue bore strong echoes of common rights which had been heard since the enclosure movement, but it was now overlaid with a rich mixture of romantic sentiment for the spiritual benefits of communion with the wilderness and hard-nosed class-based politics (which attracted the attention of the Communist Party). In April 1932 matters were brought to a head at Kinder Scout in the High Peak area of Derbyshire. A stage-managed mass trespass of the Duke of Devonshire's grouse moors, following a rally nearby, led to fighting between ramblers and estate wardens. Five of the ringleaders were arrested and subsequently imprisoned. There followed a series of organized attempts at trespass, though without further scenes of violence. Public access to private land was now placed firmly on the political agenda. A limited Access to the Mountains Act was passed in 1938, by which time all parties to the conflict had other matters on their mind. Nevertheless the 'Wild Scenes at Kinder Scout' passed into the folklore of the rambling movement, vividly illustrating another, more populist, stand in the enjoyment of the countryside which was not always apparent in the pronouncements of the leading spokesman of the preservation movement.

It is easy to recognize that the rural England so assiduously appreciated by the hiker or the motorist of the 1930s bore little relation to the rural England experienced by those who lived and worked there. However, the urban, middle-class perceptions of rustic peace were a powerful determining influence on the future development of the countryside. The attention lavished on the aesthetics of landscape contrasted sharply with the public indifference to the plight of agriculture, yet this merely reflected prevailing urban sentiment. As a result it became politically influential – as experience in the 1940s was to demonstrate. Curiously, rural England had come to present 'real' England: the Leavisite elision of elitist cultural sensibility and organic rural community allowed an idyllic version of rural life to be elevated to the status of quintessential England

and Englishness. When the Few defended the nation in the Battle of Britain it is doubtful whether they conceived of England in terms of engineering factories and municipal gasworks, but rather of church towers, thatched cottages and stooks of corn standing under a threatening harvest sky. Unfortunately, it required another war to bring home to the urban population that what counted first and foremost to the national well-being was not the amenity value of the countryside, the aesthetic appreciation of its landscapes nor even the way in which it embodied the national heritage, but its ability to produce sufficient food.

CHAPTER 9

THE SECOND AGRICULTURAL REVOLUTION

When the older generation of farmers today look back to their childhood and early adulthood, what strikes them most forcibly is the contrast between the post-war period and the conditions which predominated in the 1920s and 1930s. The lengthy agricultural depression, relieved only by the First World War and its immediate aftermath, had produced a situation in which thousands of acres of arable land lay unkempt and unfarmed, agricultural bankruptcies had soared and thousands of farm workers were unemployed or suffering from falling wages. Less tangibly, the morale of the rural population had been sapped by such a lengthy spell of economic adversity and declining population. The rural village was scarcely a centre of cultural vitality and lively social intercourse. As wartime evacuees were later to discover, many rural villages lacked the basic amenities which urban centres had long taken for granted, while social life was characterized as much by a dreary tedium as by an idyllic wholesomeness.

In a remarkable repetition of events which had occurred during the First World War, much of this was to be transformed between 1939 and 1945. More importantly, this transformation was to be sustained in the post-war period and even extended by further legislation which would guarantee, amongst other things, that there would be no return to the depressed conditions of the previous era. Agriculture was transformed by one major factor: state intervention. Under wartime conditions, the *laissez-faire* doctrines which had dominated British agricultural policy since the middle of the nineteenth century were finally abandoned – and there was to be no return once international trade had become re-established during peacetime. It was the state which undertook to reconstruct rural Britain from the ravages of over half a century of depression and neglect. Henceforward the state was not merely to guarantee the conditions which would favour enduring prosperity, it would, if necessary, directly intervene in order to ensure that this would come about. The centrepiece of such intervention was, inevitably, the agriculture industry. The need to expand agricultural production at almost any cost was not only a wartime imperative, but was given an added piquancy by Britain's reliance on imported food, following decades of free-trade agricultural policy. The intervention in agriculture was certainly the most urgent and in many respects the most far-reaching manifestation of the state's new role in the countryside, but it was by no means the only element of rural reconstruction to be undertaken. Equally influential was the state's massive involvement in physical planning, the provision of education, health and social services, the improvement of housing conditions and a whole bundle of activities concerned with countryside access, amenity and recreation (see chapter 10). Henceforth rural Britain was to be fashioned, controlled and administered through public policies, influenced albeit by the familiar hierarchy of farmers and landowners. Nevertheless these policies were to emanate not from the local Big House but from Westminster, Whitehall and – much later – Brussels. After the Second World War, state intervention was to be a permanent feature of rural life.

SUBMARINES: THE FARMERS' FRIENDS

The reorganization of agriculture was one of the most urgent tasks facing the wartime Coalition Government. As already mentioned in the previous chapter, some tentative steps towards intervention in agriculture had been taken during the early 1930s, and these were accelerated at the end of the decade when it was becoming clear that war was unavoidable. Once more German submarines became the farmer's friend. The threat to imported food supplies demanded a vast expansion in home output. Farmers were both persuaded and forced to comply. As in the First World War, farmers were offered incentives to expand production through the medium of guaranteed prices. This ensured that farmers could expand with confidence, knowing that prices would be related to costs of production and that increasing output would not be met with declining prices. But for those farmers who were disinclined to make the requisite changes – or incapable of them – the state took the necessary steps to assume direct control of food production via local representative committees. Behind the provision of attractive incentives there always lay the threat of compulsion.

The enormous growth of state intervention in agriculture stemmed initially from this compulsory element. This in turn, however, was only part of a comprehensive planning process applied to agriculture during the war years. The whole pattern of farming was drastically changed: neglected and derelict land was reclaimed, large numbers of livestock were slaughtered in order to save on feedstuffs, and a record acreage of land was placed under the plough. Compulsory cropping orders were issued and mechanization was enforced using a system of local tractor stations borrowed from Lenin's New Economic Policy in the Soviet Union. On the other hand the guaranteed prices were generous and farmers prospered; farm workers, too, benefited from wartime labour shortages and saw their incomes rise to unprecedented levels, even in real terms. Rising prosperity and the removal of uncertainty introduced by price supports created a climate of acceptance of growing state control. Although farmers and landowners were by no means uncritical, the balance of opinion had shifted decisively in favour of the state assuming a more interventionist role, even after the cessation of hostilities.

Although the principle of state intervention had been

conceded by the introduction of new marketing arrangements and other initiatives in the 1930s, the war both fundamentally altered the character of such intervention and created, almost for the first time, a sophisticated apparatus for implementing and monitoring state control. Prior to the war, most advisory and regulatory programmes were administered by county councils with universities acting as regional centres of research and specialized information. The Ministry of Agriculture possessed virtually no field officers of its own and thus was ill-prepared to offer detailed advice or to safeguard the efficient use of government resources at the local level. Consequently the Ministry created War Agricultural Executive Committees, or 'War Ags' as they were dubbed, drawn primarily from land commissioners, county council advisory staff and university personnel, leavened by exemplary local farmers and landowners. The War Ags offered advice, issued cultivation directions and allocated scarce resources such as fertilizers, feedstuffs and machinery. They had the power to evict farmers who refused to comply, and in fact some 10,000 were dispossessed (mostly non-resident owners) and 3,000 tenancies terminated. Where necessary the War Ags farmed land themselves. The War Ags also administered cropping programmes by distributing production quotas throughout the areas for which they were responsible. Their activities thus extended to each individual holding of land and, in precise detail, to the mix of commodities and husbandry methods adopted on virtually each and every farm. This unprecedented intervention in what had hitherto been the jealously-guarded autonomy of the individual farmer was, however, mitigated by the fact that the same committees were also the channel for receiving grant aid and subsidies for new forms of capital investment. In general the War Ags were administered with tact by members who were locally known and respected. Farmers found that they were willing to forgo a degree of independence in return for a sustained improvement in their economic circumstances.

The War Ags were also successful in terms of their stated objectives. British agriculture was set on the road towards technological modernization; land was being fully exploited as an indigenous source of food supplies; and, not least, output had expanded sufficiently to allow the urban population to be fed nutritiously, if monotonously, from home production. The War Ags thus provided a model for state intervention during the post-war period should the post-war Government abrogate the example of the 1920s and renew its guarantees to the farming industry during peacetime. As it turned out, no other alternative was seriously considered. Agriculture benefited from the widespread determination not to return to the depressed conditions of the 1930s and to utilize Keynesian economic management in order to ensure full employment and rising standards of living. Public opinion towards agriculture had also shifted on the basis of a renewed awareness of its strategic importance; moreover the impact of war on Britain's international trading position strongly suggested the need for a permanent increase in home production as an aid to the balance of payments. Agriculture also benefited from the public perception that farmers had made enormous wartime sacrifices which deserved rewards. There thus developed a virtual political consensus that the achievements of wartime agriculture should not be frittered away once more during the peace.

This principle was embodied in the Agriculture Act of 1947, the single most influential piece of legislation which governed post-war agricultural policy. The Act was to perpetuate the stick-and-carrot philosophy of the wartime reorganization of agriculture by establishing a comprehensive system of state guarantees for commodity prices while at the same time placing farmers and landowners under a statutory obligation to pursue good husbandry and estate management practice. The price guarantees were to ensure stability for the farmer; the pursuit of efficiency was left to reconstituted War Ags (now County Agricultural Committees), together with the incentives offered by price-support manipulation, capital grants, subsidies, etc. The Act was an ingenious piece of legislation which, with some justification, has since been revered as a model of how to harmonize and transcend the conflicting interests in the support of agricultural production. State support for agriculture was to proceed on the basis of an annual price review for specified commodities, undertaken by the Ministry of Agriculture in consultation with the farmers' interest groups, principally the NFU. The purpose of the price review was to determine the guaranteed price to the farmer of products like wheat, barley, milk, eggs, potatoes, sugar beet, beef and pig meat for the following year. If market prices fell below guaranteed prices then farmers received the difference in cash – a 'deficiency payment'. Such payments came out of general taxation revenues, allowing the consumer to take advantage of cheap food prices in the shops. The beauty of this system was thus that a 'cheap food policy' – attractive to urban consumers – was perpetuated, as in the pre-war period, but farmers achieved the support necessary for an equitable standard of living. Since the proportion of general taxation that was expended on farm support was negligible, any increase in support to farmers resulting from the price review was not immediately noticeable to the average taxpayer. Moreover, the system contained a hidden welfare element for poor families, by supporting cheap food through the payment of taxes.

Such was the immediate success of this legislation that for a generation agriculture was elevated above the everyday controversies of party politics and discussion limited increasingly to arcane and somewhat mystifying policy minutiae among a closed circle of ministry officials, academic observers and the representatives of farming organizations. In retrospect this can be seen as a dangerous and ultimately counterproductive move out of the public arena and into a conclave of unaccountable policy influentials. But for thirty years the growth of a stable and efficient agriculture disguised some of the more questionable aspects of post-war policy and its implementation. Furthermore, agricultural policy's drift into the exclusive realm of the *cognoscenti* was aided by the gradual dismantling – in fact, if not in theory – of the War Ag apparatus. Following the war the permanent staff were absorbed into the civil service and the reconstituted committees' powers of compulsion were rarely used. The 'stick' which the Ministry of Agriculture increasingly chose to adopt was the sanction of the market. By tinkering with the details of guarantees, grants and subsidies, the Ministry could influence farmers through its 'price signals' while giving the appearance of maintaining the farmer's formal independence. This placed the direction and implementation of policy further in the hands of technical experts, armed with regression coefficients and simultaneous equations, and beyond the public purview. Fundamental policy considerations were ignored or diverted.

As a result, agricultural policy was allowed to become entirely single-minded in its aims: the production of more and cheaper food. In this it was spectacularly successful: farm productivity increased fourfold in the four decades after 1939, and by 1983 Britain had become virtually self-sufficient in temperate foodstuffs. The state, quite consciously and deliberately, acted as a midwife for what has become known, with pardonable hyperbole, as the Second Agricultural Revolution, thereby transforming, too, the everyday life of rural Britain. Stripped of its rhetoric this process has essentially involved the increasing application of scientific and technological principles to the pursuit of profit in the production of food. This in itself is, as previous chapters have indicated, nothing new. All that has occurred in the post-war era is a transformation in the technology of most branches of food production, with the state granting to farmers the conditions under which they could embark upon a programme of increasing productivity and cost-efficiency without suffering from a resultant precipitous fall in prices. The consequences of this have been far-reaching indeed – and not always those which were intended.

Even the most casual observer of modern agriculture will have noticed the most obvious manifestation of the Second Agricultural Revolution: the replacement of the predominantly horse-and-hand technology, which prevailed until the Second World War, by wholesale mechanization. Tractors, combine harvesters and many other specialized items of farm machinery have replaced both horses and farm workers. Since

1945 farming has lost two-thirds of its former labour force. Equally important, though somewhat less visible, innovations have occurred in the field of genetics, producing unprecedented increases in output through selective plant and animal breeding. The application of nutritional science has also resulted in immense benefits by the scientific application of animal feed and fertilizers. Husbandry management has also been improved by the introduction of complex forms of pesticides and vaccines. In these ways agricultural production has been revolutionized to the extent that any sense of technological continuity has been shattered within the lifetime of most farmers in the period since 1945. As a result agricultural entrepreneurship has followed the precepts of rationalization apparent in other industries, and farms have become bigger, more capital-intensive and more specialized in their production. Farmers in turn have partaken in the gradual 'disenchantment' of agriculture – the replacement of intuition by calculation and the progressive elimination of the mysteries of plant and animal husbandry by exposing them to scientific appraisal. Such changes have involved, to use the cliché often employed to summarize them, a move 'from agriculture to agribusiness'.

The state regulation of agriculture has, therefore, profoundly altered both the structure of the agriculture industry and the day-to-day nature of life and work in the countryside. The encouragement of fewer, larger and more capital-intensive farms has resulted eventually in the catalogue of social and economic changes which are frequently associated with the post-war transformation of the countryside: the mechanization of agriculture, rural depopulation, the changing social composition of rural villages and the widespread changes in the rural landscape and other environmental aspects of the countryside. These changes have not been haphazard nor the result of some immutable natural law, but the result of policy decisions quite consciously pursued. The Ministry of Agriculture, for example, has promoted technological change directly through its grants and subsidies for farm capitalization and amalgamation, as well as indirectly through its manipulation of guarantees. It has also provided direct assistance through its advisory service (ADAS) and its own research establishments. It also finances research in universities and other autonomous research centres, and influences the priorities of the Agriculture and Food Research Council. A large and complex network of institutions has thus been erected in the public sector in order to effect the transformation that post-war agricultural policy has ordained. All of this suggests that while individual farmers may indeed act *as if* they were governed solely by market rationality, the state has intervened decisively and continuously over the last three decades to act as the architect of British agriculture.

The Second Agricultural Revolution has been as significant as the First, but is less associated with the inventiveness of particular individuals. The Second Agricultural Revolution has been a revolution by committee, monitored by the bureaucrat and made possible by the public official. Its impact has fallen first upon the farmer, the landowner and the farm worker and it is they who will be considered in the remainder of this chapter. However, we must also consider the broader social consequences for the population of rural England, and these, along with other aspects of post-war rural reconstruction, will be taken up in the following chapter. For it is important to emphasize that the stability and efficiency of agriculture have not alone secured unequivocal improvements in the quality of life for the rural population as a whole.

FROM AGRICULTURE TO AGRIBUSINESS

The period since the Second World War, whatever the vicissitudes, has provided the majority of farmers with a degree of stability and sustained prosperity comparable to the mid-Victorian 'high farming' era. The economic and technological contrast with the previous decades of depression is so vivid that it is tempting to regard the more contemporary period as representing a quite fundamental break with the past – a qualitative transformation which has brought about a complete break with all previous experience. The increasing technological complexity of agriculture is the most plausible example of this, and few could deny that, as a result, farming no longer corresponds as closely as in the past to the seasonal rhythm once regarded as a characteristic and immutable feature of all agricultural activity. A harvest which once took months to gather can now be polished off by a combine harvester in a matter of hours. Factory farming, a term which would have been regarded as a contradiction in terms before the Second World War, is now commonplace. However, behind the striking examples of technological change, more persistent continuities remain. Farmers have not engaged in technological innovation for its own sake, but as the means of achieving a goal which has remained the same since the commercialization of agriculture from the seventeenth century onwards: sustained profitability. Thus there is a basic similarity of purpose which links the 'agribusinessmen' of the late twentieth century with the 'improvers' of the early eighteenth century. Only the tools – literally – have changed.

To recognize that farming has become a business, even big business, cannot therefore be regarded as a wholly recent development, and the evident contrasts between pre-war and post-war agriculture should not be allowed to disguise this fact. A more appropriate way of summarizing what has occurred is to recognize that farmers have been granted the conditions under which they could realistically pursue the goal of profitability with the reasonable expectation of commensurate rewards. Those farmers who have been the most profit-conscious have thus been given the incentive to innovate, to invest and to rationalize. On this basis British agriculture has become both highly cost-efficient and prosperous. Moreover, the parameters of profitability have been set by the state in such a way as to encourage the set of structural changes in agriculture which have duly occurred. In order to remain in business in the long term, most farmers thus feel compelled to become more capital-intensive, expand the size of their holding, specialize in particular forms of production and adopt a more professional, rational and single-minded approach to their accounts. Thus, while British agriculture continues to manifest a quite bewildering degree of complexity and diversity, a developmental logic can nevertheless be discerned in the structural changes which have taken place during the post-war period.

It should be emphasized that this logic is not in itself immutable; rather it derives from the particular rationality contained within agricultural policy decisions. In effect successive governments have been able to signal what is required to farmers through the manipulation of costs and prices. By no means all farmers are completely sensitive to such signals, but sufficient farmers have been sufficiently sensitive for the policies to have been effective and for the requisite structural changes to have been set in motion. For example, in order to goad farmers into increasing their cost-efficiency, agricultural policy has consistently sought to place farmers in a 'cost-price squeeze' – that is, to fail to compensate them fully for their increases in cost. This in turn has been a spur to technological innovation as a means of reducing costs. However, not only has the new agricultural technology generally required larger holdings in order to take full advantage of it, but only the larger farms have been able to generate the resources to invest in it. As a result the larger holdings have been able to obtain cost advantages not available to the small farmer, while the latter has become increasingly marginalized: on average the size of farm required to generate sufficient income to support a full-time occupier has nearly doubled each decade since the war. The outcome is the increasing concentration of production on fewer, larger holdings. Moreoever, in order to spread the costs of new technology there has been a tendency for farms to specialize. Traditional mixed farming has declined. One by-product is that the crop and livestock rotations associated with the first Agricultural Revolution have been displaced by the second. Extensive monoculture has threatened to reduce them to farming folklore.

Economies of scale have not been universal in agriculture, however, and have varied according to the type of production and in some cases have even been negative beyond a threshold still within reach of the small, family-run farm – as in horticulture, dairy farming and sheep production. The overall pattern which has emerged in the post-war period is not, therefore, a uniform trend towards larger farming units, but rather the *slow* emergence of a dual farming structure. On the one hand a highly capitalized and large-scale 'agribusiness' sector has gained increasing control over arable and intensive livestock production. Numerically this sector is quite small – for example, 10 per cent of farms account for over one-half of production – but commercially it is in the ascendancy. This is juxtaposed with a numerically far larger, but commercially less significant sector, consisting of small, part-time and quasi-subsistence forms of agriculture existing in the interstices of the market not yet penetrated by 'agribusiness'. Small farms persist in types of production where there are few economies of scale, or where they can fulfil a specialized or local market. There is little *direct* competiton between the two sectors. This segmentation of the farming structure has helped to preserve a (reduced) small farming sector, even though in many respects its survival has run counter to post-war policy objectives. As a result it seems likely that this dual farming structure will be perpetuated for the forseeable future – although the survival of the small farmer will to a large extent be dependent upon his adaptability and tenacity.

Agricultural policy has never taken into account the social impact of the changing farm structure which it has ordained, with one exception – the special payments made to hill farmers. Significantly these were made under a separate Act, the Hill Farming Act of 1946. This recognized the threat to the social fabric of upland farming areas unless 'uneconomic' hill farmers were given special help to keep them in business. The Act allowed 'headage payments' to be made to sheep and cattle farmers in designated hill areas – essentially a *per capita* subsidy on the costs of production. The motive was social welfare rather than the promotion of cost-efficiency. Nevertheless, hill farmers were not shielded from the general tendencies of post-war policy. Payments were made on the basis of output and thus, like the deficiency payments made under the 1947 Agriculture Act, the larger the farm the greater the amount of payments that were received. Neither social need nor environmental hardship were used as criteria. One result has been that the same tendencies towards increasing scale, capital substitution, etc., have been observable in the uplands as elsewhere. It is difficult to avoid the conclusion that small farmers, whether in the uplands or the lowlands, have been an embarrassment for post-war policy-makers. In general agricultural policy has, whatever the rhetoric, attempted to remove as many small farms as quickly as possible and further promote the tendency towards the increasing concentration of production.

This objective lay at the heart of the difficulty which British agricultural policy found in adapting to the Common Agricultural Policy (CAP) after entry into the European Economic Community in 1973. The CAP was specifically designed both to keep the small farmer in production and to be used as a tool of general socio-economic development in rural areas. Both objectives were anathema to established British policy practice. Moreover, the basis of support was switched from general taxation (via deficiency payments) to consumer prices (via direct market intervention). This was guaranteed to re-politicize agricultural policy and drag the debate on farm support back from the arcane discussion of technical esoterica and into the full glare of the public arena. As far as the farmer was concerned, entry into the EEC proved, in the short term, almost embarrassingly beneficial in most sectors of production. The longer-term consequence, however, has been to reopen once more the festering resentment of consumers towards food producers which has been a historically familiar feature at all times when real food prices have risen sharply. Thus the abandonment of a 'cheap food' policy has produced a public debate reminiscent of that which existed throughout the nineteenth century – only now farmers are politically still less dominant and numerically verging on the insignificant. The political consequences of this are still working their way through contemporary society, but it is important to be aware of the fact that popular political pressure on the CAP will, if successful, provide a further push towards 'agribusiness' and further marginalize the small farmer. The social consequences of this for rural areas are rarely taken into account.

THE FOOD PRODUCTION INDUSTRY

The growth of agribusiness has produced one further historical irony which is worthy of attention. As the Second Agricultural Revolution has procceded apace, so farmers have been rendered increasingly dependent upon non-farm inputs, such as machinery, manufactured feedstuffs and agro-chemicals, and upon a wider complex of industrial companies involved in food processing, marketing and retailing. Thus when the phrase 'the changing structure of agriculture' is employed, this refers not only to the increasing concentration of production on fewer, larger farms, but also to the integration of agriculture into a complex of engineering, chemical and food-processing industries which collectively is often referred to as 'agribusiness'. The growth of agribusiness has thus occured in two senses: highly rationalized, profit-maximizing farming; and vertically integrated food production systems controlling all processes 'from seedling to supermarket'. The historical irony lies in the fact that as farmers have become merely one link in a food production chain, so they have become almost the equivalent of eighteenth-century industrial outworkers, taking in a set of inputs from agribusiness companies and frequently selling their output back to similar companies who then proceed to process, distribute and market them to the consumer. This tendency has received less attention than the changes induced in farming itself. Nevertheless, the implications are equally far-reaching, and raise important issues relating to dietary change, consumer sovereignty, public accountability and socio-economic change in rural areas.

State intervention in agriculture, in promoting a highly capitalized farming industry, has therefore, unwittingly or otherwise, promoted the interests of agribusiness companies in British agriculture. Successive governments, in supporting the farmer, have also supported large sections of the engineering industry, through farmers' purchases of farm machinery, the chemical industry (fertilizers, pesticides, etc.) and food processors, packagers and distributors. In turn, agribusiness companies have become major agents of social and economic change in rural Britain since the Second World War. They have supplemented the state agencies in setting up almost a parallel apparatus of advisory and consultative services which aid selected farmers in adopting new techniques of production while ensuring quality control over the finished product. All animal feedstuffs suppliers, for example, have provided a comprehensive advisory service, exhorting the farmer to introduce new methods employing their products, while food processors also advise their contracted suppliers on husbandry techniques and hygiene precautions. Particularly important elements in the relationship between farmers and agribusiness companies are the provision of credit facilities and advice on the purchase of new capital equipment, for in order to participate in contract farming for agribusiness clients, farmers must frequently purchase highly specialized (and expensive) equipment on which they might otherwise be reluctant to risk their investment. Where mutually beneficial commercial arrangements end, and the reduction of the farmer's autonomy begins, has often been difficult to discern. In some cases corporate agribusiness control over farming operations has been very tight indeed, but in general the influences have been more indirect. In the case of 'factory farming' the impact has been readily observable, for only agribusiness companies have been able, on the whole, to provide the wherewithal of high capital investment, technological know-how, research and development facilities and extensive marketing and advertising techniques which have made the assembly-line production of food a viable commercial proposition. More generally, however, corporate agribusiness influence over the structure of agriculture has proceeded by proxy, with agribusiness companies encouraging 'agribusiness' farming through the selective placement of contracts.

Corporate agribusiness has thus wrought its changes in farming, not so much via direct purchase and control over individual farms, but by seeking out highly profit-conscious 'agribusinessmen' farmers with whom to deal on a contractual basis. This has enabled agribusiness companies to avoid the high cost and political risk of extensive land purchases in Britain. It has also enabled them to avoid the cost of purchasing managerial expertise and of bearing some of the risks of husbandry associated with disease, weather and topography that remain part of contemporary agriculture. Nevertheless, agribusiness companies have accelerated many of the post-war trends in the structure of farming by encouraging the selective rationalization of agriculture and by enabling the trend towards specialization to become firmly established. Smaller farmers, who rarely participate in such contractual arrangements, have found themselves thereby further marginalized, while the larger farmers have found their enterprises gradually transformed by the relentless 'industrial' logic of corporate agribusiness and are encouraged to become more specialized in order to make the optimum use of their specialized technology and skills. It is possible to observe in the post-war history of agriculture, therefore, a process whereby the larger holdings have become slowly reorganized according to non-agricultural criteria, partly on the assumption that agriculture can be treated merely as a disguised form of manufacture and partly because husbandry techniques have taken less account of narrowly agricultural criteria (such as yields per acre or the maintenance of the soil structure) and more account of returns on capital invested, like any other commercial company.

The implications of these changes are widespread and have been given less public attention than they deserve. In the post-war period farmers have enjoyed the relative stability and prosperity afforded by state intervention, yet by the same token they have found themselves increasingly negotiating with large, often multinational agribusiness companies both for the provision of their inputs and the sale of their output. Farmers have simply lacked the market power to do much more than accept the bargain they have been offered. Since more of the value of food production has been captured at the processing, distribution and retailing stages, farmers have received a declining proportion of retail food prices since the war. It is not therefore clear to what extent farmers have been able to retain the full benefits of their own increasing cost-efficiency. Many farmers have certainly believed that agribusiness domination of food production has done little to alleviate their own 'cost-price squeeze'. If anything, it has further exacerbated the 'treadmill effect', whereby cost-efficiency is linked to technological innovation, which demands the generation of resources made possible only by further cost-efficiency and further technological innovation. A further twist is thus given to the process whereby agriculture becomes merely the transformation of one set of industrial products into another set of industrial products, the latter happening to be edible.

Moreover, agribusiness is unlikely to fade away. Agribusiness companies regard themselves as performing a public service by providing cheap and convenient processed foods. Cheapness and convenience are certainly the key elements in contemporary consumer demand for food. From the standpoint of agribusiness organization of food production it thus makes more sense to produce a standardized product, of whatever taste, colour or nutritional value, under conditions of semi-automated technology, and then add the colouring, flavouring and nutritional elements provided by the relatively recent science of food technology. The consumer can then be convinced of the product's 'natural' qualities through packaging, advertising and other marketing techniques. Since the war the proportion of food consumption which has derived from processed food has consistently increased and, given social trends like the increasing numbers of working women, the demand for such 'convenience' foods seems destined to continue. In addition, a new range of technologies – genetic engineering, enzyme technology, cloning, etc. – are on the horizon, which will provide a new range of innovations for the forseeable future and guarantee the continued dominance of corporate agribusiness over food production. The Second Agricultural Revolution is still under way.

FROM THE FARMING LANDOWNER TO THE LANDOWNING FARMER

The break-up of the landed estates (described in chapter 7) undoubtedly represented an important turning-point in the recent social and economic history of the English countryside. It marked the beginning of the end of the tripartite class structure which had characterized English agriculture from the eighteenth century onwards, and it also signified the abandonment of the semi-autonomous 'little kingdoms' which the estates had become at their zenith. As the twentieth century progressed, it became evident that the rural class structure and distinctive type of local rural society fostered by the estate were gone forever. By the standards of historical precedent the change was indeed startling in its rapidity, but it is important to note that even by the late 1920s, the majority of farmland in England and Wales was still tenanted – 64 per cent in 1927. In other words the landlord–tenant system, despite the upheavals of agricultural depression, war, estate duty and extensive sales, remained predominant. The renewal of agricultural depression during the inter-war years and the advent of state control during the Second World War ensured that this situation changed little over two decades. By 1950, for example, the proportion of land which was owner-occupied had risen by only 2 per cent since 1927. This is not to belittle the changes which occurred between 1918 and 1923: they did indeed represent a major structural change. But the process whereby landowning and farming became merged into a combined economic activity is one which characterizes the post-1945 era rather than the aftermath of the First World War.

These statistics suggest a rather more complex situation than the simple phrase: 'the break-up of the landed estates' might suggest. By the end of the 1970s, according to official statistics, nearly two-thirds of agricultural land was under owner-occupation, and this is evidence enough of the demise of the old tripartite class structure of rural society. In fact, for technical reasons, even this figure is an underestimate: the *de facto* rate of owner-occupation is probably between 75 and 80 per cent. The post-war period has therefore witnessed a spectacular rise in owner-occupation, yet the break-up of the landed estates is widely regarded as a phenomenon which dates from the end of the First, rather than the Second World War. This should immediately suggest that the statistics are in need of careful interpretation. Certainly any assessment of the balance between continuity and change in agricultural land-owning depends upon a judgement of who these owner-farmers are. Have former tenant-farmers purchased their holdings and become landowning farmers; or have former landowners muddied their boots and become farming land-owners?

Undoubtedly agricultural estates have continued to be broken up. There are many well-publicized examples of this, and the impecunious estate owner fallen on hard times has become a familiar caricature over the last few decades. However, the absence of any register of landownerhship or other comprehensive source of information on who owns land makes it difficult to assess the extent to which agricultural estates have suffered from a dissolution of this kind. Other things being equal, the rate of decline should have slowed down considerably during the post-war period, if only because the state has intervened to save both farmers and landowners from the worst ravages of agricultural depression. Investment in agricultural land may have continued to offer a poorer yield than investment elsewhere, but agricultural support policies have halted any major downward slide, and there have been compensating advantages in increasing capital gains. Agricultural land with vacant possession averaged £45 per acre in 1945, since when there has been an historically unprecedented rate of increase to more than £2,000 per acre by the end of the 1970s. This has been well ahead of the general rate of inflation in the economy as a whole. Moreover, attempts to tax this gain have turned out to be notoriously ineffective – a voluntary tax payable only after an untimely accident, the employment of an incompetent accountant, or both. It is important not to confuse the frequently genuine difficulties of estate owners in maintaining the upkeep of their stately homes with the viability of the surrounding agricultural land.

A consensus exists among most agricultural economists that the major beneficiaries of agricultural support policies have, indeed, been the owners of farm land (who now, of course, include a majority of farmers). Sustained stability and prosperity in agriculture has allowed landlords to charge higher rents on tenanted land, while owner-occupied land has simply been bid up in price to reflect the enhanced prospects of farming profits. This alone is enough to provide incentives towards owner-occupation, whether by sitting tenants buying up their land or by landowners taking land 'in hand' (that is, farming it themselves) at every available opportunity. Indeed there are good reasons to believe that since the Second World War, estates have become not so much fragmented among an array of purchasers, as consolidated in the hands of their existing owners. The system of taxation alone has provided incentives for this. Income from rents has not been subject to earned income relief, so there are considerable fiscal penalties involved in letting land as opposed to farming it. Furthermore between 1947 and 1958, and again since 1976, legislation concerning the hereditability of tenancies has granted virtually complete security to tenants, leaving landowners with a further disincentive to let. Both of these factors have encouraged landowners to farm more land themselves, irrespective of the other advantages to be gained, such as those from economies of scale and a more rationalized structure of landholding. Consequently landowners have taken more land 'in hand' and this probably accounts for much of the increase in owner-occupation.

It seems likely, then, that the ownership of agricultural land has not changed hands to the extent that a superficial reading of the statistics on tenurial status might suggest. Tenacity as much as diaspora has characterized the situation of the estate-owner since the 1920s. It is misleading, then, to over-emphasize the decline of the landowning families who controlled rural England down until the First World War. Many landed estates have indeed been broken up and some of the former stately homes of England are now put to more mundane uses as convalescent homes, trade union head-quarters, recreation centres and the like. Nor can the land-owner expect any longer to conduct a life of leisured gentility surrounded by a vast army of servants. However, many of the estates remain, albeit usually reduced in size, with the Big House no longer hidden from the gaze of a prurient public willing to pay the cost of admission. The landed aristocracy, in particular, has survived remarkably well. Only the gentry, traditionally less adaptable and with fewer resources to fall back upon, has suffered extensively. The post-war period has not, unlike analogous periods of decline in previous centuries, produced a new gentry to replace the old – only a new class of landowning (yeoman?) farmers.

INSTITUTIONAL LANDOWNERS

There has been one significant exception to this trend towards owner-occupation: the rise of institutional landownership. By the end of the 1970s the top ten landowners in Britain included only one private individual, the remainder being a variety of public or quasi-public institutions. Their holdings had nearly doubled during the previous one hundred years to account for approximately 8 per cent of the farmland in Britain. The largest institutional holdings are those of the local authorities, followed by the nationalized industries, the Forestry Commission, the Crown (including the estates owned by members of the royal family as private individuals) conservation bodies (for example, the National Trust) and the churches. It will be apparent that such institutional ownership is by no means new. The monarchy, the churches and the older universities, for example, have all been involved since medieval times. During the 1970s, however, public attention (including one committee of inquiry) was drawn towards the question of increasing institutional involvement by the renewed interest of financial institutions (pension funds, insurance companies, unit trusts, etc.) in the purchase of prime quality agricultural land. This led to much speculation as to whether a landlord–tenant system was about to re-emerge in British agriculture, with the twentieth-century tendency towards increased owner-occupation being merely a brief historical interlude in the 'natural' situation. The increased activity of the financial institutions has potentially far-reaching consequences; it is not surprising that they have aroused interest as, over the decade since 1970, they have proved to be the fastest-growing landowners in Britain. Perhaps as a result they have also attracted a good deal of mythology which has not always contributed to an informed assessment of their role.

Between 1971 and 1976 alone, the financial institutions doubled their agricultural holdings to 350,000 acres. It was this startling rate of increase which at the time aroused so much comment. Their involvement needs, however, to be kept in perspective. The renewed interest of the financial institutions was undoubtedly a product of the high rates of inflation during the 1970s and the poor performance of the equities market over the same period. Agricultural land offered a safe investment with the prospects of long-term capital growth – a characteristic almost underwritten, as indicated earlier in this chapter, by state intervention in agriculture during the post-war period. The financial institutions have never devoted a large proportion of their investment portfolios to the purchase of agricultural land. On the contrary, it has frequently consisted of the small change of their investment accounts – although this has been quite sufficient to have a major impact on the land market. Since these institutions have also been concerned with long-term capital growth and not year-on-year yield, they have not, on the whole, been interested in farming the land themselves. Their intervention therefore needs to be kept quite distinct from the growth of agribusiness described in the previous section of this chapter. Although it is not beyond the bounds of possibility that a financial institution *could* link up with an agribusiness company in a joint farming venture, this has not occurred. The precise ownership arrangements are in fact quite variable, involving orthodox agricultural tenancies, lease-back arrangements with former owner-occupiers, equity partnerships and so on. In their day-to-day practice there has been little to distinguish the activities of financial institutions from other large landowners, whether private or public. Indeed much of the land is actively managed by the same agents who offer similar services to private landowners. Far from being the rapacious, remote and ruthless investors which prejudiced comment often tried to depict them, the financial institutions have, if anything, conducted their activities with studied moderation and a careful attention to rural sensibilities.

This has not, however, prevented the financial institutions being perceived as a threat to established patterns of land-ownership (which, as has been indicated, are not themselves so 'established'). The financial institutions have certainly benefited from advantages concerning capital taxation, and can muster huge resources which all individuals and most other institutions cannot match. But opposition from within the farming industry has extended beyond pointing to these apparent inequities. Whatever past historical experience may suggest or other sectors of the economy indicate, farmers have become rapidly convinced during the post-war period that a division between ownership and control would be against their interests. Their fears stem partly from a concern over a possible loss of independence, partly that institutional owner-ship would be a stalking horse for land nationalization, and partly that the financial institutions are inadequate stewards of the land in particular and rural society in general. There are certainly few convincing *economic* arguments against insti-tutional involvement, given the huge investment resources upon which the financial institutions can call. Thus those who wish to champion the cause of the private, individual owner have been forced to fall back upon less material and less tangible considerations. Indeed, by denegrating the exclusive pursuit of economic rewards and elevating a notion of personal service to the rural community and a protective atavism for the land itself, they have echoed the gentlemanly values of the nineteenth-century landowner. They, too, have 'returned to Camelot'.

The key element of continuity here is the concept of stewardship – the emphasis on altruism and service associated with the ownership of land. Stewardship places great importance on the sense of duty to the rural community – a potent factor when considering the gentlemanly ethic (see chapter 3). This imples that farm land is not so much a factor of production to be used to generate profit, as part of a wider national heritage which the landowner regards as his duty to protect. The landowner thus regards himself – and wishes to be regarded by others – as merely a caretaker, holding the land in trust for the nation before handing it on to the succeeding generation, preferably in a better state than when he received it. He is therefore not 'really' an owner, but a custodian, a protector – a steward. This notion continues to be evoked in order to defend the existing pattern of landownership against any radical changes. When deployed against the financial institutions it has become an idiom in which to express a quite simple xenophobia towards urban outsiders – an antagonism to city ways as well as City money.

This is not to state that the concept of stewardship does not have a peculiar affinity with the ownership of land which is often absent from the ownership of other forms of capital. The benefits which accrue from the land are frequently of a long-term nature. Even the financial institutions recognize that the major value of landownership lies in long-term capital growth rather than short-term yield. Moreover the production cycle of agriculture is frequently a lengthy one and the fertility of the land may easily be harmed by the short-sighted pursuit of immediate gains. In this sense the notion of stewardship need not be an entirely anachronistic ideal. However, these considerations, since they apply to all owners of agricultural land, irrespective of whoever they may be, apply equally to the financial institutions. It is in their interests, too, to be good 'stewards' by being mindful of their investments. As a consequence, good stewardship and self-interest coincide, just as they have for the private landowner for centuries.

THE FARM WORKER: A PLACE IN THE SUN?

The Second Agricultural Revolution has had a paradoxical impact upon the life of the farm worker. The working conditions of most farm workers have indeed been revolutionized: hundreds of thousands have left the land since the end of the Second World War and technological change has transformed the employment of those that have remained. On the other hand, the relative position of the farm worker, either within rural society or nationally, has barely changed at all: they have remained among the lowest-paid of all workers and have encountered remarkably few opportunities to increase their standard of living relative to the rest of the population. It is certainly difficult to maintain that the farm worker has reaped any substantial benefits from the Second Agricultural Revolution in comparison to farmers, landowners or even food consumers.

For a time during the 1940s, however, a social – as opposed to a merely technological – revolution within agriculture appeared to be within the grasp of the farm worker. After the traumas of the 1923 strike, the membership of the NUAW was mostly to be found in its East Anglian stronghold, where a rump of some 25,000 adherents clung on and preserved the union's identity. The most tangible achievement of the inter-war years had been the reintroduction of statutory wage control by the short-lived Labour Government of 1924, although as the result of a Liberal amendment this was organized effectively on a county basis. A further notable success was achieved when, in 1936, a special scheme for unemployment insurance for farm workers was introduced, removing for the first time since 1834 the fearsome threat of the workhouse for the old and the indigent. Meanwhile the much-reduced union membership bided its time in the hope that more propitious circumstances might return. Eventually the outbreak of the Second World War ensured that they did so. Wages and conditions – and with them the prospects for agricultural trade unionism – became once more transformed.

Later shortages on the land again enabled the NUAW to achieve large wage increases. This in turn stimulated union membership, which was to be quadrupled by the end of the war. In 1940 the Central Wages Board had returned to it the power to decide on a national statutory minimum wage, a measure later consolidated in the Agricultural Wages (Regulation) Act of 1947, which created a newly-organized Agricultural Wages Board. Such were the wartime shortages of labour and the importance granted to food production that the farm worker was able to make enormous and unprecedented strides towards the union's ultimate goal: parity of wages and conditions with the urban worker. By 1946 this had almost (though not quite) been achieved. All that remained was to abolish the tied cottage system and equality of status could be proclaimed. At the end of 'the Union's greatest Year', in December 1946, an editorial in *The Land Worker*, the NUAW's journal, proclaimed:

The story of the Union is at once a record of enormous gains for the workers and a romance. A new country life has been born. Minimum wages are now fixed by law. The earnings of farm workers are now comparable with those of many other workers. It is mainly due to the efforts of the Union that the land worker is now treated not as a serf, but as a citizen.

The architect of this 'new country life' was the Union's president, Edwin Gooch. He had shepherded the NUAW through the difficult years of the 1930s and, in an act of some political courage, had been prepared to break with the Labour Party's policy of supporting free trade. The lesson which Gooch drew from the 1923 strike was that direct action was no longer feasible in agriculture; his more conciliatory approach to labour relations had brought dividends during the war when the NUAW was admitted as a full participating member to most of the wartime agricultural committees. In this way Gooch hoped to ensure that the farm workers' interests were taken account of in policy-making and that the future status of farm workers would be guaranteed – that they would find, in his words, 'a place in the sun'.

This time the portents were encouraging. Sustained state intervention in agriculture was to ensure that there would be no repeat of the retrenchment of the early 1920s. As it turned out, however, even the guarantee of agricultural prosperity was not sufficient to retain the wartime gains of the farm worker. Once normality was restored in the rural labour market, so the familiar underlying realities began to reassert themselves. The 'drift from the land' not only recommenced but was accelerated: mechanization meant that labour supply chased labour demand in an ever-decreasing spiral. Gooch's conciliatory policy with farming employers during the war left the leadership disinclined to engage in militant action to preserve their recent gains. Between 1949 and 1955 real wages actually fell, and throughout the 1950s and 1960s the 'earnings gap' between agricultural workers and workers in manufacturing industry widened alarmingly. During the late 1940s, agricultural wages attained a peak of over 75 per cent of average industrial earnings; by the late 1960s this figure had slid to under 60 per cent. Wages Board decisions ceased to act as more than a safety net for the most exploited employees: the vast majority of workers fared better out of individual 'negotiations' with their own employers. Negotiations over a wages structure involving higher rates for the more skilled workers, first mooted in 1945, dragged on for no less than 27 years until it was introduced in 1972. By this time there was growing discontent among union members with the role of the Wages Board, which was clearly following, rather than leading, the successes of farm workers in improving their pay and conditions, but having struggled for so long to establish the Board and having been such a supporter of its role in the early years, the union leadership was locked into its structure of decision-making, for good or ill.

As the number of full-time workers fell from nearly 750,000

in 1946 to less than 200,000 thirty years later, so the NUAW found itself under increasing pressure to retain a viable membership. A demonstrable lack of success at the negotiating table did not help. Over the same thirty years the membership of the union was halved, despite vigorous recruitment in the agricultural ancillary industries, a factor which was recognized in the change in title to the National Union of Agricultural and Allied Workers in 1968. As the membership fell, so the difficulties of obtaining the resources to sustain a strong union increased. Uppermost among these was the sheer scale of the problem of recruiting, organizing and servicing the membership in the face of a declining labour force by no means conducive to unionization. Agriculture not only retained a structure in which it had more employers than virtually any other industry, but the workers were increasingly scattered in ones and twos across the countryside, often in isolated and inaccessible areas. The NUAAW was thus forced to spend large sums of money simply in maintaining an organizational infrastructure in rural areas – a structure running to thousands of small branches. Equally debilitating was the changing context of farmer–farm worker relationships: more personal, more informal, more intimate and more benevolent – though not more equal – than in the past. Falling numbers of workers per farm *and* the decline of villages as agricultural communities brought farmers and farm workers closer together: the intervention of the union in this relationship was not always considered necessary or desirable by either party. The return to chronic poverty among farm workers did not, therefore, produce a commensurate tendency to engage in collective action to mitigate it. Eventually it was financial pressure rather than a farmer's lock-out which was to terminate the second, and most lasting, attempt to bring farm workers into an independent union. By 1980 the NUAAW reluctantly recognized that it could not continue in its traditional form. From that date it became an independent section within the Transport and General Workers Union, whose industrial backing might give the farm worker a more realistic chance of narrowing the gap between industrial and agricultural wages.

The absence of any strike activity in agriculture since 1923 has enabled farm workers to retain their social invisibility to the public at large. For the struggle to find 'a place in the sun' has always meant much more than equitable pay and conditions. It has also involved a demand for equality of status and a claim for public recognition of the role of the farm worker in food production. All farm workers have remained acutely sensitive to the suggestion that they are merely unskilled and unintelligent yokels whose work requires little versatility, initiative and judgement. It is here, indeed, in the nature of the actual tasks that are performed by the modern farm worker, that the Second Agricultural Revolution has had its revolutionary impact. The onward march of mechanization and other technological innovations has turned the farm worker into a highly skilled technician. Although the rhythm of the seasons has remained an important factor in most branches of agriculture, the pace of the work has altered dramatically. Mechanization has also removed much of the physical effort and routine drudgery that used to be involved in farm work, and by allowing many workers a greater variety of tasks it has not necessarily produced any loss of job satisfaction either. The major drawback has been a growing sense of isolation. The camaraderie of the field, whereby workers laboured alongside one another and took their meal breaks together beneath the hedgerow, has now disappeared. The rural working-class subculture of the past, which thrived on such workplace conviviality, has tended to disappear.

It is at this point that the paradox of change and continuity in the life of the farm worker becomes most clear. Throughout the post-war period his social and economic situation has continued to be regulated by the kind of disciplines that have been familiar to successive generations of workers on the land – poverty, the lack of alternative employment opportunities, the dependency for jobs and housing on local farmers. Yet wider cultural influences have exposed the farm worker to a range of alternative possibilities and raised his aspirations beyond what has conventionally been defined for him as his proper place in the natural order of rural society. Previous chapters have illustrated the extent to which the social horizons of the farm worker were limited largely to his immediate locality, especially the village community of which he was a member. Most of his social cues and expected behaviour were derived from this relatively enclosed social world. It has never been a static world, nor has the farm worker ever been entirely unaware of the wider society beyond it. However, in the period since the Second World War there can be little doubt that the farm worker has been drawn into a much greater participation in this wider society by virtue of changes in education, transport and the mass media and, as will be considered in detail in the following chapter, by virtue also of changes in the social composition of the village community itself. The farm worker has remained socially and geographically isolated, but he has also become less bound by custom and habit and, as a result, is more impatient with his traditionally inferior social status.

Yet change in this area has been the most difficult for the farm worker to engineer. The extension of citizenship rights and welfare benefits to the farm worker have come about less through his own efforts than through the trickling down of measures introduced at a national level. Even the stigma of the tied cottage remains, despite greater security of tenure introduced by an Act of 1976. Farmers have not encouraged the participation of their employees in the modern world: on the whole they have been hesitant, distrustful, and grudging. There is, then, a contrast between the technologically modern and progressive character of the agriculture industry wrought by the Second Agricultural Revolution, and the backward and conservative social relations in which it is embedded. The traditional and the modern continue to collide in contemporary agriculture in a manner which to the outside observer may seem strange, but is regarded as unexceptionable by the participants. The farm worker is largely aware of the widening gap between his own standard of living and that of the mass consumer society which surrounds him. Yet the relationship with his employer remains generally amicable. For all the rapid changes at the workplace and in the village,

the established patterns of authority remain remarkably
unchanged and unchallenged. The new independence coexists
with the old dependency. In this respect, as Joseph Arch
would recognize, the farm worker still has to find his place in
the sun.

CHAPTER 10

THE ECLIPSE OF THE RURAL WORLD

The post-war reconstruction of rural England was not limited to the creation of an economically viable and technologically advanced agriculture. The whole fabric of rural society had been affected by decades of social and economic decline and there was a widespread recognition that agricultural assistance needed to be complemented by a range of other measures which would improve the quality of life for all rural inhabitants. Part of this social reconstruction involved the provision of a wide range of public services on a national basis and from which the rural population benefited accordingly. The clearest examples of this are the introduction of the National Health Service in 1948 and the reorganization of secondary education, embodied in the 1944 Education Act, together with the creation of the modern welfare state following the recommendations of the Beveridge Report. One consequence of such legislation was that English rural society was drawn more and more into the mainstream of English society as a whole. It was a pattern to be repeated in many different ways, not only in the provision of public services and welfare, but in the continuing absorption of rural life into a mass consumer culture, influenced by the spread of new media of communication like radio and television, but prompted more than anything by the rising standard of living of the entire rural population.

Other measures were specifically aimed at rural areas, however, many of them the continuation of relief measures first mooted in the 1930s. Some of these were quite mundane, but nonetheless essential. For example, the programme of rural electrification was extended to even the most remote rural areas, and although electricity poles and pylons were widely regarded as a disfiguring element in the landscape, the fact remained that the service which they carried to villages and farmsteads across the length and breadth of the countryside was one which considerably improved living standards for all concerned. Other improvements in the infrastructure of rural areas, such as roads, water supplies and sewerage, were no less significant. A determined effort was also made to improve the standards of rural housing, which, despite a series of Housing Acts during the inter-war period, remained a national scandal. Legislation in the 1920s and 1930s had been aimed at increasing the sheer quantity of housing available to the rural population, thereby relieving overcrowding and improving the state of repair of the housing stock. Despite financial support from central government, however, the housing drive had met with a disappointing response in rural areas, where local authorities proved reluctant to co-operate – so reluctant, in fact, that specific legislation aimed at alleviating the plight of rural workers was introduced in 1935. This reluctance was partly due to the agricultural depression which had left many rural areas bereft of a rate base and so depressed agricultural wages that not even local authority rents could be afforded. A further factor, though, was the continuing political control of rural local authorities by farmers and landowners who were unwilling to raise local expenditure in order to provide subsidized council housing for farm workers who might thereby be tempted to vacate their tied cottages. Even when, in 1935, rural councils were offered no less than 80 per cent of the cost of construction, many still proved to be recalcitrant and progress was slow. As a government report concluded in 1942: 'Thousands of cottages have no piped water supply, no gas or electric light, no third bedroom and often only one living room with no separate cooking and scullery accommodation. For the great majority of rural workers a bathroom is a rare luxury.' There was a new determination after 1945 that conditions like these could no longer be tolerated.

In the reforming climate which influenced post-war policies towards the countryside there were high expectations that all matters relating to the social and economic development of rural areas could be placed within an overall framework of town and country planning. This notion, that rural society might require some form of rational planning, stemmed from two, somewhat contradictory, considerations. The first came from a belief in the need for a modicum of progressive social engineering in order to achieve an improvement in the living and working conditions of those in the countryside. In part this was born out of attempts to solve the social problems associated with rapid urban growth – lack of hygiene, overcrowding, poor sanitation and so on. By the late 1940s this had come to be accepted as a legitimate concern of government, and rural planning, as a minimum requirement, was concerned with extending and improving the quality of public service infrastructure in the countryside. The second consideration was the desire, increasingly voiced towards the end of the 1930s, to protect the countryside from urban growth (see chapter 8). At its simplest this meant the desire to limit the development of agricultural land for industrial and residential purposes, thus ensuring that the countryside retained its 'natural' character by preventing the incursion of urban industrialism. In its more utopian form planning involved the merger of these two aims by promoting socially engineered rural communities which were healthy and vibrant, yet untainted by urban encroachment. There were, therefore, high expectations surrounding the centrepiece of post-war legislation in this field, the 1947 Town and Country Planning Act.

THE RISE AND FALL OF RURAL PLANNING

The mobilizing of influential public opinion in favour of rural planning had begun in the 1930s (see the final section of chapter 8). During the early 1940s this resulted in a flurry of government committees and reports aimed at setting the stage for the regeneration of rural England once peace had been restored. Central to these deliberations were the recommendations of the Royal Commission on the Geographical Distribution of the Industrial Population, better known as the Barlow Commission, which was appointed in 1937 and reported in 1940. The Barlow Commission was concerned with two major policy objectives. The first, clearly given urgency by the depressed economic conditions of the 1930s, was the correction of the manifest regional imbalance which had arisen in the distribution of employment and population. The second objective was that of urban containment, to which the problem of regional imbalance was believed to be indissolubly linked. By controlling the growth of the largest conurbations, especially London, it was believed that employment and industrial renewal could be directed towards the depressed areas in the North of England, Wales and Scotland, thereby also sparing the fertile agricultural land and threatened countryside of the Midlands and the South East. In this way a humane desire to improve the distribution of industrial development and improved living standards in the urban centres was combined with a fairly rigid preservationist approach to the countryside. Given the acute agricultural depression of the 1930s this might seem strangely myopic, but it was engendered by the essentially arcadian vision of rural England which proved to be so influential during the 1930s, particularly among the middle classes of the Home Counties. In this regard the Commission had proved to be receptive to the views of one of its members, Patrick Abercrombie.

The Scott Report on Land Utilization in Rural Areas, published in 1942, reinforced the recommendations of the Barlow Commission on the need to impose physical controls on urban growth. It also sanctified the prior claims of agriculture both over land use and labour in rural areas. Written under wartime conditions, when the very survival of Britain appeared to be at stake, its general approach could be summarized in the phrase 'every acre counts', for the Report put forward a new planning principle for rural areas – that the onus of proof must lie with the prospective developer to show that 'a clear case of a national advantage was made out' before planning permission could be granted. In the context of 'Dig for Victory' (the wartime slogan which exhorted the nation to produce more food), such a view was understandable, but whether it represented a sound basis for the future planning of English rural society was open to some doubt. In a Minority Report, Professor S. R. Dennison had pointed out that such a policy might, among other things, restrict the location of new industry in rural areas and thereby further depress rural wage levels, increase rural–urban migration and hinder the viability of rural services – that is, exacerbate the problem of regional imbalance that the Barlow Commission had been so intent on redressing. Eventually, however, not only did Dennison's colleagues on the Scott Committee ignore his arguments, but the general presumption in favour of agricultural land use in rural areas was incorporated into future planning practice. This commitment to rural preservation was based neither on marginal utility economics, nor on any rational calculation of costs and benefits which would equate a ubiquitous agriculture with an efficient agriculture. Rather, it was based on a gut feeling that the English countryside needed to be protected, rather than planned in any positive sense. The custody of the countryside could safely be left in the hands of farmers and landowners; all that was required was to contain the spread of urban sprawl.

The provisions contained within the 1947 Town and Country Planning Act largely reflected the dominant philosophy of the Barlow and Scott Reports. Under this legislation development control was linked to the construction of local plans, which in rural areas sought to limit the spread of urban growth into the countryside by designating 'white land' where agriculture should remain undisturbed. In this respect the Act turned out to be successful, the rate of loss of agricultural land being reduced to half the pre-war level. The Act also sought to check urban encroachment in other ways – for example, by controlling the proliferation of outdoor advertising in rural areas and by granting only short-term planning permission for caravan sites. Since, however, there was a prevailing assumption that the conservation of the countryside could safely be left in the hands of those *in situ*, and there was no wish to pick a fight with either the NFU or the CLA, from the outset 'the use of any land for the purposes of agriculture or forestry' was excluded from the provisions of the Act. With the exception of very large or very tall buildings, beyond the requirements of any normal farm at that time, farmers were granted a freedom from planning restrictions enjoyed by no other industrial activity. This doctrine of 'agricultural exceptionalism' proved to be a resilient one, even though, as will become clear below, it was eventually to come under increasing attack.

These steps taken to protect the countryside were reinforced by accompanying legislation in the immediate post-war period, most notably the National Parks and Access to the Countryside Act of 1949. This was the culmination of the aspirations of the recreation and access lobby (see chapter 8) to establish a comprehensive system of protection for those areas with the most outstanding amenity value. Their introduction into England and Wales followed the production of the Dower Report in 1945 and the Hobhouse Report in 1947 which had dealt with conservation and recreation issues. Dower initially defined a National Park as:

. . . an extensive area of beautiful and relatively wild country in which, for the nation's benefit and by appropriate national decisions and action,
(a) the characteristic landscape beauty is strictly preserved,
(b) Access and facilities for public open-air enjoyment are amply provided,
(c) Wildlife and buildings and places of architectural and historic interest are suitably protected, while
(d) established farming use is effectively maintained.

Ten National Parks were subsequently designated, but the task of achieving all of these aims simultaneously proved to be extremely difficult – and was not helped by a somewhat haphazard system of councils and committees established to run them. Nevertheless the injunction that the landscape of the National Parks should be 'strictly preserved' meant that development control was to be particularly draconian – at least in principle. In practice control was often much more loose and ineffective than the Dower Report had envisaged, with large-scale mineral extraction and, later, the construction of new roads and motorways providing continuing threats to landscape preservation. A National Parks Commission was established to act as a watchdog and to ensure a minimal degree of administrative co-ordination. In 1968 this was renamed the Countryside Commission, and its remit was expanded to include general responsibilities for the promotion of environmental conservation and recreation in the countryside.

The 1949 Act also attempted to guarantee public access to the countryside by requiring county councils to publish footpath maps which might eventually provide a definitive guide to public rights of access. The Act also enabled long-distance footpaths to be painstakingly assembled by linking together existing paths and, where necessary, negotiating new sections. Since successive public access might be too much of a good thing for the preservation of wildlife, Part III of the Act made provision for National Nature Reserves, under the control of the Nature Conservancy, a research and advisory body created by Royal Charter in 1949. Public access to these was not to be encouraged. The Act also gave the Nature Conservancy a duty to notify planning authorities of land which was ecologically of 'special interest'. By the time the Nature Conservancy was reorganized into the Nature Conservancy Council in 1973, over 3,000 such Sites of Special Scientific Interest had been designated. Other provisions within the Act encouraged tree planting and the removal of eyesores in order to restore derelict or disused land.

What emerged from both the 1947 and 1949 Acts was a hierarchy of land-use and landscape designations whose purposes were primarily negative: to preserve those rural areas considered to be of irrefutable national importance from the prospect of intrusive development. This approach was essentially defensive and protective. There was little attention paid to positive management or appropriate forms of development. At the pinnacle of these designation categories stood the National Parks, all of which were located in the uplands (the one lowland area which was proposed, the Norfolk Broads, never being established) and therefore less inclined to encounter, so it was believed, conflicts between landscape preservation and agricultural change. Below them stood Areas of Outstanding Natural Beauty, where public recreation was not encouraged and where the emphasis was on landscape conservation. Here designation was based on frankly aesthetic criteria and included areas like the Cotswolds, Dedham Vale, the Quantock and Mendip Hills, the Downs, and so on. The third rank were Areas of Great Landscape Value, small sites of local importance which were controlled under the Town and Country Planning Act. The 1947 Act also ushered in Abercrombie's scheme for creating Green Belts around major towns and cities. Here the purpose was to contain urban growth rather than preserve landscapes (many of which were of little value in themselves). Development controls were, nevertheless, as severe (if not more so) as those pertaining in the National Parks. This control was also associated with the designation of New and Expanded Towns which would form concentrated nodes of development in the rural hinterland of metropolitan centres, thereby restricting unplanned suburbanization and allowing rural areas 'worth saving' to be equipped with stringent development controls.

In theory, then, the system of town and country planning created by the legislation of the immediate post-war period involved a radical reform of the *laissez-faire* approach to land use which had brought unwanted and sometimes unintended changes in the countryside. The underlying political aims were liberal and progressive, a fabian desire to eradicate the worst irrationalities and social injustices of industrial and residential development that had been mostly derived from the unrestricted application of market forces. The practical results, however, turned out to be rather different. By the late

1960s 'the planners' had become a byword for remote bureaucracy and heartless inhumanity, and although these feelings were more often prompted by the consequences of urban redevelopment programmes, they were echoed in rural areas over sensitive issues like reservoirs, motorway development and 'key village' policies (the concentration of services on larger settlements while others were 'left to die'). To some extent planners merely became convenient scapegoats who could be blamed for problems which often lay beyond their control; moreover, if the ideals of the original architects of the British planning system were not always fulfilled then the fault sometimes lay elsewhere, in the political distortion of the early objectives and in economic and social changes that no one could have anticipated. Each of these factors has to be taken into account in attempting to explain one of the central paradoxes of the rural planning system as developed in the late 1940s: the fact that the idealized blueprint contained a strong element of planning for the least forunate, whereas in practice it had almost systematically the reverse effect.

The reasons for this state of affairs rapidly became institutionalized within the planning profession. Because planning was originally defined in terms of land use there were only sporadic attempts to relate such physically-defined policy objectives – zoning, design and so forth – to the *social* needs or demands of the rural population, except by default. It was in this way that planning policies often worked in a manner that was counter to many of the social policy objectives that were supposed to be their ultimate ends. As far as rural planning was concerned, social objectives were translated into the preservation of the countryside from urban encroachment and the provision of basic public services. By such means, it was believed, the 'traditional rural way of life' could be retained, but there was no attempt to monitor how these policies might affect the distribution of resources and opportunities *within* the rural population, if only because planners were neither trained, nor particularly inclined, to investigate such matters. Instead an influential but unexamined assumption prevailed that 'the rural community' was essentially a harmonious and homogeneous entity while the 'traditional rural way of life' was beneficial to all rural inhabitants. Consequently, planning policy framed the objectives of rural planning in terms of the protection of an inherently changeless countryside and a 'rural way of life' – a perspective which overlooked important social differences within the rural population.

The most obvious manifestation of this was the presumption that the countryside should be preserved, almost exclusively, for agriculture. Yet this occurred at a time when the farming industry was shedding labour at a rapid rate, as a result of mechanization. By directing new industrial development away from rural areas, conventional strategic planning policy restricted the economic growth of the countryside and perpetuated a low-wage rural economy for the reduced number of workers who were employed there. A parallel sequence of events occurred with respect to housing development. New housing was to be restricted – in both the public and the private sphere – so that a planned scarcity of housing duly emerged. Even where housing development was allowed, the insistence on ostensibly technocratic design practice features (density, layout, materials, etc.) ushered in an era of social exclusivity. By the 1970s not only was public housing in rural areas in short supply, but so too was cheap private housing. In the case of both development control policy and housing policy, attempts to preserve the rural status quo turned out to be redistributive – and in a highly regressive manner. Moreover, such changes were accompanied by a wholesale social transformation of rural communities which was to exacerbate these socially regressive changes.

CHANGE IN THE VILLAGE

The post-war period has been marked by very rapid and widespread changes in the rural population. In chapter 4 I described how, by the mid-nineteenth century, most rural villages had become occupational communities, based upon agriculture and with a clearly defined social order. Although changes in the structure of landownership immediately after the First World War tended to remove the influence of the Big House, the essentially agricultural character of the rural village was to remain up until 1939. Although in the Home Counties the countryside had been 'discovered' between the wars, leading to the growing presence of an urban commuting population, for the most part rural England remained agricultural England, and the village an agricultural community. In the first two decades after 1945 this was to change dramatically.

During this period the English village as an occupational community was virtually to disappear. The social changes which had first become apparent in the Home Counties were to spread out across the whole of lowland England and to penetrate deep into the uplands. The harbinger of this transformation was the internal combustion engine, the effects of which were to destroy the village as an agricultural community and lead it to succumb to the twin assaults of creeping urbanization and the drift from the land of agricultural labour. On the farm the introduction of tractors and combine harvesters brought about a vast decline in the number of employment opportunities and provided an added stimulus to the rural working population to move to the towns in search of jobs. They were replaced in most villages by an urban, overwhelmingly middle-class population which was attracted by a combination of cheap housing (until the planned scarcity began to affect prices in the late 1960s) and an idealized view of rural life (see chapter 9). Widespread car ownership enabled this new rural population to enjoy their pastoral havens without being confined to them. The transformation of rural villages into non-agricultural settlements thus took place in a series of waves out along the lines of transportation from the major urban centres, particularly, in the first instance, from London. By the end of the 1960s the motorway network had linked up most of the commuting areas between the major conurbations, and the in-filling of commuter villages between such radical transport routes had virtually been completed. Only a few areas, isolated by bad

roads and non-existent railways, remained relatively untouched, but even these, by virtue of their isolation, were
often susceptible to the equally voracious demand for holiday
homes and weekend cottages.

Rural England, which had been agricultural England,
swiftly became middle-class England. The new 'immigrants'
brought with them an urban, middle-class life-style which
was largely alien to the remaining local agricultural population. Unlike the 'locals', these newcomers did not make the
village the focus of all their social activities, for their possession of a car enabled them to maintain social contacts
elsewhere and to make use of urban amenities while living in
the countryside. Their entertainment, their socializing, even
their shopping, tended to take place outside the village. This
influx of strangers quite rapidly affected the nature of village
society: suddenly, so it appeared, everybody did *not* know
everybody else. The newcomers, moreover, did not enter the
village as lone individuals who had to win social recognition
among the locals in order to make life tolerable. Instead, they
arrived in such large numbers that urban, middle-class
patterns of sociability were quickly established in the village
itself and there was less necessity to adapt to the hitherto
accepted *mores* of the village society. There therefore arose
new social divisions and cleavages within the rural population
which cut across the clearly demarcated class boundaries
which were characteristic of the old agricultural community.
On the one hand there were the closely-knit 'locals', the rump
of the old occupational community, increasingly enclaved in
the council house estate or scattered among tied cottages. On
the other hand, there were the ex-urbanite newcomers,
affluent, by no means wholly insensitive, but to some extent
disruptive of established ways. Inevitably conflict ensued and
frequently the 'locals', faced with an invasion of 'their'
community by outsiders, tended to retreat in upon themselves, forming a community within a community, suspicious
of and resistant to any intimate social contact with the
commuters and second-home owners who now formed a
substantial proportion of the village population.

In view of these changes it is not surprising that new dimensions of social conflict arose to replace the rural class antagonisms of the old occupational community. Typically, there have been two issues over which such conflict has been generated: housing and the environment. Each has, in its way, contributed to the social polarization of the village population which has become a marked feature from the 1960s onwards. Housing is obviously a crucial resource, and one for which, moreover, the whole rural population – locals and newcomers – are competing. In general this does not apply to local employment, because the newcomers either retain their employment in nearby towns and commute or they have come to the countryside to retire. Both they and their children tend to compete in an entirely separate – usually professional and managerial – labour market from the 'locals'. Housing, however, is another matter. Here newcomers do compete with the locals, contributing to a higher demand for rural housing which, together with the restricted supply, has led to inflated prices. Resentment among local people has grown at their inability to find housing for themselves and their children. Yet they have also found that the newcomers have frequently opposed the construction of new housing, especially council housing, on the grounds that it is 'detrimental to the character of the village' and detracts from the rural environment.

In certain respects, therefore, the provision of housing has linked up with the second issue which has provoked conflict – a range of problems associated with environmental conservation. The environmental movement will be considered in more detail in the following section of this chapter, but here it can be noted how the growth of environmental concern in the countryside from the mid-1960s onwards was itself associated with the changing social composition of the rural population. This was because the newcomers often possessed a set of stereotyped expectations of village life which placed a heavy emphasis on the quality of the rural environment. Consequently they have held strong views on the desirable social and aesthetic qualities of the English village, which they wish to see conforming wherever possible to the prevailing urban view – picturesque, ancient and unchanging. The expectation that the countryside should conform to a certain idea of the picturesque and that it should present an unchanging spectacle to the appreciative onlooker led, for example, many new-comers to be bitterly critical of the changes wrought by modern farming methods. Because they regarded the countryside primarily in aesthetic and recreational terms, friction soon developed with the local farming population. An already wary relationship between the farming population and the newcomers was easily strained by such encounters, reinforcing the division between the two sides. Individual petty disputes rapidly accumulated to add to the differences already apparent in terms of background and life-styles.

For those newcomers who moved to the countryside in order to seek the social intimacy of a happy and integrated community life, the reserve (and worse) of the local in-habitants may have been a disappointment. Many of the newcomers arrived full of goodwill and good intentions, but failed to perceive the often unanticipated consequences of their arrival on the lives of the local inhabitants. The sense of having been 'taken over' was, at times, difficult for the locals to avoid and, moreover, the newcomers provided an easily visible scapegoat for factors – such as the rural housing shortage – which lay beyond their control. What is also clear, however, is that, despite the disruption which they brought with them, had the urban migrants *not* chosen to live in the countryside, the consequences might have been even more severe, and might have entailed the complete destruction of both the social and the physical fabric of many villages. Some of this can, indeed, be observed in those areas which, by virtue of extreme remoteness and the idiosyncrasies of landownership, have remained entirely dependent upon agriculture.

There has, in consequence, been a good deal of uncertainty about whether the newcomers to the countryside have wrought a deterioration or a revitalization of the village community. Indeed, the transformation that has occurred within a single generation in most rural areas has been so rapid and far-reaching that it is not surprising that, from the 1960s onwards, many writers and observers were beginning to question whether the village could survive as a 'community' in the traditional sense. Most of these observations were pessimistic, almost elegiac in tone, concerned to document 'the decline of the village' and to enunciate the last rites over any lingering 'community spirit'. In fact, much of the evidence described in earlier chapters of this book would question whether the rural village has declined as a vigorous community: there is surprisingly little evidence to support this view, except where a locality has been subject to wholesale depopulation. It is equally clear that rural village life, rather than representing some unchanging arcadian past, has been subject to considerable fluctuations in social and economic circumstances. Furthermore, judgements in relation to the 'community spirit' of the contemporary village are inherently dependent upon the values and priorities of the observer. Should account be taken of only the material standards of village life, or should more decisive qualities, such as the sense of identity and belonging, be included? And from whose perspective should any assessment of gains and losses be taken? As there is no consensus, either among or between the different groupings which now comprise the village population, any overall conclusion about a 'loss of community' in rural society is impossible: it all depends on what is meant by 'community'.

ENVIRONMENTAL CONSERVATION AND RURAL CHANGE

As the English countryside became the residential location of the English middle classes, so the desire to protect what was regarded as quintessentially 'rural' about the countryside grew apace. The technological revolution which had transformed agriculture during the post-war period thus confronted the social revolution of the English village on the battlefield of

what came to be known, somewhat loosely, as 'the environment'. Consequently, a wide range of what had previously
been considered to be mundane or esoteric problems concerning the countryside were thrust to the forefront of public
attention. As awareness of 'the environment' grew, what had
begun as a specific and separate set of issues involving such
matters as landscape change, pesticide use, urban and industrial development, resource depletion, recreational demand and the preservation of wildlife habitats were linked
together in a much more comprehensive debate about environmental matters. Such was the wide-ranging nature of the
discussion over the future of the rural environment, that it
encompassed not only technological issues relating to modern
farming methods, but also the much more nebulous concept
of 'amenity' – a mixture of social, aesthetic and even philosophical questions about the direction of change in English
rural society and in the countryside which reflected this
underlying social character.

In part, this concern for the environment was fuelled by a set
of considerations which lie well beyond the scope of this book
– for example, a growing anxiety about the future of modern
industrial society and a lack of faith in social and economic
progress which was in marked contrast to the confidence of
Victorian Britain. However, the growth of the environmental
movement was not merely part of the 'politics of decline' of
the 1970s onwards. In some respects it was an extension of a
much older phenomenon, for, as has been demonstrated
earlier in this book, ever since the Industrial Revolution those
who could afford it have sought to escape from the squalor of
the urban industrial world, fearful of the breakdown of social
order in the cities and wishing to remove themselves to more
aesthetically and socially congenial surroundings. By the
1960s the ability to leave behind this unpalatable existence had
simply passed a little further down the social scale, so that the
urban middle class could now aspire to a share of rural
England rather more modest than their nineteenth-century
nouveaux riches predecessors. What many of the newcomers
found, however, was frequently something less attractive

than their idyllic (and often unrealistic) assumptions had led them to expect. Modern agricultural practice was busily transforming the 'traditional' countryside, removing hedge-rows, ploughing up heather moorland, filling in ponds and destroying plants, insects, birds and small mammals with pesticides. Moreover increasing accessibility to the country-side, due to increasing car ownership and greater leisure time, was threatening the peace and tranquility of this rural retreat from an entirely different direction. The countryside, so it seemed, had to be preserved from both farmers (hitherto considered reliable custodians of the rural environment) *and* 'the public'. The countryside had become what Fred Hirsch, in his book *The Social Limits to Growth*, was to call a 'positional good' – that is, something which is fixed in supply and whose consumption is dependent upon one's position in society. It followed that many of those who cared for the amenity quality of the countryside also believed that this quality could only be retained if access by other social groups could somehow be restricted.

Concern for the rural environment thus became a public issue partly because there was now residing in the countryside an affluent and articulate population, no longer dependent upon local farmers and landowners for housing and employ-ment, and which was capable of mobilizing itself politically. Viewed historically it is possible to recognize that eighteenth- and nineteenth-century agricultural improvements created equally drastic changes in rural landscapes and ecology, and that the 'traditional' field boundaries of lowland England frequently date only from the Enclosure Movement. During the decades after the Second World War, new capital-intensive farming methods have certainly dramatically altered both the appearance and the ecology of the countryside, and they have done so at an accelerating rate, but it is doubtful whether these changes would have met with such fierce opposition had not the *social* composition of rural society been so thoroughly transformed also. The social character of the environmental movement therefore explains the priorities which it has assigned, reflecting as they do the values and judgements of its predominantly middle-class membership. This has led to charges of elitism which cannot altogether be discounted: more fuss is made over the siting of electricity pylons than the existence of houses without electricity; more has been heard about landscapes than low pay in the countryside; and so on. Farmers have also accused environmentalists of hypocrisy, of demanding cheap food, but wishing to deny them the wherewithal to produce it. Such accusations have not been entirely without foundation, but underlying this inevitably inconclusive conflict of values, there has also been revealed a great deal of objective scientific evidence which has documented in an alarming fashion the impact of modern farming methods on the ecology of the countryside.

This threat was first perceived in the early 1960s when evidence began to accumulate on the impact of pesticides on the food chain of mammals and predatory birds. Public attention was brought to bear by the publication in 1962 of Rachel Carson's *Silent Spring*, which envisaged an alarming future of a countryside devoid of some of its most cherished bird species. As a consequence much stricter controls were placed on the use of pesticides and the problem was largely brought under control. By the 1970s the debate had moved on to consider changing agricultural landscapes, a somewhat more contentious issue since this was ultimately dependent upon subjective aesthetic judgements. Widespread mechanization in agriculture had brought about the removal of many hedgerows and other field boundaries, especially in the cereals-producing counties of lowland England. Concern was also expressed about the 'improvement' (i.e. ploughing up and reseeding) of areas of semi-natural vegetation used for rough grazing, especially the heath and moorland of south and south-west England. Many farmers had been encouraged by government grants and subsidies to undertake such changes in pursuit of greater efficiency and the maximizing of production. There thus developed a considerable conflict of interest between farming profitability and landscape conservation. Various palliatives failed to prevent the transformation of large parts of East Anglia and the Eastern

Counties into 'prairie' landscapes – cereals monoculture largely devoid of trees, hedges and similar natural features. Not until after 1980, however, with the publication of Marion Shoard's remarkable polemic *The Theft of the Countryside*, did public opinion begin to swing decisively against farmers on this issue – by which time, in many cases, it was too late and the damage had been done.

ENVIRONMENTAL PRESSURE GROUPS

The growth of the environmental movement during the 1960s and 1970s not only created a new set of political issues to be debated in the countryside, but it also ushered in a new political style. This was the age of the environmental pressure group. Both the number of environmental organizations and the size of their memberships increased dramatically between 1960 and 1975. Partly this was the result of a spontaneous grass-roots movement, with amenity societies and conservation groups being formed locally to pursue some particular interest and only later joining one of the nationally-based 'umbrella' associations, which could put them in touch with other like-minded groups. Elsewhere, however, the growth of environmental concern was expressed in the transformation of older-established national organizations, such as the National Trust, the Council for the Protection of Rural England and the Royal Society for the Protection of Birds. By the late 1970s it was estimated that environmental pressure groups as a whole could count on a membership of two million individuals. One by-product of this was that hitherto obscure corners of rural England could find themselves the focus of national attention by virtue of the interest created by an environmental pressure group determined to take a stand on some particular instance of environmental degradation. A further, and more far-reaching, consequence was that the 'politics of the countryside' was becoming a national (which is to say, urban) concern, as opposed to a minority interest indulged in only by farmers, landowners and their representative organizations.

The success of the environmental movement in forcing

conservation onto the national political agenda was not, however, due to the sheer weight of numbers represented in the membership. The quality of leadership and the tactical political skills of its active members have been equally important. Many of the organizations have developed a degree of technical expertise which has led them to be sources of valued advice to decision-makers at both the national and the local level. In some cases their views have been incorporated, formally or informally, into the procedures surrounding planning controls, greatly assisted by the vogue for participatory planning during the 1970s. As a result, the environmental movement's influence increased considerably during this decade, particularly at the local level through consultations between planning authorities and local amenity societies. Nationally, though, the environmental movement continued to show signs of its relative immaturity. National co-ordination remained ill-defined and sporadic, occasionally undermining the ability of the movement to act concertedly to further its goals. Certainly the environmental lobby lacked both the national organization and the sustained political influence which the agricultural organizations had long enjoyed. Indeed, the continuing exemption of agriculture from most planning controls was both a testimony to the continuing influence of the NFU and the CLA and a monument to the political weakness of the environmentalists. By the late 1970s the credibility of the farmers' claims to be the true custodians of the rural environment had been widely called into question, yet planning legislation continued to be based on this prescription. The 1981 Wildlife and Countryside Act attempted to provide a modicum of control over the most precious sites, but still the principle remained. Nevertheless, there were clear signs that the tide of public opinion was running in favour of conservation and that the days of unfettered agricultural land use might be numbered. Were this to be achieved it would add the finishing touch to the thoroughgoing urbanization of rural England which has been such a feature of the decades since the Second World War.

While the environmental lobby has, then, provided a

political counterbalance to the hitherto unquestioned supremacy of farmers and landowners over rural affairs, the social
profile of the environmental movement does raise the
question of political equity. There is little doubt that the
political mobilization of environmentalists has, in some cases,
accentuated the already existing disparities between the living
conditions and life chances of the affluent and those least
educated. The latter have experienced the greatest difficulty in
protecting their interests and in convincing the conservation-
ists, for example, that rural council housing or industrial
development are additions to, rather than detractions from,
the quality of rural life. Farm workers have found it extra-
ordinarily difficult to ensure that such bread-and-butter issues
as their wages and conditions of work be given the attention
which they feel they deserve (see chapter 9). The environmental movement has not, of course, been responsible for this
state of affairs, but the social composition of its membership,
together with the values and aesthetic judgements which often
characterize its interpretation of 'the environment', can hardly
be said to have enhanced the position of those rural inhabitants
already lacking political and economic resources. The field has
therefore been left clear for a somewhat particular and partial
definition of 'the environment' to dominate public discussion,
one which, unchecked, will take rural communities in the
future even further away from the balanced social composition which was envisaged in the immediate post-war
legislation.

RURAL ENGLAND – PRESENT AND FUTURE

By the mid-1970s a number of the factors referred to in this
chapter which were influencing the direction of social change
in rural England had come together. The technological
revolution in agriculture had substantially reduced the labour
force employed on the land and had removed from the village
most of its former agricultural inhabitants. Most villages were
instead inhabited by large numbers of ex-urban professional

and managerial households who, having sought their rustic retreat, were disinclined to favour further 'intrusive' industrial and housing development. A whole new balance of political forces now underlay rural planning policy and its implementation. However much the newly-arrived rural population might support community development in the abstract, they have frequently voiced strenuous opposition – on 'environmental' grounds – to new development in *their* village. A similar process can be observed covering the whole range of public and social services. The intervention of government to provide a basic service infrastructure for rural areas was, as has been noted, one of the key elements of the post-war reconstruction. However, the changing social composition, and therefore political balance, of the rural population has meant that there has been increasing pressure to preserve only those services which are self-financing. The affluent majority of the rural population has been able to overcome any problems which arise by stepping into their cars and driving to the nearest town, whereas the poor, the elderly and the disabled have been particularly vulnerable to any decrease in the provision of local services, and especially of public transport. A sharp division has arisen between that section of the rural population which is in need and may be suffering from multiple social deprivation, and that which has benefited from living in the countryside and for whom access to a full range of services does not present a problem. Numerically it has been the latter group which has been in the ascendancy, and which has achieved a firm grip on the levers of local decision-making. As a result the deprived members of rural society have found it increasingly difficult to obtain recognition of their requirements, let alone divert a larger proportion of available resources in their direction. The affluent majority of ratepayers have demonstrated an understandable reluctance to foot the rapidly-rising bill on behalf of their less fortunate neighbours.

Such political realities have formed a barrier to attempts to alleviate the socially regressive effects of rural planning policies referred to earlier in this chapter. Even though, by the early 1970s, some of the drawbacks of conventional rural planning policy were well recognized within the planning profession, it had become difficult to find the local democratic support to overcome them. Local sentiment was inclined to be less favourable towards a relaxation of planning controls to allow new employment opportunities to be created. The affluent majority also chose, quite democratically, to accept lower levels of service provision in return for lower levels of taxation. Planning therefore ceased to be the instrument of balanced community development which had been envisaged in the late 1940s; instead it was more likely to be a means of reinforcing social exclusiveness. What had emerged was an alarming degree of social polarization, involving not merely the subjective differences in living standards between those who had chosen to live in the countryside (and this included not only the ex-urbanites, but also most farmers and land-owners) and those who had been stranded in rural areas by social and economic forces over which they had no control and which were frequently reinforced by public indifference to their plight. Two nations in one village was increasingly the norm.

Of course to many this deprivation was not new. As this book has attempted to show, the history of most villages is a history of poverty. In the past, however, when poverty was chronic, the experience of deprivation was one that could be shared by the majority of the village population, whereas in the contemporary village poverty brings with it a sense of exclusion rather than mutuality. This form of social polarization has been a slow but inexorable process during the post-war period. While there can be little doubt that the material conditions of the rural poor, the elderly, the disabled and other deprived groups have undergone a considerable improvement in absolute terms since the war, in relative terms they have encountered little improvement. A stark contrast exists between them and more affluent – and visible – neighbours. Many, the rump of the former local working population, are tied to the locality by their (low-paid) employment, by old age and by lack of resources to undertake a move. They have become increasingly trapped by a lack of access to alternative employment, housing and the full range of amenities which the remainder of the population takes for granted. A life-style, once only distantly and fleetingly observed, is now frequently encountered at first-hand among the new inhabitants of 'their' village. They have found, somewhat disconcertingly, that they and their needs are increasingly regarded as residual – or even unacknowledged. Their new minority status hardly lends itself to making a fuss, nor to the expectation that they can achieve any tangible change if they attempted to do so. Generations of inherited experience form an accurate guide here. Instead, like their predecessors, they mostly 'make do'.

It seems most unlikely that rural planning will be able to redress this social imbalance, even if the political will were there for it to do so. Planning policies continue to militate against the location of industrial and commercial development in rural areas, with, for example, county plans continuing to advocate no-growth or low-growth policies for rural districts. In any case strategic planning has come to mean less and less in practice during the 1980s under the impact of widespread economic recession. For similar reasons it seems unlikely that the necessary instruments to ensure a degree of social balance in rural communities will be made available to planners. All of this suggests that traditional 'top-down' planning is unlikely to offer many solutions. The future of English rural society seems, instead, likely to be determined by a much broader range of influences which stem from the future shape of the British economy as a whole. Whether this will alleviate the social polarization of the countryside is a moot point, but if the future composition of rural society is to be determined by any one set of factors these are unlikely to be found within rural planning policy decisions, nor even in the economic trends of the agriculture industry (referred to in chapter 9), but in the changing role that rural areas will play in the industrial and economic structure of Britain in the future.

A post-industrial rural world?

In the latter sense, a widespread, but less frequently acknowledged, transformation of rural England is already under
way. The results of the 1981 Population Census confirmed
that, the prescriptions of rural planning policy notwithstanding, the British economy had, during the previous decade,
manifested pronounced centrifugal tendencies. Not only had
there been a flow of population into rural areas, but there had
also been a substantial decentralization of economic activity.
The industrial restructuring of the 1980s is exacerbating these
trends. Urban areas have suffered from a massive decline in
manufacturing employment, whereas rural areas and small
towns, especially in East Anglia and the South West, have
witnessed an increase in manufacturing. Rural areas have
benefited from the virtual completion of a national motorway
network, which has greatly altered the balance of advantages
and disadvantages of locating manufacturing and assembly
plants on 'green-field' sites. Similarly, there is little doubt that
the availability of a pool of cheap and relatively quiescent
semi-skilled labour in rural areas has been an attraction. Much
of this labour has been female; thus the siting of some
manufacturing branch-plants in rural areas has improved the
hitherto negligible employment opportunities for working
women in rural areas and increased household incomes – even
though individual rates of pay tend to be low. Nevertheless,
the benefits have been spread very unevenly. Manufacturing
employment tends to be unstable, and multi-national and
multi-regional comparisons show that investment is switched
with great rapidity. Many rural plants turn out to be
peripheral in an economic as well as a geographical sense.
Plant closures demonstrate the extent to which decision-
making over rural employment opportunities is often far
removed from local hands.

Another important factor which has contributed to rural
manufacturing growth has been the presence in rural communities of an affluent, middle-class population with high
disposable incomes. It is a population which has created its

own buoyant market for certain kinds of manufactured goods – mostly high quality products manufactured on a small scale. Similar factors apply to the service sector. Rural newcomers have created or revived demand for a whole range of personal and domestic services which has in turn created local employment opportunities. More recently still, those services capable of taking advantage of new developments in information technology and associated forms of computer networking have also located themselves in rural areas, where new 'cottage industries' in computer software, database management and other micro-electronic applications have emerged. These developments indicate that the prospect is now opening up a vast reduction in the significance of location and distance as constraints on economic and social development. Consequently, for the first time since the Industrial Revolution, rural areas may participate in a technological breakthrough on an equal footing with urban centres. The relationship between hitherto 'rural' and 'urban' areas is likely to be fundamentally altered by these processes.

Such futuristic possibilities for the rural 'post-industrial' society sit oddly with the bleak portrayal of social polarization presented earlier in this section. The current processes of change are, indeed, paradoxical and the eventual outcome will depend very much on how far the benefits of future economic development will be diffused among all sections of the rural population or will be retained within the more affluent sector. It is becoming clear, nonetheless, that in order to appreciate the impact of such changes a new way of looking (literally as well as figuratively) at rural society will be required. For example, 'rural' will become more and more dissociated from 'agricultural'. Only in terms of land use will rural England be agricultural England. In all other senses – economically, occupationally, socially, culturally – rural England will be (and in many cases already has been) comprehensively 'urbanized'. This also suggests that the *future* of rural communities cannot be predicted on the basis of a straightforward extrapolation from the past. This book has argued that the *history* of rural communities can, with a few minor qualifications, be understood in terms of factors that were rooted first and foremost in changes in agriculture. In the future, rural England will no longer be an agrarian society and it is very doubtful indeed whether any future changes in agriculture will have any significant effect on the social fabric of the countryside. Harsh though it may sound, agriculture now has only a residual significance on the economic and social structure of many 'rural' areas. This is the measure of the change which has occurred in rural England since 1945 – a change which is likely to be no less profound, even when viewed in a longer historical perspective, than the Agricultural Revolution with which this book opened.

FURTHER READING

This section not only provides an opportunity to guide the reader to a more specialist literature but also to acknowledge the source of quotations and other references made in the text.

A most accessible introduction to the feudal period is M. M. Postan's *The Medieval Economy and Society* (Penguin, 1975). The broad sweep of economic change which marked the transition from feudalism to capitalism – and the role of agriculture within it – has long been one of the central debates of British and continental European historiography. A helpful summary, for those already aware of the general lines of argument, is Keith Tribe's *Genealogies of Capitalism* (Macmillan, 1981). For those who wish to catch up on the debate itself (drawn largely from the 1940s and 1950s) a handy collection is Rodney Hilton (ed.), *The Transition from Feudalism to Capitalism* (New Left Books, 1976), although not all the contributions are relevant to the study of agrarian change.

As I mentioned in chapter 1, the history of the Agricultural Revolution is not without pitfalls for the unwary. For all its faults, Lord Ernle (formerly R. C. Prothero) sets the scene in his magisterial *English Farming, Past and Present* (sixth edition, Heinemann, 1961), in a manner which remains highly readable. The stress on technological innovation can be found in Eric Kerridge, *The Agricultural Revolution* (Allen and Unwin, 1967); G. E. Mingay, *English Landed Society in the Eighteenth Century* (Routledge and Kegan Paul, 1963); and *Enclosure and the Small Farmer in the Age of the Industrial Revolution* (Macmillan, 1968). The work of E. L. Jones is also an important contribution – see his collected essays in *Agriculture and the Industrial Revolution* (Blackwell, 1974). The social and cultural – as opposed to the narrowly economic – aspects of the agricultural revolution are dealt with in a number of essays in Jack Goody et al. (eds), *Family and Inheritance* (CUP, 1976), especially in the contributions of Joan Thirsk and E. P. Thompson.

The most sustained analysis of the countryside in English literature from the eighteenth century onwards is Raymond Williams, *The Country and the City* (Chatto and Windus, 1973). Ideas about landscape and the picturesque in the eighteenth century are examined in the first two chapters of John Barrell, *The Idea of Landscape and the Sense of Place, 1730–1840* (CUP, 1972). The work of landscape gardeners is also discussed in Edward Hyams, *The English Garden* (Thames and Hudson, 1964) and placed in a broader context in Heather Clemenson, *English Country Houses and Landed Estates* (Croom Helm, 1982). Reference should also be made to Mark Girouard's delightful *Life in the English Country House* (Penguin, 1980).

William Cobbett's *Rural Rides* continues to inspire generations of professional rural-watchers. The unrest which he observed is vividly portrayed in Eric Hobsbawm and George Rudé, *Captain Swing* (Lawrence and Wishart, 1971). Life in the Big House is authoritatively described by F. M. L. Thompson, *English Landed Society in the Nineteenth Century* (Routledge and Kegan Paul, 1963). There are extended discussions of the gentlemanly ethic in W. L. Burn, *The Age of Equipoise* (Allen and Unwin, 1964); J. F. C. Harrison, *The Early Victorians, 1832–51* (Panther, 1973); and G. Best, *Mid-Victorian England, 1851–75* (Panther, 1973). Mark Girouard's *The Return to Camelot* (Yale, 1982) traces the rediscovery of chivalry and its influence on Victorian morality.

The nineteenth-century village remains *terra incognita* for many parts of the country. A good overview is W. E. Tate, *The English Village Community* (Gollancz, 1967). Rowland Parker's *The Common Stream* has its followers, but possibly more authentic voices are those of Flora Thompson in her *Lark*

Rise to Candleford (Penguin, 1973) and M. K. Ashby, *Joseph Ashby of Tysoc, 1859–1919* (CUP, 1961). A useful collection is Raphael Samuel (ed.), *Village Life and Labour* (Routledge and Kegan Paul, 1975). Pamela Horn takes a panoramic view in *The Rural World, 1780–1850* (Hutchinson, 1980). The new sobriety of village life is discussed in David Morgan, *Harvesters and Harvesting 1840–1900* (Croom Helm, 1982), and more extensively by Bob Bushaway in *By Rite* (Junction Books, 1982).

Agricultural change during this period is dealt with in somewhat conventional fashion by J. D. Chambers and G. E. Mingay, *The Agricultural Revolution 1750–1880* (Batsford, 1966). There are also detailed studies, with much more besides, in Mingay's sumptuously-produced two volumes of *The Victorian Countryside* (Routledge and Kegan Paul, 1982). The years of depression are charted in P. J. Perry, *British Agriculture, 1870–1914* (Methuen, 1973); and in C. S. Orwin and E. H. Whetham, *History of British Agriculture, 1846–1914* (OUP, 1964). A detailed account of the land question is in Roy Douglas, *Land, People and Politics* (Allison and Busby, 1976).

The life of the farm worker has not been neglected by agricultural historians. Classic accounts include J. L. and Barbara Hammond, *The Village Labourer* (Longman, 1966). The best recent account is Alun Howkins, *Poor Labouring Men* (Routledge and Kegan Paul, 1985). The early history of unionization can be found in J. P. D. Dunbabin, *Rural Discontent in Nineteenth Century Britain* (Faber, 1974); Pamela Horn, *Joseph Arch* (Roundwood Press, 1971); and Reg Groves, *Sharpen the Sickle!* (Porcupine Press, 1948). Crafted examples of oral history can be found in the writings of George Ewart Evans, especially *Ask the Fellows Who Cut the Hay* (Faber, 1956); *The Horse in the Furrow* (Faber, 1960); *Pattern under the Plough* (Faber, 1966); and *Where Beards Wag All* (Faber, 1970). Some of the recent history of the farm worker is also covered in Howard Newby, *The Deferential Worker* (Penguin, 1979).

The inter-war years are rather poorly covered by recent social historical research, although the appearance of a volume in the *Cambridge Agrarian History* series, edited by Joan Thirsk, has helped. The most readily-available histories of the period barely refer to agriculture, but the changing pattern of leisure activities is a more pervasive theme. A most useful essay is John Lowerson, 'Battles for the Countryside', in F. Glover-smith (ed.), *Class, Culture and Social Change: New Views of the 1930s* (Harvester, 1980).

The post-war period is covered more extensively in my companion volume, *Green and Pleasant Land?* (Penguin, 1980; Wildwood House, 1985). However, brief mention can be made here of a few general references. The post-war reconstruction of agriculture is surveyed in Tristram Beresford's *We Plough the Fields* (Penguin, 1975), while the parallel work associated with town and country planning is considered in Peter Hall's *The Containment of Urban England* (Allen and Unwin, 1973). Marion Shoard's strident but effective *The Theft of the Countryside* might be described as *The Silent Spring* of the 1980s. A personal favourite, which knits together both conservation and social objectives in the countryside, is Richard Mabey, *The Common Ground* (Hutchinson, 1980).

INDEX

Abercrombie, P., 177
access, to private land, 175–8,
    216–17
agribusiness, 75, 187, 188–93
Agricultural Development
    and Advisory Service
    (ADAS), 188
agricultural engineering, 73–4;
    see also farm machinery;
    technology
Agricultural Revolution (18th
    century), 6–28, 29, 34,
    189, 190, 237
Agricultural Revolution (20th
    century), 180–210, 185,
    190
agricultural prices, 68–75,
    104–19, 156–60, 166,
    170–73, 182
Agricultural Wages Board,
    164–5, 166, 168, 205–10
agricultural workers, 69, 76–
    103, 120–37, 149, 158–79,
    204–10
agriculture
    and commercialism, 6–28
    passim, 33–4, 69–75, 95
    import of urbanism, 54–5,
    110–15, 154–5
    medieval, 7, 8

and politics, 110–15, 138–
    56, 157–79, 180–210
Agriculture and Food
    Research Council
    (AFRC), 188
allotments, 124, 149
almshouses, 86
Amalgamated Labour League,
    123
Amersham, 174
arable agriculture, 11, 20,
    33–4, 73, 80–81, 106–8,
    118, 140–41, 170–73
Arch, J., 78, 122–32, 141,
    167, 210
Areas of Great Landscape
    Value, 218
Areas of Outstanding Natural
    Beauty, 218
Argentina, 106
aristocracy, 58–65, 139, 150–
    56, 200
arson, 38–47 *passim*, 83, 101
Ascot-under-Wychwood
    (Oxon), 126
Ashby, M.K., 240
Asquith, H., 151
Australasia, 105
Australia, 44, 46
Ayrshire, 109

242

Howitt, W., 94
Howkins, A., 240
Hyams, E., 239
Hythe (Kent), 40

improvement (in estate
management), 13–28
passim, 68–75 *passim*, 189,
228
Ireland, 142–4, 146–7
Irish National Land League,
143–4
Irish National League, 144

Jeffries, R., 116–19
Jones, E.L., 23, 238

Kent, 39, 40, 43, 45, 163
Kent, William, 18
Kerridge, E., 7, 238
Kinder Scout, 178
Kyle of Lochalsh, 145

labourers, farm, 10, 29–52
passim, 55, 56, 76–103,
120–37; *see also*
agricultural workers
Labourers' Revolt, 38–47
Lake District, 146
Lancashire, 109, 162, 163
land, 9–28 *passim*, 68–75
passim, 89–92, 106–8,
114, 124, 138–56, 180–
210 *passim*
Land Enquiry Committee,
152
Land Nationalization Society,
148, 149
land reform, 138–56
Land Reform Union, 148
Land Restoration League,
148–9

land use planning, *see*
planning
landlords, 14–28, 56, 69–75,
81, 82, 83, 86–8, 89–92,
97, 108, 129, 137, 138–56,
163, 180–210 *passim*, 215,
227, 229
landownership, 9–13 *passim*,
14–28, 55–6, 58–75, 89–
92, 108, 124, 138–56,
163, 180–210
landscape architecture, 17–20,
89–92
Lea Valley, 110
Leamington Spa, 122, 123,
124, 129, 131
Leavis, F.R., 178
Leicestershire, 121
leisure, 92–6, 174–9; *see also*
sport
Lenin, V.I., 182
Letchworth, 174
Liberty and Property Defence
League, 149
Lincoln, 129
Lincolnshire, 109, 121, 123
Lincolnshire Farmers Union,
163
Lisle, Edward, 1–2
Llanidloes, 98
Lloyd George, D., 151
lock-out, 127–32, 162
London, 41, 49, 51, 64, 65,
123, 129, 167
London Season, 64, 65
Loudon, J., 90–91, 174
Loveless, G., 47
Lower Hardres (Kent), 40
Lowerson, J., 175, 176, 241
Lucas, Lord, 158
Luddism, 44

246

Parker, R., 239
pastoral agriculture, 11, 62,
    80–81, 107, 140–41, 150,
    191–2
pastoralism, 1
paternalism, 45–46, 50, 58,
    65–8 passim, 72, 78, 86–8,
    91, 94, 125–7, 138–9
pauperism, 7, 13, 23–4, 29–52
    passim, 83–8
Peak District, 177–8
peasantry, 8, 20–24, 27, 112,
    148
Peel, Sir Robert, 43, 52
Perry, P., 134, 240
pig production, 111
planning, 174, 213–20, 231–4
poaching, 39, 65, 79, 83, 101
politics, see agriculture and
    politics
Poor Law, 34–52, 64, 83–8,
    171
Postan, M.M., 10, 238
poultry production, 106, 111
poverty, see pauperism
power, 58–69 passim, 82–3,
    122–32 passim
prices, of farm products, see
    agricultural prices
primitive Methodism, 45,
    100–3, 121, 122, 123, 161
property, rights of, 14–15,
    62–5 passim, 138–56,
    177–9
Prothero, R.E. (Lord Ernle),
    107, 113, 238

Quantock Hills, 218

railways, 97–8, 123, 222
Ramblers Association, 178

rambling, 178
rates, 34–47, 100, 212
Raynham, 14
recreation, 175–8, 200
religion, 63, 79, 82–3, 94,
    99–103, 142, 143, 145–7,
    161–2
rent, 9, 51, 69, 72, 84, 108,
    113, 138–56 passim
Repton, Humphry, 18–19
Revolt of the Field, 122–32
Richmond, Duke of, 43
riots, 29–33, 35–6, 51, 74, 78,
    80, 178
romanticism, 1, 18, 178
Romsey (Hampshire), 42
Royal Society for the
    Protection of Birds
    (RSPB), 229
Rudé, G., 26, 36, 101, 239
Rutland, 62
Rutland, Duke of, 125–6, 129

St Faith's, 162
Samuel, R., 240
Sandringham, 162
sanitation, 84–5, 212
schools, 63, 68, 86, 98–9
Scotland, 140, 142, 144–7
    passim, 174, 214
Scott, Sir Walter, 66–7, 144
Scott Report, 214–15
serfdom, 10–11
servants, farm, 32–3, 120
Sheffield, 177
Shoard, M., 229, 241
Shropshire, 64
Skye, 144–5
smallholders, 10, 124, 139,
    148–9
Somerset, 163